HIGH PRAIS
LEARNING T

LEARNING

TO

LEAVE

A WOMAN'S GUIDE
REVISED EDITION

Lynette Triere with Richard Peacock

WARNER BOOKS

A Time Warner Company

The chart on page 200 was compiled by T. H. Holmes and R. H. Rahe from the *Journal of Psychosomatic Research*, vol. 11, 1967. Reprinted by permission of Pergamon Press.

"Incipience" by Adrienne Rich on page 21 is reprinted from *Poems: Selected and New, 1950–1974* (New York: W. W. Norton and Co., Inc., 1975, 1973, 1971, 1969, 1966.)
Reprinted by permission of the author and the publisher.

Warner Books Edition

This Warner Books edition is published by arrangement with the authors.

Warner Books, Inc., 1271 Avenue of the Americas, New York, N.Y. 10020
Visit our Web site at http://warnerbooks.com
Ⓦ A Time Warner Company

Printed in the United States of America
First Warner printing: June 1993
10 9 8 7 6

Library of Congress Cataloging-in-Publication Data

Triere, Lynette.
  Learning to Leave.

  Bibliography: p.
  Includes index.
  1. Divorce.   I. Peacock, Richard.   2. Title.
HQ814.T74   1983   306.8'9   83-10283
ISBN 0-446-39483-1

Cover design by Michèle Brinson

Contents

Introduction

When the first edition of LEARNING TO LEAVE was published some years ago, it met with mixed reactions. For many women, the book was the first direct confrontation with the tough and painful issues which the divorce process brings up for them. The writing offered genuine understanding and specific advice. Hundreds of women responded in letters. "Your book is a *lifeline* through this chaotic period of my life" was a typical sentiment. In a time of emotional isolation and an uncertain future, women caught in the dilemma of divorce welcomed the book.

Counseling professionals did too. Although practicing psychologists have been trained to help solve a person's struggle with past and present emotional turmoil, the flood of special issues which accompany the decision to end a relationship can be an overwhelming puzzle. Problems surrounding divorce often entail legal and economic conflicts which many counselors and therapists are not readily equipped to address. LEARNING TO LEAVE became a handy and basic primer to recommend to women, a useful adjunct to whatever on-going personal help the counselor was giving. "This is the most practical and helpful guide for women in any aspect of divorce that has been written," wrote Elizabeth Campbell, Ph.D., former president of the Association for Humanistic Psychology.

Media reaction was not so uniformly receptive. As we toured the country when the book was first published, we appeared on an array of television and radio talk shows, and were interviewed for numerous newspapers and magazines. It became clear that the book triggered some deep-seated biases. While it is true that the media thrives on controversy, and that TV talk shows have replaced the back fence as the place to carry on outrageous gossip, LEARNING TO LEAVE frankly discussed the strategic realities of divorce solely from a *woman's perspective*, and gave unshrinking advice. This seemed to stretch the limits of proper media morality. When we stressed that leaving the relationship with her personal dignity intact was ultimately rewarding for all parties, it did not seem to ease the insecurity of media producers.

We had inadvertently touched into perhaps our nation's strongest taboo. Although the public fusses over sexual transgressions and frets about increasing violence, a book advising women who want a better way to end the bonds of marriage was seen as almost dangerous. Many male program co-hosts seemed to take personal offense. Before and after the shows, even though the discussions with other women had been lively and surprisingly harmonious, the ideas of the book were sometimes treated gingerly, as though they posed a serious threat to the well-being of the society.

It was as if the book sent out shock waves that could not be easily measured and contained: an alarming situation. The widespread existence of divorce is a reality with which the society has still not come to grips. Today, simplistic doctrines mislabeled "family values" seek to punish women who choose a better life for themselves. Pious sentiments clash with the truth of many women living in the tough and thankless existence of a bad marriage. For women going through a breakup, our book was an anchor of sanity and solace; for some other people, it was quite unsettling.

Since the book first came out in the early eighties, some things have changed. The hard economic times have made the struggle for women in the workplace even more complicated. And although strides continue to be made in making society increasingly responsive to women's issues, progress is painfully slow. In addition, men have become more savvy regarding divorce, and many of them are demanding a greater say in child custody questions. The positive side of this new male awareness is that men are beginning to recognize their lifelong responsibility to their children.

But certain things in the leaving process are universal and will never change. Leaving a relationship is a very personal and profound time of one's life. The hurt, the fears, and the self questioning are the same for most people. The deeply felt emotions that are triggered in divorce must be managed by each woman and man involved. How each of you decide to handle this fragile turning point will profoundly shape both your present plans and future dreams.

Although this book is primarily geared to women who are choosing to *leave* a relationship, it has much to say to women who are *being left*. Many women who did not initiate their divorce have turned to the book and found an objective insight into the problems they face, and a direction out. For instance, whether a woman is leaving or being left, she still has to deal with her anger and letting go of guilt. Both share concern for their health and sexual needs. Both have to look at old dependency patterns and get ready for new emotional and economic independence. And a fair and peaceful resolution is in the best interest of everyone, no matter what situation you find yourself. Certainly there have been enough nationally publicized cases showing the extremes to which divorcing couples can go to sound a general warning. In the end, it matters little who decides to quit the marriage first. If you don't do your divorce well, it will come back to haunt you.

The text of this new edition has been changed extensively to reflect more recent statistical information and source material, as well as further insight gained into the divorce process over the years. However, having contacted thousands of women through seminars, lectures, and personal discussion, the experience only reaffirms belief in the basic soundness of our original book.

Divorce is a passage in life that is profoundly intense for everyone connected with it. Many women struggle alone and in silence.

This book reaches out with understanding and advice. Read it with growing certainty that things get better when you wisely take charge of your life.

Lynette Triere
Richard Peacock

CHAPTER 1

The Reality of Divorce

Leaving a marriage is hard. Probably the hardest single thing a woman will do in her lifetime. This is not an idle exaggeration. A sudden or tragic death in the family is a blunt shock and the trauma that results from it may last a long time. But eventually it is attributed to "fate" and is ultimately seen as being out of one's control. The pain of childbirth is consuming, but it is also a natural function of a woman's body and the process has a limited biological time span. However, a woman's decision to leave a marriage—and the act of doing it—is a totally free choice. Fate and biology have nothing to do with it. The final responsibility for her action, despite help and advice she might get from others, is hers alone. No one can sign the legal papers but her. And that sense of being alone in her decision, the reality of it, can be overwhelming.

Other important actions of life provide some guidelines. Certainly there were plenty for getting into marriage. But leaving a relationship is a relatively uncharted and hazardous course that women enter into with little preparation and few forecasts. If the breakup is badly mishandled, through mistakes, lack of knowledge, or misfortune; the pain can last beyond months into years.

Jean-Paul Sartre once said that each man and woman is "condemned to be free," and the truth of that philosophic irony is never more strongly felt than when a woman decides to leave a relationship. When a woman is on the edge of that momentous decision, she may feel both charged by a new range of choices, and imprisoned by the need to make these choices. Freedom, after all, is not a value that women have traditionally been encouraged to experience. Despite some media images of carefree girls romping confidently and effortlessly through a stream of handsome males in gleaming cars, the more accurate reality is that of an unsure and circumspect young woman attempting to find acceptance. In high school, this was found by going with the right boys. Her identity was often tied to the person she was going steady with and that bonding was her passport to social mobility.

This early conditioning for a committed relationship set a pattern for many women. They came to view marriage and motherhood as their ultimate careers. Their role as wife and mother was what principally defined who they were. The threat and opportunity of divorce demands a redefinition for the woman about who she is, what she does. For the first time, in many cases, a woman is faced with the possibility of consciously and freely choosing her destiny. Her training may have made this kind of thinking quite alien.

Naturally, many women don't fall into this pattern. But even for those who resisted the stereotyping of sex roles, women leaving marriages must deal with many of the popular myths of our culture. They can be subtly powerful. The promised magic of what marriage is supposed to bring is presented to us at every turn. Images of young lovers in fields of flowers, of a gay wedding festival, the bride glowing in white innocence and the groom in formal black, the moonlit terrace of a honeymoon hotel, the drive back to a cozy apartment in which begins a lifetime of love and sharing—who would dare destroy the dream? Television, magazines, and Harlequin Romances repeat endless variations on this idyllic theme, and the barrage of messages creates a solid belief system that is almost impossible to resist. And perhaps it's not a question of resistance. Love does spring eternal and all the world's academic social realism will not dispirit two people romantically involved. But they have to be willing to pay for the luxury. The romantic ideal promotes such notions as love being a changeless state of bliss and marriage as having the supernatural grace and power to permanently ensure it.

But the cold truth is that for every two marriages, one will end in divorce. Marriages begun since the late '60's will last an average of seven and one-half years. For many, the initial innocent joy will turn into the sad realization that the two were badly mismatched, that they had mistaken each other, but now they feel unalterably bound in spite of their physical and mental anguish. There seems to be no way out, no clear passage once the fantasy dissolves. This is not to say that relationships cannot and do not survive first disillusionments or later hardships. Indeed many partnerships grow stronger after the gloss of the initial attraction and in the working out of mutual problems. But for many couples it is not a question of finding new solutions to a building list of conflicts. With some women and men, there is a fundamental difference in life goals, ways of communicating, belief systems, rhythms of living, temperament, and concepts of pleasure. Faced with such basic incompatibility, women are now breaking out of their more common conservative roles and have become more frequently the initiators of divorce.

But this realization is usually not an immediate one and the decision to leave is rarely hasty. The very idea of divorce is so radical that some women refuse to even consider it at first. In fact, stages of awareness can be outlined in the average movement of a woman toward leaving a relationship. First, many women report that they only "subconsciously" felt the stirrings to leave, that these feelings would never be articulated even to themselves. A surprising number have said that they harbored the secret for five years or longer before moving to the next stage of privately but deliberately thinking about leaving. These thoughts might take the form of fantasy, the dream of living in another place alone or with another person, the desire to break out into a new style of living, the pursuit of a challenging career, perhaps a passion for travel. This stage can be a consuming one. A few women get stuck at this point and become permanent daydreamers. But most will move on to relate their desires to a close friend, often a sympathetic woman who has experienced a similar situation. They may at this stage seek out a professional therapist to confide in, or take the bolder step of seeing an attorney.

However, the simple outlining of what generally goes on does not begin to afford a guide for what to do when caught in this train of thinking and action. There is hardly a place to look for help. After all, society gives us no models from which to learn leave-taking. There may be an ideal marriage but there is no ideal divorce. Most situation dramas on television do not present the inner conflicts and external problems as they are experienced in the everyday world. When realistic conditions are exposed, they are neatly resolved by the end of the show. Even though there are thousands of couples in every community who have been or are being divorced, there is still no institution in our society that has especially geared itself to deal with this very human problem. Indeed, the stigma of failure is still reinforced at every turn.

The problems that a woman faces in the process of deciding to leave her husband and in the act of getting a divorce are twofold: She must face the reactions of others while coping with her personal emotions and self-questioning. Among the external elements that she will find herself responding to are her family and relatives, her close friends, the community in which she lives. She will also come to grips with the economic realities of her situation. On top of that will be the everyday complexity and confusion of modern life.

Parental expectations, for instance, may be a very important factor when a woman is making her decision to leave her husband. The message that many women grew up with was that they should be "good girls." It's a loaded term. It sets up as moral virtues such culturally taught habits as deferring to others in important decisions, the quiet rewards of self-sacrifice in placing everyone else's needs ahead of their own, and the constant concern with pleasing others. These values run counter to those most needed by a woman deciding her future.

A woman may even find it hard to turn to old friends with her troubles. Divorce is viewed by some people as a kind of infectious disease—it's best to stay away. Married friends see themselves as especially susceptible because the turmoil of a failing marriage may trigger similar but latent conflicts in *their* relationships. The quarantine may be more subtle than total desertion, but still felt in a hundred ways. Conversations will often be less natural, more touchy. There may be a shying away from any "heavy" subject in fear that it might lead into a very personal—and therefore threatening—discussion. Fortunately a woman in this situation does usually find a confidant to share her world, and this outlet can become an extremely valuable, even lifesaving, one for her.

The community is often a stronger critic, and less forgiving. Naturally this depends on the circumstances of where one lives. Certain parts of the country are renowned for their ability to keep people in line. A small town can be a watchdog of what it considers standards of female behavior. Even in a city, most people exist within some subculture and seek out acceptance and approval of others. At the vulnerable point of her life when she is struggling with essential problems of her existence, a community can impose century-old attitudes of how a woman should act and react toward an unhappy marriage. An independent woman is still given the closest scrutiny by everyone around. To be unhappy is one thing; to take the initiative and leave a permanent relationship is quite another. If the community is a tight one, the issues of the divorce may be a daily drama played out for the neighbors. Social acceptance is still a powerful force in a person's thinking.

The economic problems that a woman faces when she decides to leave can at first seem staggering. Whenever there is a divorce, the life-styles of the two partners will be seriously affected. Simply put, two people living apart cannot live as cheaply as two together. Duplication of services and facilities eats up money. If more money isn't earned in some way, a woman will often find herself struggling to maintain the standard of living she may have previously enjoyed. For a woman who spent her days in marriage caring for home and family, it will mean a whole new set of concerns. She will most likely have to find outside employment and this experience is often one for which she is unprepared. Her background and capabilities as they relate to the job market become important. Even if a woman is currently employed, she may find herself rethinking her present job situation in order to bring in a larger income. The time, energy, and preparation this calls for is extensive.

Children, obviously, are an important part of the whole scheme of things. The complications that come from merely trying to support oneself and maintain a healthy family life can be enormous. A woman may find herself arranging a new and complex schedule of daily activities which now may include child care centers, instant dinners, late evening grocery runs, and weekend housecleaning. Added to this may be a range of things the male partner may have handled. These vary greatly from situation to situation but it may mean that a woman must learn the intricacies of the personal financing or the regular repair of the lawn mower. In short, she alone must take on the maintenance of all aspects of her life.

As hard as all of this may be, the greater problems are the internal conflicts by which a woman is torn. By the time a person reaches maturity, and certainly by the time a woman has reached her decision to leave a marriage, the messages of the culture have become part of her conscience. (Even so, it is interesting to note that in 1989, the Catholic Church granted 69 thousand *annulments*.) Yet overall, religion has been very damning toward divorce. Bible passages seem to abound with lessons for women on the importance of female humility and wifely duty. The Sunday morning airways are often filled with males exhorting women to subjugate their earthly desires for passing happiness in favor of fulfillment in a world beyond. The dangers of the wayward woman are repeated with such constancy that these sexist and archaic attitudes are still capable of even infiltrating the consciousness of the nonbeliever.

These and a hundred messages like them are delivered to women from every source of information in our culture. Whether it's the wife in the television coffee advertisements feeling anxious and guilty about not giving her husband the perfect blend, or a high school instructor automatically paying more attention to the boys in a calculus class, the messages transmitted become the emotional and spiritual storehouse from which a woman will draw her opinions and responses in life. In the months during which a woman is strongly considering leaving her mate, she must use every bit of her good sense, reasoning, feeling, intuition, and judgment to answer questions of herself that she may never have faced before. The bombardment is incessant:

"Do I really love him?"
"Did I *ever* love him?"
"What went wrong?"
"What part was my fault?"
"Did I give it a real chance?"
"Is there something I haven't done yet?"
"When I find out what it is, can the marriage work?"
"What if I changed?"
"Can he change?"
"Do I really want him to change?"
"What will this do to the kids?"
"Will they blame me?"
"Can I survive by myself?"
"Can I make enough money?"
"Is this a stage I'm going through?"
"Should I just swallow the suffering and make the best of it?"
"Will I wind up a bag lady?"

There are usually no clear answers, because many women were never prepared to expect such problems and, therefore, are ill-equipped to solve them. At the same time, these questions cannot be avoided.

MARRIAGE PATTERNS

When you walk down the block in your neighborhood, you are confronted with rows of houses or apartments that are impersonal fronts for what goes on inside. From the outside, it all seems so ordinary, calm, and predictable. But if by some miracle you were given psychic powers to pierce the walls, you would most likely find a man and a woman intertwined in a unique and very complex set of behavior patterns that create strong personal bonds. They most probably would be joined by children, possibly a relative, perhaps some animals. This mix of things would complicate the patterns even more. Daily life in any single house would be composed of the blend of each individual's style based on his or her emotional needs, physical characteristics, family history, social and employment pressures, expectations, or simply whatever good or bad happened to them in the last hour. The dynamics of each household form its distinct flavor. No two are quite alike.

And when marriages begin to come apart, each breakup also has a separate style. The infinite variety of elements that have gone into the making of a relationship now become the forces that unravel it. Some couples who have had an orientation toward hard work and financial gain often find themselves burned out and spending months in court fighting about their money; partners who searched out intellectual pursuits in their marriage may nitpick ad nauseam over inconsequential matters; still others who devoted themselves to leisure and recreation now find new playmates. Just keeping track and making sense of the separate threads in the unwinding is a major task. If you or any woman on the block would claim "There's never been a marriage like mine," you'd probably be right.

But you are not alone. There are things about your marriage and divorce that you share in common with other women. Again, if you were to consider that same street in your neighborhood and if you could imagine that by some strange fate every woman on the block decided to leave her marriage, and further, if those women met as a group at the local YWCA, they would find it very natural to break into three groups:

Childless Marriages

Offhand, we tend to view a woman thinking about a divorce in a marriage that has no children as having it easy. Compared to other types of marriages, the issues appear cleaner, more manageable, easier to resolve to one's own benefit. After all, the woman is relatively free of responsibility beyond her own life. She is most often young, and her options are considerable, whether it is getting into a college or training program, seeking out a new relationship, or finding a job for financial security.

Also, the marriages are usually of a shorter duration. A woman married for three months may wake up one morning to the stunning realization that the relationship is "all wrong" and simply want out, rather than drag it on through years of needless hassling. The more common situation, however, is a woman who has been married for three or four years and has slowly come to discover that there is a basic incompatibility between her and her husband. Of course, there are some women without children who have been married for many years. But for all of these women, the issues of the divorce are not complicated by the complex concerns that are built into marriages with children.

However, it's not all that simple. The pain and difficulty of divorce is always a relative thing, and for a woman in the distress of an unhappy marriage, it is of little use to point to more complicated crises and ask her to be thankful. A relationship of any kind has the innate capacity of becoming incredibly wrenching and unacceptable. The emotional strain on a woman in this kind of marriage can be just as personally overwhelming as anything felt by a mother struggling with her issues.

For one thing, a woman in a childless marriage is often young and alone. The beginning of marriage is not only about learning to live with a man but is an experience of life that brings to it a hundred new ways of acting and interacting. Youthful marriages have a way of cutting off a woman from the world that she once knew. The support systems of women friends, parents, and others close to her often become oddly distant as she finds herself tucked into a small apartment in a strange neighborhood. It is new and unknown to her, yet she feels the responsibility for creating the basis for a home and family to come. For some women, it is an isolating experience. Her reliance on her husband for companionship can become exaggerated to the point of seeing him as her essential link to the world, the only reality to be dealt with. It is obviously an unrealistic and potentially volatile situation.

There are not as many variables to be considered in the problems of a marriage without children, and oddly, that's what makes it so hard. The problems that do exist are dealt with in an intensity and tension that offers little release. A woman with children may sometimes find temporary relief in a troubled relationship by simply talking and playing with her kids. To hold a small child can be therapeutic. But many women without children have no place to turn and in frustration turn back into the web of the failing relationship, only to become more enmeshed.

The idea that this divorce may the first in a long and continuous series of unsuccessful relationships is one thing that haunts a young woman wanting to leave. Popular magazines are filled with images of former Hollywood starlets who have gone through eight marriages and who now, at age fifty, simply look tired. The prospect is frightening, but at least they did it with some glamour. However, it's nothing like this divorce. The idea lingers that because a marriage, begun with such youthful hope, didn't work, leaving is the first step in a long, aimless search for the unattainable. It is sad to witness a relatively inexperienced young woman become life-weary at age twenty-five.

Marriages with Children

It could be argued that the biggest decision of a woman's life is not whether to get married, but after she is married, whether to have a child. Marriage puts two people in a house together and demands they interact. If the couple doesn't eventually do it successfully, they can somehow break the agreement and be free. However, the biological bonds of childbearing quickly become, for a woman, spiritual and physical links that never completely dissolve. The concept of having a child may mean many things to a woman, but the reality of it is usually a surprise. Even though she has prepared through many months of pregnancy for the care that the child will demand, until she actually delivers the child she will never really know what it means to be responsible for another human being twenty-four hours a day, week after week, month after month, year after year.

There are obvious joys a woman will experience in having children. They hardly have to be gone into here. For many, the special mother/child relationship is reward enough.

For some, the lure of marriage is essentially that they can have and raise children in a condition of shared joy and responsibility coupled with a sense of security. So that when there is a problem with the marriage, and when that problem seems to be irresolvable, no one is more concerned or more affected than the woman. These days she hardly has to be reminded of the seriousness of the prospect of divorce. She lives every day with the raw reality of her needs surrounding the care of children—the need for food, clean clothes, warm beds, and a safe environment.

The image of a slightly wacko mother in hair curlers who suddenly decides she's "had enough" and, with little thought to anything else, turns off the game show, packs up the kids, and takes off in the car, has little truth in reality. It may be the stuff of a "Saturday Night Live" comic sketch but most women rarely act in that way.

Children so intertwine a man and a woman that, at times, it seems almost impossible to separate all of the conflicting needs. You may be able to fairly split the furniture, the stereo equipment, sell the car, and even work out support payments, but what do you do about the kids? How can the time, the love, and the sheer energy of it all be weighed? The courtrooms of this country quake with the anger and frustration of sincere women and men fighting it out for custody.

Despite this, many women move rather than stay stuck in a life without meaning or at the very least, a life without abuse. Children bring incredible detail into a woman's life and they bring parallel complications to a divorce. But some women rightfully and instinctively know that the best course for them and their children is to break out and start a new life. Whatever difficulties may come to them, it is necessary if life is going to be something better than mechanical motion.

Marriages with Grown Children

There are people who see a scandal in every divorce. The one that is often associated with a woman wanting to break away from a long-term marriage could be stated something like this: "She probably read too many romantic novels and exotic travel brochures. It's a fling."

The idea that a woman, after living with the same man for many years and raising children, would want to substantially change her life is beyond the reach of the imagination of some people. Conventional wisdom says, "Be satisfied. If you think this is bad, what you face out there, *at your age*, is even worse." It is less unusual to hear of a man who, at age thirty-nine or forty-seven, became suddenly disaffected with his life, and in what some call The Middle-Age Crisis, leaves his wife to live in California with his secretary. For a woman to do a similar thing is seen as not only careless and risky, but possibly an act of self-destruction.

The fact is that most women don't leave long-term marriages for such reasons or in that style. They leave because they simply want peace and independence. Divorce is not just an adventure or a search for her last chance at the fountain of youth. That's not to say that women are not alive to life, or strongly sexual persons with natural motivations, but the years of living in serious disharmony and emotional distress with a man have built to an unbearable point.

Again, for most women in these marriages, the decision to leave is not a spur of the moment one. It is not prompted by a phase of life she is "going through." It is usually a much more conscious struggle that has been considered for years—in some cases for ten, fifteen years, or longer. What held most women back was their commitment to their children, and the insecurities that surround that question—namely, "How would I provide for these children as a single mother?"

In discussing this, history cannot be denied. There was a time when women were raised in a generation when certain conservative attitudes dominated the society. Those values went unquestioned by most people. A man was the head of the household; his wife was the anchor of the marriage and held the family together with care and cooking. If, for instance, a woman worked outside the home, it was probably to help buy needed living room furniture or save money for a down payment on something. The idea of a career was beyond the scope of all but the most highly motivated and gifted women, although nursing and school teaching were traditionally proper vocations.

Times have changed. Not only is the neat, assured definition of marriage being questioned, but more broadly, women have reexamined the boundaries of what they have been taught to expect out of life. They realize the need to have a voice. Women are discovering that, in relation to men, they have distinct ways of taking in and understanding the world. Some women may want to independently search for new depths of their sexuality, while others seek a life in another relationship built upon respect, common interests, and love. Women are discarding the tired, old molds that required acceptable behavior at designated ages, and are discovering their own individual time clocks whose accuracy depends on how they feel about themselves. They are learning to express their wants and need no apologies. But most importantly, many have found that their original choice of a partner all those years ago no longer works. After all the books, the therapy, *and* the compromises, their marriage is still intolerable. If it was not wrong at the beginning, it certainly is now.

But because of the duration of the marriage, special problems exist for a woman in this situation. They seem insurmountable at times. The weight of it all is crushing. This is best pointed out by the fact that for every one woman who breaks out of an unhappy long-term marriage, there are many times that number who cannot find the resources, strength, or support to do it.

I am a woman who personally experienced divorce. I left a marriage after nineteen years. The breakup was a harrowing affair. I had to draw upon my knowledge and experience from personal therapy, and being in training as a therapist, in order to help myself survive. Despite whatever help this was in giving me basic emotional security and a sense for problem solving, I made almost every serious mistake a woman can commit when she decides to leave a relationship.

However devastating some of the experiences were for me in the breakup of my marriage, I don't present the story as one that

I believe is unusual in its events or intensity. In my research and consulting since that time, I have encountered innumerable women with stories that are similar, each playing out a variation of the theme of a dying relationship. The description of my feelings is in no way meant to discount the suffering of my ex-husband. But in the final analysis, we are all left having to deal with our own version of reality.

An outline of my marriage history is almost too ordinary. From being the naive winner of several beauty contests at age sixteen, I quietly followed the path most common to girls of that day and got married two years later. During the next nineteen years we lived first in Chicago and later in a rural suburb of that city while raising four boys amidst the joys and hassles of modern family life.

The background and details of the conflicting issues of our marriage are complex and the stuff of another story. What is instructive is the final process of my leaving the marriage.

The idea of leaving was like a low hum that pervaded much of my married life, but I kept it to myself believing, as many women do, that my responsibility to my children and my goal of creating a good home for the family was the most important thing I could achieve. Personal fulfillment was a random item somewhere down the list of things to do. Besides, my husband was a good father and said he loved me. But during the last five years of our marriage, these vague feelings grew to become an almost constant preoccupation. Even then, I wouldn't fully admit my discontent because I didn't trust my sense of what was good for me. Instead, I suggested to him that we go to marriage counseling and group therapy together. Ironically, over the years it proved to be a lifesaver for me, but not for my marriage. The result was that it clarified the differences in our ways of viewing the world and sharply contrasted the ways of conducting our lives. It became quite clear that we were two people going in opposite directions—quite clear to me at least.

I finally came to a point where I could frankly tell him that I felt distant—that in fact I didn't love him. I told him that I wanted a separation. After a heated discussion, he wouldn't agree. My alternative was that we would have a separation within the marriage; that is, we would live together for three months but would not be sexual. It seems strange now but at the time it was the only way that I felt I could get through that period emotionally. At the end of it, we would see if our relationship could be renewed.

My husband didn't seem to take the whole thing seriously. Although we were not physically close, he was unwilling to recognize my deep unhappiness, my call for radical changes in the way he dealt with our finances, my need for increased independence, or my desire for a career. Instead, he suggested that we take a business vacation to Florida. I felt frustrated but I acquiesced. The vacation was pleasant enough and the feeling between us revived somewhat. It was a time without the responsibility of children and Key West was beautiful. But when we came home, old resentments surfaced again, especially in regard to financial mismanagement which had plagued us all along.

I felt permanently stuck, bogged down in a marriage that I realized had not given me happiness for years. At thirty-seven years of age, I was faced with the prospect of having my middle years slip by in a routine that would prove deadly. Physical ailments already had become common for me and I was on my way to developing an ulcer. It was not that I consciously wanted another man. I had been completely faithful for the many years of our marriage. But my increasing interest in psychology, specifically in the area of transactional analysis, had opened a way of looking at life—my life—that I hadn't previously considered. The ideas and experiences that came out of the groups that met weekly presented me with the possibility of real change for the first time. And the newly discovered personal contacts with vital women and men both challenged me and gave me support. I invited my husband to join me in this, but he found it impossible to be committed to it. The concepts were alien to him.

But he must have felt the growing estrangement because a few months after our first trip to Florida, he suggested another, this time with the boys and our camper. We couldn't afford it but as usual that didn't stop us. The trip lasted a month and was a nightmare. The confinement of the camper, given the way he and

I had been getting along, proved too much for me. Ideally, I suppose it was to be a practical lesson in the warm rewards of being a good wife and mother. It was not. He resorted to childlike nagging behavior until I felt like the only adult in the group. I couldn't wait to get home.

I had been scheduled to assist in a four-day group marathon on the day we came back. The contrast of those days that followed could not have been greater. Although I was confined with a group of people again, this time I found sanity. The experience challenged me to make some serious and strong decisions in my life. When I left the group I was very troubled. But even then, it took three restless weeks of fighting with myself. My duties as a mother and the responsibility of managing a small pottery business were no longer diversions.

I finally decided to act. My husband and I had been seeing a marriage counselor and at our next meeting I would tell my decision in her presence. In the office that night, I struggled for the right words. How, after nineteen years of involvement with a person, do you say it's all over? The moment froze. By announcing my decision, I knew that from that time on, my life would be unalterably changed.

"I want a divorce." I said it as firmly as I could. He seemed astonished and disbelieving.

"You just can't do this!" He was very agitated, shaken by the announcement. I remember finding it hard to believe that it came as a total surprise to him. Our marriage had not had normal warmth, companionship, or sexual caring for years. Yet I knew that the concept of divorce was completely foreign to him. He had always given special importance to the role of father. During an emotion-packed discussion he offered to make some of the changes that we had talked about for years. He argued that we should give the situation more time, that after nineteen years he deserved this. He demanded that I give the relationship six more weeks.

"I can't go along with this unless you do!" he said.

I wasn't sure what he meant by that, but at this stage I was still in the frame of mind in which I could be intimidated. On the face of it, it was a reasonable request. But having already gone through years of disappointment, I was inwardly cynical. At his request, I agreed not to tell our children, family, or friends about any of this.

The following weeks dragged by. It was a nightmare for both of us. Foolishly, I didn't plan ahead, and the time evolved in a formless way. I was simply too worn out to seriously try again. We could no longer pretend to be natural with each other. I felt guilty about hurting him and carried the burden of breaking up our family to fulfill my own "selfish needs," as he put it. I searched for a way to make it all easier. It was too late, however, to be a partner with him in marriage, or to give myself to him physically. My hope was that we could make a mutually friendly split, and I felt that it was possible if I just hung in there long enough, didn't act in an overtly hurtful way, and did enough of the "right" things. I had expected his initial anger but thought that the tide would change and we could begin to be accepting and even supportive of our separate futures.

My hope was totally unrealistic. Living in such close contact, things became quite volatile and I found myself dealing with an ever-increasing level of tension. Finally after some weeks of this, I told him that I wanted to go to California for a few days to talk to my parents and my sister who lived there. I needed relief as much as anything.

When I arrived in the coastal village where they lived, I wasn't prepared for the response that I got from my parents. I had naively hoped that they would automatically support me in my decision. Instead they couldn't really believe that my marriage was ending. Like many others, my husband and I had for years put up an image of the all-American couple. When our secret was exposed, my parents were not only surprised but embarrassed. The gap in a generation of values was too great. I was failing to keep my marriage together and their primary message was to stick it out for the children's sake.

Fortunately, my sister gave me a great deal of love and caring. She listened and offered advice. When I was about to leave, she offered to share her home with me and the children if I decided to leave my husband and come out. The idea was appealing but the change was almost too great to contemplate. However, the memories of sitting on a high bluff watching a calm orange sunset over the Pacific at a meditation center in Encinitas stayed with me on the night flight back to Chicago.

When I saw my husband again he immediately wanted to know what I had decided. I thought it was clear and repeated the fact that I wanted a divorce. For some reason, he acted as though he was astonished by the news and couldn't believe that my parents hadn't brought me to my senses. When, after a long time, he finally accepted the intensity of my determination, he asked what I now expected to do. I asked him if he would move out. He flatly refused, saying that if I wanted a divorce I would have to move out. What's more, the children would stay with him.

The blunt proposition stunned me. I had given no thought to arranging another place to live, had little money with which to survive, and was emotionally unprepared to have any thought of giving up my children. My career was not yet established and I had no immediate financial means of taking care of anybody. The whole world was swiftly coming down around me. There were times during the next few days that I thought I was going crazy. The level of hostility increased and there seemed to be no way out. But I held on somehow, finding an inner strength and welcome support from a few close friends.

My husband was finding it harder. He completely broke down. One day in the fury of anger, he demanded that if I indeed wanted a divorce that the children should know—immediately and all at once. We were in the bedroom. He rushed downstairs and called the boys in from playing. In a scene that I won't relate in detail but one which I will never forget, he completely devastated me in front of them. I stood accused and had no recourse but to take it. The situation was so charged that all I could do was to keep some shred of perspective in hopes that the children wouldn't be plunged into even deeper confusion. It was the most hellish time of my life.

The situation continued in varying states of madness for the next eight days. Our home life was completely shattered by the experience. At the end of it, I packed my bags one morning after he had gone to work, drove by school, picked up my two youngest boys, and headed for the airport. My oldest son was no longer living at home. Leaving my second child, Tim, was a heartbreaking decision but I knew he felt that he should stay with his father. And at this point, it was a matter of survival, not just for me but for all of us. The plane took off for California at 11 A.M.

Looking back, there are many things that I would have done differently. In the period that has intervened since my departure, I learned a lot from simply having time to reflect on the experience. But more, I've learned from others. In my early work as director of the Women's Center at Palomar College, in the hundreds of interviews with women at drop-in clinics and battered women's centers, in listening to the experiences of women in my support groups and classes since 1980, in talks with military wives and impromptu conversations held on airplanes, at Christmas parties, or in doctor's waiting rooms, I found an amazing consistency of experiences. There are certain situations in the divorce process that a woman can expect and prepare for. Divorce is not an easy thing. But neither does it have to be a permanently crippling one. The purpose of this book is to provide a guide for a woman at this most crucial time of her life. If a divorce can avoid the many pitfalls that so often mark it, the benefit is to both partners. A smooth transition is obviously better than a difficult one.

This book in no way blindly advocates divorce. Marriage can be a wonderful experience and the problems that periodically arise when two people live together are certainly normal and can, in fact, contribute to a deeper understanding. Life inside or outside of marriage is not smooth. There is no utopia. But every woman— and man—should seek a life that affords maximum fulfillment and meaning. If that can be found in the present relationship, then it is in the best interest of a woman to rediscover her marriage and with her husband find a way to make it work. On the other hand, there is no reason that a woman should be bound for life to a mistaken choice she made at age eighteen, twenty-four, thirty-three, or forty-one. It is an unreasonable principle to uphold.

Divorce should not be taken lightly and few women do. The very nature of this book indicates the gravity of the problem. The book assumes, however, that the reader has already given it serious thought, has made some basic decisions about her life, and now wants some practical and immediate direction.

On the positive side, a divorce may well be a turning point, a time when looked back upon can be seen as the central decision of a lifetime. Sartre's statement about the modern human need to confront the issue of freedom is important for women. There is joy in emancipating oneself. Like many real problems that a woman will face in this difficult period, it is worth it. In a sense, there is no other choice, for to live in the constant state of unhappiness, anxiety, or abuse that some marriages foster is to court both mental and physical illness. Breaking into a different life can be a great source of renewal. Ordinary daily activities take on a different aspect and previously annoying things may become insignificant. As hard as breaking up is, it is sometimes even harder to stay together.

For some, divorce is a symbolic act as well as a practical one, the culmination of a personal revolution. The best primer for women can be found in our country's early political papers. Perhaps a woman should accept as her own the philosophic truism that she is endowed with certain inalienable rights, that among these are life, liberty, and the pursuit of happiness. For many women, the act of leaving is truly a declaration of independence. It was for me.

CHAPTER 2

Indecision

To live, to lie awake
under scarred plaster
while ice is forming over the earth
at an hour when nothing can be done
to further any decision

to know the composing of the thread
inside a spider's body
first atoms of the web
visible tomorrow.

to feel the fiery future
of every match stick in the kitchen

Nothing can be done
but by inches. I write out my life
hour by hour, word by word
gazing into the anger of an old woman on the bus
numbering the striations
of air inside the ice cubes
imagining the existence
of something uncreated
this poem
our lives.

Adrienne Rich, "Incipience"

For a woman distressed in her marriage, the pressure to find an answer to the simply stated question "What should I do?" is magnified in her everyday life in the same way as Adrienne Rich's imagery. The anxiety that breeds from indecision has a way of distorting the most common things. Life does seem to be measured by inches, "hour by hour, word by word." A child's complaint, misplaced keys, a late appointment, a broken appliance, become the stuff of daily disasters. These crises multiply each day. Whereas before such things would be accepted as small misfortunes, they now become recurring symbols of the growing tragedy of your existence. The vicious circle that indecision creates is mentally and physically exhausting. If you hadn't noticed, you're tired a lot lately, even though you haven't done more work than usual.

Indecision, of course, is a part of life. By her choices each day, a woman decides, in big and little ways, the course of her future. Should you push for a vacation at Myrtle Beach or go to the Blue Ridge Mountains; look for a transfer to another department or put up with your present boss a little longer in hopes he will get transferred first; visit your mother on Sunday or spend the day in bed; buy your daughter new shoes or save the money for her overdue dental appointment; buy Crest or Tom's Natural; risk the hassle of asking one of your kids to do the dishes or do them yourself in quiet anger.

Decision making is not necessarily an unpleasant activity. Some answers are self-evident, almost automatic. We move through them effortlessly. Others are enjoyable. If you have the money, it is a pleasure to go shopping and play with all of the possible alternatives.

Obviously, the weightier the question, the more important the decision. And the more important the decision, the greater the chance for indecision. There are no more profound choices that you will make than the ones concerning divorce. The consequences of your action could radically change the course of not only your life, but everyone else's around you. When the reality of that begins to ring home, you need a strength and clarity of purpose that may, until this time, have been untested.

As much as we might like it to be otherwise, not much in life is white or black. If your relationship with your husband had been totally rotten, if everyone you knew agreed with that assessment, if he as a person gave no hint of worth or goodness, if you were totally confident in yourself as a skilled worker and an attractive person, and—yes—if you had plenty of money, indecision would not be a problem.

But we live in a gray world, and we must make choices that refuse easy delineation. Barbara, a woman of thirty-four, was convinced that she no longer loved her husband, but leaving him was not that simple.

> I knew I wasn't happy but I wasn't sure about divorce. So I spent a lot of time each day fantasizing this single life while I busied myself with a job, part-time school, and as a parent, being involved with my husband in the kids' lives. My husband and I didn't get along in many ways. We fought about money—there wasn't enough; we fought about my emerging style of living—I was becoming more independent. We didn't get along philosophically or as lovers. But we were fairly good friends and we were very good parents—we were great with the kids. We did really neat things with them.

What should she do? Barbara felt that she had explored every avenue of reconciliation but was still stuck with a situation that had positive and negative elements, and no clear answer. In fact, she stayed with the relationship through eight years of indecision before finally leaving.

Such a prolonged period of decision making may seem excessive, but it is not uncommon. A good percentage of the women with whom I consult have been struggling with their desire to leave for years. Some people might find it easy to be impatient with their unresolved lives but it is important to recognize their immense struggle in making a decision that matches their experience and ethical values.

Even with the most rational approach, the process of making up one's mind under such stressful conditions is liable to be mind boggling. The normal way of working through indecision is to look for an answer in logical thought. The hope is that if you coolly set forth all the facts and feelings of the problem, think them through, and just follow the lines of your reasoning to their final conclusion, you will reach the right decision. So you try and try, but doubts creep in. Premises that you once blindly accepted have now become suspect. Those things you once took for granted—the goals in life that you were sure would give complete satisfaction—have gradually changed. What starts out to be a search for an answer becomes a requestioning of the very process you are using to get there. The neat and orderly workings of the mind can become a house of distorting mirrors.

So, instead, you turn to your intuition. If only you could open up and become totally sensitive to your inner feelings, a sudden answer would "come." However, the mounting tensions of your life have so exaggerated every emotion that you are at a point where you feel that you can't trust yourself. And your generally heightened emotional response to things around you seems to confirm this. You find yourself less patient, inconsistent, and more prone to crying.

This is not meant to discount the value of either human reasoning or intuition. In the end, it is about all we have to go on. But recognize that whatever process you use in making your decision is vulnerable to the stress and weight that the questions carry. It may be that what worked for you so well in the past—your ability to reason quickly or your special sense of just "knowing" the right path—may not come as easily now.

Immobility

Faced with the dilemma of having to make such a life-altering decision, many women simply sit, frozen in the awesomeness of it all. Movement becomes impossible in the paralysis that indecision brings. The late nights alone in dark thoughts are followed by bleak mornings that promise nothing and afternoons that stretch on endlessly. Some women experience this and move through it. Others become imprisoned by the yes/no/yes/no that swims through the brain.

Fran is a woman who experienced this for long periods. The remembered pain came through as she spoke.

> Most of my indecision, lack of ability to make a decision, was that everything seemed so insurmountable. I had so many things that I was facing, that I couldn't take just one step at a time. I couldn't sort it out well enough to take one step at a time. At that point, I couldn't cope with a spilled bowl of sugar without cracking up, I mean, just coming unglued. The prospect of dealing with where I was going to live, what kind of income I was going to have, was beyond me at that point. The most trivial thing would set me off, the least little thing. And here were all these major decisions. I couldn't make a decision—I couldn't decide if I wanted to go to the grocery or not. I can remember sitting and pondering that kind of trivial thing and . . . well, I didn't know what I wanted. I found myself becoming more and more of a recluse. That way I didn't have to deal with anything.

The imagery is personal but many women, in their own way, experience the horror of a situation that seems to have no exit. Instead, they retreat into themselves.

Escape

And *escape* is the word here. It is the other side of coping. We all have developed certain coping skills for stressful situations. For some it means spending time alone, reading a book, watching television, seeing a friend, going to a therapy session, taking a drink, or just relaxing. At times of extreme stress, however, what had been the means of coping can become ways of escaping. Whatever method you use in dealing with your problems will probably be escalated at this time.

Unfortunately, the most popular form of escape for women over the past forty years has been the abuse of drugs and alcohol. As an example, one woman in my seminar admitted to drinking great quantities of coffee during the day, and taking eight Tylenol tablets nightly as a way to finding relief. Another woman relapsed into a destructive eating disorder, using food to "swallow her feelings." Add to this mix the frequent abuse of alcohol and such illegal drugs as marijuana or cocaine. Kathy's account of this period is becoming a frequently heard story.

> Dick left for work about 7:30 each morning. I would start smoking dope to relieve my depression. I smoked, listened to records, and watched TV. He got home at 6:30. I was stoned all the time. It was a reflection of my state of despair. It's like sleeping too much. Pretty soon you just can't wake up at all. You're just there all the time. . . . That was a horrible situation. I look back and realize that I was truly ill. I was ill for a long time.

It goes without saying that drug abuse has reached epidemic proportions. Ironically, many women are introduced to drugs by the very person they entrust with their health—the doctor. Statistics from The National Council on Alcoholism and Drug Dependency show that physicians prescribe two thirds of all legal drugs to women, and more than one million women are dependent on those drugs. As our former first lady Betty Ford relates from her own drug addiction, "Doctors have a strong tendency to overmedicate women. It is easy, when a woman suffering from stress comes in their office, to write a prescription for a tranquilizer." In a typical situation, a woman in a depressed state goes to her doctor for help. Instead of dealing with the source of the problem, the physician takes thirty seconds to write a prescription in hopes of covering up the problem.

The range of prescription drug abuse is well known. In consultations with Philip A. Sanderson, M.D., with the Del Mar Medical Clinic, and Stephanie Covington, Ph.D., the program designer at the Betty Ford Center, the following drugs were listed as the most often abused: Xanax, Valium, Seconal, Librium, Dalmane, Serax, Restoril, and Halcion. Dr. Sanderson reports:

> Like alcohol, these drugs are a trap. The problem is that you are depressed, so you take Valium and feel better. For half an hour, two hours, four hours . . . you get a good feeling. But all the anti-anxiety

medicines, including alcohol, are *depressants*. When the underlying problem is depression, you get a buzz, and then are more depressed than you were in the first place. So now you need to take it to feel better, and you do feel better for a short period of time. But when you finish, you're more depressed. So you take it again. It just sucks you in.

Continued use of prescription drugs, without vigilant monitoring of dosage and counseling for the underlying causes of stress, is a freeway to abuse. Dr. Covington suggests that "If a woman has been using alcohol and/or drugs to cope, it is important that she get an assessment from a chemical dependency specialist. She may have crossed the line from abuse to addiction. In most cases, a physician will be unable to make this diagnosis."

Drugs seem to afford an immediate getaway in the blind hope that sometime soon things will magically change. In the haze of drugs, decisions won't have to be made, or guilt about leaving will disappear. Tragically, it turns out to be yet another means of self-punishment.

Acknowledging Your Doubts

A woman's awareness of her desire to leave a relationship can be considered as a two-stage process. The first is when she intuitively allows herself to even consider the question of separation as an option in her life; the second stage is when she moves from testing her private thoughts to actively planning, in detail, the many things that must be prepared for in divorce. Often this latter stage will be shared with a close friend.

When was the first time that you let the half-formulated idea "I don't think this is going to work" arise to your consciousness? It was probably a shock—half heresy—when you first said it to yourself. Depending on your cultural and family situation, the very concept may have seemed, in a practical sense, out of the question. Your relationship before this may have been rocky, the hurts cutting deeper, and the confidence of your original commitment weakened, but you saw it as a part of the growing pains of a relationship. Somewhere along the way, those pains became not a sign of growth but of sickness, possibly fatal to the marriage. Still, at this early stage of awareness you may have felt a sense of disloyalty in harboring such secret thoughts yet behaving normally. But the first stirrings made the question a reality.

Jackie was finally divorced after sixteen years of marriage but her first awareness was long before.

> When I first thought about getting out of my marriage, I remember my thoughts weren't very realistic. Sometimes I fantasized that my husband would *die*, and that would solve all my problems. And then I'd get distracted for a couple of months, get busy with other things and wouldn't think about leaving. And then something would happen to remind me how unfulfilling my life was.
>
> The first time I really thought I wanted to leave our relationship was when I was married four or five years. I was about twenty-three years old and I wasn't happy. I was pregnant with our second child at the time; my self-esteem was in the basement. I felt fat and ugly and middle-aged and saw this as how I was going to go through life. I was going to end up a housewife like my mother, or my husband's mother—you know, sitting in the house waiting for everyone to come home. I didn't *want* that. I wanted more but I didn't know how to get it.
>
> I found myself being sexually attracted to men. I watched some of them outside our house repair electrical lines one day. It was shortly after I had the baby and I felt attractive. I used to flirt with them, find excuses to go out and talk to them, or drive by and smile. They didn't think I was "housewifish." I spent hours fantasizing running away to some sunny beach and being free and making love. I'd just fantasize this unreal world every day.
>
> However, I didn't really believe there was any way to get out of our relationship. I didn't know how to do it and I didn't know anyone else who had done it.

In many ways, the dreams are harmless enough, but in Jackie's case seeds were planted that would germinate for years. At this stage, a woman usually sees her unhappiness either as a temporary phase, or fatalistically, her lot in life. And it is often striking how long some women will quietly play with the idea of divorce before they act. That patience and endurance have been culturally encouraged qualities for women is evidenced in their ability to hold on. The long-suffering woman's motto might be, "I may be having troubles, but all things pass."

Religion or other cultural beliefs reinforce this. Joyce, brought up as a devout Catholic, was one of these women.

> The idea of divorce was not viable, but after the fights, it would take a little longer to recover each time. I thought things would work out but they didn't. I guess maybe seven or eight years ago was one of the first times I thought "How can I get out of this mess?" But I immediately thought there was no way.

The later stage—the one on which this book is based—is when you recognize that your present life is intolerable, that something must be done very soon, and you ask yourself, "How am I going to do it?" This is when you begin to investigate the need for emotional support systems, a lawyer, and economic planning.

Jackie, twelve years later, finally acted on what she knew.

> It was about a year and a half before I left. I not only knew I wanted out, I was actively thinking about it—what could I possibly do for a job? How would I manage the house? What kind of life would I have as a single woman? And I spent a *lot* of time thinking about it. At the time I hadn't told anyone, but I made it a point to talk to women who were divorced to see how they managed.

But at this juncture, as your commitment to change becomes real, so do the waverings of a new intensity of indecision. Previously, whatever the pros and cons of your thinking, it was still in the stage of idle speculation. Now, on closer inspection, every action is fraught with difficulty. Nothing seems simple. For every action there are two reactions. If you leave and move to the other side of town, Johnny will lose his newspaper route and there is no public transportation from there to where you work. You want to rent a new place but it has no refrigerator or stove. Life at this time becomes extremely complex.

Vacillation

> I cried when I saw the beginning of *Kramer vs. Kramer* because I
> knew exactly where the lady was, and I knew what it was to feel that
> way. There were times when I felt like instead of having to make
> decisions, I'd rather just . . . kind of . . . let go. It was a gut level type
> of feeling. There were times when I knew that decisions had to be
> made and I didn't want to make them.

Vacillation is indecision in action, in motion. It is the pull of
opposite directions, the grand tug-of-war. Every answer presents
a new problem and any affirmation is immediately slammed down
by a negating argument.

In its most ordinary form, it might go like this. At the height of
your marriage troubles, you spend an evening at the movies with
your husband and it is surprisingly warm and enjoyable. Eating
out afterward reminds you of earlier, more hopeful times in your
relationship. Your silent reaction throughout the night is, "Oh, if
only it could always be like this. Maybe it can." So you gear up to
reinvolve yourself in the dynamics of the relationship in hopes of
salvaging it. But a day later you get into a violent argument that
vividly reminds you of the chasm between both of you, and inwardly you respond with, "How could I possibly want this?! It's
not what I want. I hate it. I hate him." This experience, in its
myriad forms, is one of the most taxing, frustrating, and monoto-
nous things about leaving a relationship. It's like being caught in
some cosmic Ping-Pong game.

And yet it is important to recognize that vacillation is a *process*,
an inevitable and necessary part of leaving. Vacillation is the impact of the past and future on the present. The forces holding
you back are indications of the seriousness of the questions for
you. If the strong pull in either direction won't subside, it means
that attention must be paid to it.

Connie was interviewed at the time when she felt stymied by
the whole process.

> You know, this kind of indecision was actually going on with me for
> the last two years. Hardly a day went by when I didn't think, "Am I

going to get the hell out of here today or am I going to wait until tonight and try to talk to him again?" It was always back to that same thing.

"Yes, I want to go"; "No, I will stay." Every woman goes through this to some degree. It is important to investigate the depth of your feelings in this process. Even though your sanity at times cries out for inner peace and quiet, it is not enough to simply hope the feelings will go away. The process of vacillation is, in a sense, shaking you loose, defining and refining the world as you know it. Despite the pain, in that way it is useful. Eventually it brings out the issues more clearly.

During this time of flux, there is often a strong need to make things right again. If only a few things could be changed, or just patched up, then indecision would give way to conviction. A woman, in her desperate attempt to be free of the quandary, sees the main block as a lack of ingenuity on her part. If she could only hit on that magic formula for marriage.

Peggy felt this strongly:

> I was always thinking I must be mistaken. Maybe if I can just do this or that, things will work out. Maybe if I can just hang on for another year or two and Alex changes his job or gets a raise, or if we do move out of New York or I do have a baby . . . perhaps it will prolong it so I can understand him better. Yeah, if I can hang on for six more months it will get better. So I hung on and on and on, and after I was out of it I thought, "Why did I do that?" But when you're there, you know why you do it—because you haven't exhausted every possible resource yet.

The point is not that there is any intrinsic value in staying around for two more years in a marriage that clearly has no possibility for revival, but that some degree of delay and vacillation at the end of a relationship will simply happen. Expect it.

Also realize that your personal needs regarding how you leave may not make much sense to anyone but yourself. We all have our own ways of dealing with crises. Gail, a mother of two girls, is now out of her marriage. Looking back and reflecting on this period she said:

> I'm feeling so positive now. For such a long time I'd say, "Why didn't I do it sooner?" But you know, I wasn't ready to do it sooner. We all get to that point—the point of no return. It just took me longer to leave than most people. It took me longer to fully realize how the marriage was negatively affecting the kids. For a long time, I thought I was selfish, wanting all those things for me. Wanting attention and love and affection. I kept thinking that was selfish. I should live my life without those things as long as we had a roof over our head and the kids had a dad there all the time. It took me a long time to realize that I couldn't live that way.

The sources of your vacillation reflect the world you live in. The attitudes of your family, friends, church, neighbors, and co-workers are important and greatly influence conviction or hesitancy. Whether or not we are willing to admit it, none of us does well with disapproval. And at this precarious time, we feel especially vulnerable. Often it is the indirect criticism that carries the strongest message.

Kathleen remembers it vividly:

> I was worried about what other people would think because they were going to think I was crazy. I was telling my girlfriend that I was going to have to face everybody coming down on me, because Mike always seemed like the ideal husband.
>
> Then one day my aunt came over and said she heard I was getting a divorce. "Why are you divorcing him? He doesn't beat you, does he? He doesn't cheat on you, does he? Why are you leaving him?"

If Kathleen's husband had beaten her regularly, her aunt would have approved of the divorce. The church would approve the separation if her husband were an unrepentant adulterer; if he spent all the food money on booze, her friends would have understood.

You may feel gravely unfulfilled in your marriage. That concept could be completely foreign to the value system of your family or church as grounds for separation. But the issues of divorce are seldom simple, and the subtleties of your relationship can never be fully explained to an outsider, especially one that may have fundamental values threatened by what he or she hears. No one knows what your life is like but *you*. As the movie title states so directly: *Whose Life Is It Anyway?*

Let yourself know that this stage of leaving is a process, and in it you will experience extremes. Each day may be different. One day you will feel light and airy, the next you will feel like hiding under the covers. This is the way it is going to be for a while, so be accepting and not unduly hard on yourself. Your critical self may call you wishy-washy. It's not that. It is a stretching, a testing of the extremes. And in that, there are things to be discovered, parts of yourself that have been too long dormant and need to be exercised, new ideas that you have until now refused to integrate into your life.

As much as you can, step out of the tension of the situation and seek a discernible and coherent pattern to your life right now, and also a movement. You might feel that because of your indecision, you have become stuck in one place when in fact there has been gradual but steady progress. Where are you compared to last month? What issues were you avoiding that you are now actively dealing with? What parts of your life have you resolved or partially resolved? There may be more positive things happening than you recognize.

The fact that you cannot come up with an easy answer should not surprise you. As one woman put it, "It's kind of like . . . you're going to have moments of doubt and it's going to go against everything you've ever been taught."

Dependency

Sadly, many women have never made an independent decision based solely on what they think and feel. That may be a strong statement to accept, but my experience bears it out. Things are changing, but historically women have not been encouraged, in this culture, to think for themselves. In families, a girl has traditionally been given less independence than a boy, with the result that she is often not completely comfortable without the protection of a father or mother. The role then passes on to the husband. However, somewhere in the process it no longer feels as cozy. And when she finally begins to take charge of her own life, she runs into resistance.

In the family, many women are shut out of a role in making important decisions whether it be *how* money will be invested, where, or for what purpose. Who *really* decides if you need a new car? If the family should move to Boston? If there is enough money for you to start back at night school? When you aren't exercising the power to decide issues that seriously affect your life, then another person is controlling your destiny. Many of the messages women get from our culture quietly encourage that surrender.

It is little wonder that college extension catalogs inevitably include classes titled "Assertiveness for Women," "How to Be Your Own Boss," and such. It is significant that women are now recognizing that in order to overcome 5,000 years of training to be submissive, deferring, and marginalized, they need to rebuild their consciousness.

Historically women have few models to imitate as decision-makers and the ones that were significant in the women's movement have either been quietly neglected in our history books or, like Joan of Arc, burned at the stake at age nineteen. In the professions, apart from primary and secondary school teachers, women make up a notoriously low percentage in jobs that demand decisions. Pages of statistics could be quoted but the following are typical: 8 percent of the engineers in the United States are women; whereas women make up 90 percent of the clerical work force, only 3 percent hold top jobs at the Fortune 500 companies; 20 percent of the lawyers and judges are women. The last figure is interesting because it is this profession that interprets the rules of the game that we must all play. In the 200 years of this country's existence, only now has a woman been seen fit to decide the meaning of a law as a member of the Supreme Court. Who said it isn't a man's world?

But as the opportunities in society continue to open up for women, new roles will follow. It is important right now that you continue—or perhaps begin—on a personal level to know that you have the right and duty to make the important decisions that affect your life and future. Whatever injustices may have befallen you, whatever combination of bad choice and bad luck, the only way that you will find an answer is when you decide to act on your own behalf.

Sometimes It's Easy

To give some balance to this section, it must be noted that some women have little problem with indecision regarding their separation. They may have hassles with finances or getting a good lawyer or finding a new place to live, but they are quite clear that they want to end the present relationship and feel no regrets beyond some very natural sentiments. For these women, when the relationship, as they saw it, came to an end, there was simply no reason to stay on.

In some cases, the situation determined it. The marriage was such a total disappointment that leaving it was just a relief. Whatever leaving meant, it did not conjure up guilt, shame, anxiety, fear, or any other haunting emotion, but was more the discarding of a heavy burden.

Often, however, the woman's individual personality will determine the ease with which she deals with indecision. A woman raised as an independent and self-sufficient person is not as likely to get caught in the mesh of unending inner conflicts.

Stephanie is a woman who had little trouble leaving her relationship. She is a person used to taking care of herself, having lived at a boarding school in Canada when she was growing up. Although the school was heavily authoritarian, survival in it remained a very individual effort. Nobody was going to take care of her, whether it meant protecting her clothes or getting extra food. She had to learn to rely on her own judgments and realized that results were determined by her effort. She was finally well rid of school and after several jobs, moved to the States where she married. After five years, it was clear to her it was not working.

> It really wasn't a matter of indecision. Part of me had been carrying along with the feeling that I was duty-bound to make this relationship work. There was still a little part of me that kept saying, "Gotta try a little bit harder," "Gotta be a better wife," or, "Joe has to be a better husband." I would say to him, "Look, things have got to change," and we would try, but two days later things were the same again. I think it was really a surprise to him when I said, "This is it; this is really *it*."
>
> The breakup was not actually difficult for me; in fact, it went very smoothly in a sense. I mean, it took a long time to be able to say that this is what I wanted, but when I did, by the time I did, there was absolutely no doubt in my mind. My whole being knew it. There was really no thought of going back.

The issues that Stephanie faced in breaking up were simpler than those that most women experience. She had no children, had confidence in herself as a skilled office worker, was twenty-six years old and attractive, and was excited about trying out a new life in the arts. Not all women are so fortunate, and yet we are all better off in terms of our reserve of independent spirit than we give ourselves credit for. The strength and sureness that Stephanie exudes in personal contact is well within reach of all women.

DEALING WITH INDECISION

Only you can make the important decisions about your marriage. It is not the purpose of this chapter to tell you what you should or should not do in that regard. However, the ideas and exercises that follow will ask hard questions. The intention is to stir your thinking and give a fresh perspective so that whatever you decide, it is done with more self-knowledge and conviction. The answers to your problems lie within you. Take this time to seek them out and take them seriously.

Don't try to complete all of the exercises in one sitting or approach them as you would a personality quiz in *People* magazine. Take your time and give each one as much effort as you can. If you are anxious to get on with the book, read the following chapters and return to this section when you are ready.

Certain exercises require you to write things down. The special value of putting a thought on paper is that it then takes on an existence of its own. You can see it, touch it, come back to it, and rethink it. It is the inner self externalized. The work that you put into this will be immediately rewarding in clarifying your feelings to yourself.

Of course, when dealing with indecision, the value of a good therapist cannot be underestimated. That person can give objective assessments, reassurances, and guidance when you may not have anyone else that you trust or can open up to. You might use some of the exercises that follow in conjunction with this therapy.

In addition, group therapy is a way to gain new awareness and knowledge. One of the best resources available to you at this time is contact with other women, particularly women who have been through a breakup, or are going through one now.

What Is Your Real Intention?

The initial thing you must do is to clearly determine your intention. The first question you would want to address is, "Are you really serious about wanting to break off your relationship with your husband and are your actions geared to that end? Or are you just using all of this to shock—in hopes that the threat of divorce will awaken him to the empty state of your relationship?" In the first case, you want *out*; in the second, you want *change*. The two motives are very different and it is essential that you know what you want.

Such confusion may seem naive, but it is very easy to be unclear about this. It's not hard to lose touch with your more subtle and original purpose during this time of high tension, and get lost in its drama.

Many husbands and wives have never learned to communicate their feelings honestly and directly. You may complain bitterly about the constant noise of his power tools when you actually want to ask him to turn them off and spend more time with you. In the opposite manner, you tell him that you really want to finish watching the late TV movie when you mean that you don't want to go to bed together. The process of communication becomes an elaborate game that could use a full-time interpreter.

Finding out your real intention is not as easy as it first sounds. The obvious question a friend might ask you when hearing about your problem is, "Do you still love him?" Be wary. Avoid a prolonged philosophic discussion on *the nature of love*; we all know it's a loaded word. Many feelings are called *love*, and they run the gamut from lusty nights in bed to caring times of sickness to respect for another's talents. (You also *love* your cat, your Boston ferns, your high school sweetheart, and a good rainstorm.)

During this period of indecision, feelings toward your husband may fluctuate. Nostalgia can be a powerful draw and many women find that memories of better times wash over them when they're in doubt. It is often hard not to admit to some kind or degree of love. That's really not the point. As one woman said of her husband, "I love him. I still love him. But it got to be like living with a brother you can't get along with."

The basic question is not whether you love him, it is this: Do you love him in such a way that you want to *live* with him every day? There are many people whom you love or care for strongly, but the act of living in daily contact that intertwines two people in every way is something you only want with someone very, very special. If you choose to test your intentions by asking the question "Do I still love him?" follow it up with another question, "And is this relationship meeting my needs?"

Stephanie, after five years of marriage, put it this way:

> I feel that it took that long for it to surface so that I could deal with it. I was then able to say, "Look, this is it; it's not going to work. There's no way it can, because on an important, deep level, we don't match; we don't have enough."

If you find that you want to be free of your relationship, let yourself know it even though it may not be the time to say it to him.

One more thought: At this point it may be too late for such advice, but the tactic of using divorce as a threat is not recommended when what you really want is a change in the relationship. By using divorce as a scare tactic, you are setting up or continuing a game that will eventually be played back against you. Nobody likes to be fooled and people instinctively recognize insincerity. If you suddenly announce, "I'm splitting—unless you do this, this, and this," the shock may work at first. Your husband's behavior may change drastically for a while as he bargains for time. But when he is put in such a corner, he is stuck either with having to give in to your ultimatum or with taking responsibility for having broken the marriage. Coercion seldom works for long, and, if you weren't being sincere, don't expect to get the results you want. The level of the game just becomes more heightened.

Be as straight as you can be with your partner. But first, know your intentions.

- Write down your definition of marital love. First take your time and think about it for a while. This writing is only for you and it must satisfy only you. After you have finished, set it aside for a while, then go back and reread it. Is there anything you wish to change or add? How does your definition match with your life?
- Time yourself. For two minutes, write down on paper your feelings about your husband. The reason for the short time span is to get down as much as you can in an uncensored manner. When you have finished, study the list. Is there anything to be learned from it? How did you feel as you were writing the positive and negative responses?
- On a wide sheet of paper, divide the page into four columns, and give each column the following titles:
  Column One: "Qualities I Want in a Partner"
  Get in touch with what you want in a partner. Use realistic standards. Movie star qualities are fun in daydreams but are

seldom found walking down the street. Ideally, what do you want in a relationship?

Column Two: "Positive Things in My Present Relationship"
List all of the things you like about your present life. Include everything that means anything to you—financial security, a common love of nature, shared attitudes toward the children, etc.

Column Three: "Negative Things in My Present Relationship"
List everything you dislike, whatever it might be: verbal abuse, little support for your thinking, refusal to help in the house, etc.

Column Four: "Things I Want but I'm Not Getting"
This will be a recording of your unfilled wants. Some of them you may have had earlier in your relationship but are no longer there: good sex, special attention, help with the kids, etc. Can any be negotiated? Put a mark next to the items that you think could be changed within your relationship, perhaps through mutual discussion and effort.

- Go back over Column Three—"Negative Things in My Present Relationship." Circle the items that you think carry some hope for change, if you were to work on them together, preferably with the assistance of a marriage counselor. Put those things on a "Positive Possibilities" list.

If you are or already *have been* working on these in therapy, and to no avail, make note of that too.

Simply study the lists. Compare them. Think about what the chart tells you. Put it in a safe place and go back to it later. Discuss the list in your support group, with a therapist, or a close friend who you can trust to be straight with you.

Be Realistic

Before deciding what you are going to do about your future, take a hard look at the present. What does your daily existence really consist of? After all, the basic question you are presented with in making your decision is whether your present life is working well for you. But part of your indecision is because you can't get a clear perspective on your marriage and life. Being enmeshed in it, it is difficult to see what is going on. Days, weeks, months slip by and it is hard to tell what is happening. Much of your energy is taken up searching for the reasons for your unhappiness.

Strip away, for the moment, all of the reasons that your marriage is in trouble and for the purposes of this section, simply look at what exists in your life. As psychologist William Glasser says, "People often avoid facing their present behavior by emphasizing how they feel rather than what they are doing."

Look at what you *do*. Not what you *hope* to do, *like* to do, have the *potential* to do, not the *reasons* for doing it or the *necessity* of doing it—but look at what your husband and you *do* in your marriage.

As a person, it can be claimed that you *are* what you *do*. You may think that you are a person of good humor, but if you haven't smiled in the past few weeks or had fun, then you're not. You may have the potential for it, but you are not acting in a humorous way.

The same judgment can be applied to a relationship. Get tough and look at the surface reality of your marriage. By surface, I do not mean superficial. We live on the surface of life much of the time. Your house is a certain shape and size, and within it you get up, brush your teeth, supervise the kids at breakfast, leave for work, return, wash clothes, hold conversations, have arguments, mop floors, etc. It could be argued that your life is the total accumulation of these small events. They may be drudgery, or charged with joy, or something in between. When you look at your daily activity, ask yourself: "Who *am* I—who have I become?"

The idea here is not to find fault or initially make judgments but merely to accurately see what you are doing as a person and in a marriage. If your marriage is evidently not working, then that reality should be faced objectively. One of my clients did this and went on to talk about it realistically:

> You've got to let people be themselves. If you happen to be with a
> man who you realize is not going to adapt himself to your needs, or

can't, or either can't or is *unwilling,* you've got to respect that, too. What business do you have tying up the rest of his life? If it's not going to work for you, it's not going to work for him.

Try the following exercise:

- Write down events over the past six months that you would classify as pleasurable. Be specific. These may not be spectacular events—even small activities can be very special if you enjoyed them. How many of them were done with your husband? How many without him?
- Write down specific unpleasant experiences during the past six months. Which of them involved your husband?
- Think about what happened in your life yesterday. Write down, hour by hour, what you did during the day and evening. Don't skip over small details; they are *the reality of your existence.* Read about your day. Do you want to do what you are doing? How can you change it?

Be Patient

The advice to "be patient" may be almost unwelcome at this time. Because of the constant stress, everything seems to have an urgency, and the impulse is to get things decided and over with one way or the other. Patience is hard to summon up in a situation marked by sudden fights, unpredictable behavior, simmering emotions, and general uncertainty. But I will repeat the advice: Be patient.

Chances are that the situation you find yourself in did not happen overnight. The grievances have been a long time coming. Don't try to solve everything at once. When a woman begins to acknowledge that she wants to leave her relationship, she often feels that she should be able to resolve everything immediately and make a final decision. If it doesn't happen so easily, she criticizes herself for being slack.

But because of the nature of this particular decision, don't add to the pressure by feeling the need to rush on. It is OK to take your time. It also makes sense. The idea of actually leaving is still new and with the number of very practical things to be considered, it is unrealistic to expect that you will be perfectly clear about what you want. You have enough pressure in your life as it is. Don't be hard on yourself.

Diana, a woman with four children and much on her mind, worked through it in this way:

> I used the period of indecision as a way to buy time until I worked some things out. I don't think I consciously said to myself this was happening. But I used to wonder about living alone and how that would feel. Now *that* was an unacceptable thought. But I know that it was a way for me to get used to the idea. I must have been preparing myself without knowing it. So you could say my indecision bought me some guilt-free time to work through some of my problems.

It is good to nurture yourself by taking time at this point. You may have lived for years in a poor relationship, and although you might feel like you've "had it," do not force your decisions and risk making some rather disastrous mistakes.

One version of this is what I call "looking for the straw that broke the camel's back." A woman leaving a relationship wants a good reason. The better and more visible the reason, the easier it is to leave. If your husband is already doing something overtly abusive or hurtful, you don't need to find a reason; he has provided it. But if your grievances are bound up in the accumulation of a hundred less significant events and interactions, it becomes more difficult for you to justify your leaving. To satisfy yourself and the imagined judgments of others, you need concrete reasons that are "good enough" to leave. A tabulation system is started, a mental listing of all the things he is and isn't doing. This is normal—a part of the process of letting yourself know how you feel.

Many people have a private agenda of grievances toward their partner that has been stored away for years and never fully exposed. At this time when you are looking for justification for deciding to leave, it is tempting to lie in the bushes and wait. The inner dialog goes something like this: "If he does *that* one more time, I'm leaving."

But some of us feel we need more than that—a "biggie," that one last incident that will certify forever the rightness of our decision. Sometimes we don't even have to look for it. The scenarios are well-known: He drives home drunk once more, but this time is arrested by the police and booked; or he loses most of his paycheck in a card game with the boys; or he beats one of the children; or he stays out all night and you know he's with the woman from work. Incidents like these are often the final straw and any action that follows from them seems justified.

Some women, under stress and impatient, will *create* an incident. Initiating a fight is most common. At times, it may even mean prodding him to violence, or it may take the form of the woman having an affair with another man and doing it so blatantly as to be easily discovered. These situations show their extreme need for a reason to leave that is acceptable. In the turmoil, the last straw is finally broken.

A warning: Although such drastic measures have their peculiar usefulness, it is unwise to seek them. If your marriage is not working, it is not necessary to bring the issues to a head in some near-tragic conflict. The troubled state of your relationship speaks for itself. The source of your problems is not in the isolated incident, no matter how dramatic it is, but rather in the entire landscape of your relationship. You have legitimate human needs that are not being respected or even acknowledged in this marriage. You are totally justified in using that as the reason for your desire to leave. Some fights are inevitable. It is what people do to initiate distance. But don't press them. It can be dangerous.

There is a solution to your problems, even if you don't know what that might be at this time. Focus on that solution. It's out there, so to speak. If you decide that you want to break off your relationship, there is much to do. Conserve your energy for times and events that are more productive. The next two items will help you understand and deal with your feelings.

- Analyze the *content* of your last argument with your husband. What was it really about? What was your part in either initiating it or keeping it going? Did something good come of it or was it a further drain on your energy?
- A cause of impatience is the feeling of unrelieved pressure. Give yourself ways for healthy escape. Do something that you have always found to be fun. Take time each day to read an absorbing novel. It can literally take you out of your small world. Be physical. A thirty-minute aerobic workout, jogging, yoga are excellent ways to relieve tension. A later chapter is devoted to this.

Continue to Make Small Decisions

Facing the life-altering decision of divorce, some women slip into literally doing nothing. As described earlier, the classic picture is of a weary woman in a robe, drinking coffee and passively watching her house fill up with the junk of her life as the world comes apart around her. The simplest tasks take on momentous proportions and most things seem to be either bewildering or just not worth the effort. Depression fogs any decision making, and lethargy immobilizes the woman. Even the ordinary and necessary choice that make up everyday life—from grocery shopping to visiting a sick friend—are put off. This may be an extreme description, but most women are affected by some form of it.

It is essential that you do not ignore the small things that keep life going smoothly, that elemental kind of caretaking that assures some order. Because of the nature of the present situation, it is hard to resist that distorting inner voice that says, "Most decisions I ever made turned out badly." And because of your present trials your confidence is very low resulting in the fear that any choice will be the wrong one. However, if you don't feel capable of making decisions on the larger issues that confront you, don't stop making the lesser decisions. This, in itself, is a continuing affirmation of your ability to take charge of your life.

In a sense, life demands a hundred decisions each day. No one of them has earthshaking consequences, but if they are ignored, you soon find yourself buried in what seems to be meaningless detail. It may sound ludicrous, but if you can't, for the moment, tell your husband what you want for your future, you can at least decide to pay a bill, see a friend after work, go to the hairdresser, wash clothes, or write the paper for that night class you are taking. Some of these tasks may be part of the drudgery of your life, but looked at in another way, they are simple things that can be accomplished with some small satisfaction. Not only is your mind working but your body is active. Movement is important, even routine movement.

When your thoughts are continually being drawn toward the anxiety of the future, as they tend to be in this period, choose activities that focus you in the "here and now." If you have a job, for instance, it is important to stay competent. The world goes on—let yourself be part of it. Try the following exercises:

- In the morning, make a list of things you want to do that day. Choose the day's tasks and realize that you are making decisions that will create your particular schedule. Plan ahead how they will be accomplished. Don't be self-defeating by listing an impossible number of things to do. Be good to yourself. The idea here is to win.
- Choose one small thing each day that you normally wouldn't do, but could with a reasonable effort. It may be going through your clothes and taking stock, or simply taking time to appreciate something beautiful in the world around you—some artwork in a store window on the way to work or flowers in a garden you pass. The emphasis is on regularly expanding your interest, breaking out of your routine. Relish in each accomplishment.

Use Your Time Positively

This period can be very productive. Because it is a period of change and you find yourself thinking and acting in ways that may be new, take advantage of it and get into some activities that have always held your curiosity or that have challenged you, but that you have never taken time to investigate. In doing this, you are creating an interest outside of your marriage and the rewards are twofold: It gets your mind off your troubles at a time when you need to regularly, and it rejuvenates your spirit by involving you in things you like.

A client of mine was at the impasse of not knowing what to do about the future of her marriage and it was affecting every part of her life. After a few consultations, she came back several weeks later and from the moment she walked in the office, the change was apparent. She had enrolled in a ballet class, a computer technology course, and an acting workshop.

> Me, the person who couldn't get up and talk in front of anybody: I figured as long as I'm going to be changing myself, I might as well go all the way.
>
> You wouldn't believe what a difference all this has made. I feel funny saying it, but I'm happy. It wasn't like that the last time you saw me. My whole life is different. I get up in the morning and I have something to look forward to. I pick up the house, send the kids out the door, and I'm off to school. My day is filled from beginning to end. At night, I even have homework sometimes.
>
> I really feel good about myself. I still don't know what I'm going to do, but I'm enjoying life in the meantime.

The object is to stay active so that when hard decisions are to be made, you are alive and ready to respond. Try this:

● Pick some activity that you always were interested in and do it. Don't make the excuse that you haven't time. See it as a survival technique. Ideally, do something that takes you outside the house and is both physically and creatively rewarding. For some, this will mean returning to school for a degree or accreditation. Most high schools offer adult education classes for a nominal cost. Colleges have a variety of career-oriented classes offered at different times during the day and evening. By signing up for something, you will be making it a mandatory date on your weekly calendar.

For working mothers, such suggestions are pure luxury. They only wish that they had some free time to do *the necessities*. Their day consists of putting in eight hours at work, then tending to the chores of life that never cease. There is a car to be serviced, plants to be watered, cooking, laundry, doctor appointments, cleaning, shopping, bills to pay. And because of the care children require, multiply those tasks by some number and add overseeing homework, taxi services, baths, and bedtime. In general, it's being responsible for all human life around you. As one woman put it: "Now we get the jobs all right, *all* the jobs—at home, with the kids, and at work." For a woman in the throes of indecision, she doesn't need to find something to do with this schedule.

In that case, move to "Plan B"—slow down. Seriously, your sanity is your strength. In this case, using your time positively means taking time from the nonstop rush of life to center yourself in your body. An overcrowded personal schedule can be maintained only so long, and then something gives, either your mental balance or your physical health. Both are essential to you at this time of your life. This exercise could help:

- Wake up fifteen minutes earlier, before everyone else, and give that time to yourself. It is essential to give yourself a quiet time each day. Use it to do meditative breathing, yoga, stretching, or some other form of a relaxation exercise. Rather than an extra burden, you will find it invigorating and it will clear your head. Some of you will want the time to simply read the morning paper, undisturbed, with your coffee. Other options are to take a pleasant walk on your lunch hour, or as one woman sharing her best-kept secret suggests—delay your homecoming by thirty minutes and do something for yourself.

Get in Touch with Other Women

There is a bit of the martyr in everyone. When a woman isolates herself from others, refuses to share her problems (or doesn't know how), and chooses to go it alone through this period, she may be satisfying an inner need but she is also making life harder than it has to be. Don't hesitate to look for help. It can come in many forms: the warm and concerned understanding of a woman friend, a new awareness gained from reading, or energy derived from an organization of women.

The voice of another woman who has successfully gone through the process that you are now caught up in can be very valuable to you. You will want to seek out someone who cares for you as a person but is willing to be honest and frank. Your instinct will find the right one. Peggy recounts her appreciation of a friend at this time.

> During the last two months, my woman friend from next door told me a little bit about her divorce. She was very reassuring and supportive. She'd say, "Hey, I know. I support you and it's OK." And I knew with just two people (another woman had helped me), it was going to be all right. I doubt if I would have had the strength, alone. Then my friend said, "Look, it's going to be rough for a while, but hang in there; it'll work out."

Naturally, this calls for an openness on your part at a time when you are feeling vulnerable. Trust that newfound friendships with other women can be a generating force, not only to carry you through this period but for the rest of your life.

Often women, by the nature of their activities, become isolated from the world and see life from a very narrow angle. The culture itself has not, until recently, encouraged them to broaden themselves. Even working women may not have contact with a significant number of people with different viewpoints (or time to talk to them). For women at home, it is more limited.

Part of what would help you right now is information about new ways of looking at old material. A fast way of gaining it is through reading women authors in magazines and books. Not all of them have something to say, unfortunately, and some merely apply a more feminine version to staid male wisdom. But in the last decade, great numbers of women with something of their own to give have found many more publications open to them. It used to be that women's magazines treated women only as consumers of cake mix and hair tint, while gently chiding or teasing them with half-baked ideas on extramarital affairs, or lessons on how to be the perfect mother. Many still continue in this same tradition. But certain women's magazines are fruitful sources for getting in touch with new attitudes toward marriage and female independence.

Certainly since the 1960s, women have been active in organizing themselves into groups to both raise their consciousness and effect change. They learned that there is strength and power in numbers and they rediscovered what earlier women's movements knew. Men, of course, have known it all along and continue to try to frustrate women by ridiculing their attempts to organize and hence direct their own lives. You may find the following suggestions helpful:

- Do some feminist reading. If you haven't done any before, forget the negative propaganda and pick up some literature. *Ms.* magazine is still the most popular voice of the women's movement, but also check out *Feminist Issues; Heresies: A Feminist Publication on Art and Politics; Signs; Women and Work; Women's Review of Books.*
- Read a book by a woman known for her insight into female consciousness. Simone de Beauvoir's *The Second Sex* is the bible, but also look into the work of Mary Field Belenky; Bonnie Anderson and Judith Zinsser; Jean Shinoda Bolen; Paula Caplan; Andrea Dworkin; Betty Friedan; Susan Forward; Carol Gilligan; Barbara Ehrenreich; Emily Hancock; Natalie Rogers; Adrienne Rich and Barbara Walker.
- Attend a meeting of an organization dedicated to women's issues. Overcome the fear that these are "radical feminists," as the nightly news would describe them, but women with the desire to take control of their own lives, and improve the quality of life for women. You have something in common with them. Check out: The National Organization for Women (NOW); Women for Change, San Diego; American Association of Uni-

versity Women (AAUW); and the meetings and seminars sponsored by college women's centers or local feminist bookstores.

Check Your Early Messages

> Woman is determined not by her hormones or by mysterious instincts, but by the manner in which her body and her relationship to the world are modified through the action of others than herself.
> Simone de Beauvoir, *The Second Sex*

About now, a woman might justifiably complain, "How did I get into this mess . . . and how do I get out of it?" Perhaps a place to start is by questioning the very way you have been shaped to respond to the world around you. Your past is always intruding on your present. As a woman, you are a storehouse of past messages that were given to you in early childhood and which you now use in a modified but still detectable form to make the decisions of your life.

From the moment you were born, and before, you have been a highly refined sensor of the world around you. A baby in a crib is like a finely turned radar receptor that is continually scanning its environment, picking up every signal that is out there, from the taste of the mother's milk to a noise outside the window to the texture and warmth of the blanket. Some of the messages it receives from the parents are intended, others are picked up as naturally as one breathes. A baby may hear the soft words of love but also feel the impatient way in which she is being carried. Both messages are recorded.

Later, parents and other teachers will quite consciously and emphatically tell a child what they want it to know, especially as the young girl gains some facility with language. As the child grows, she learns to cope with her world by incorporating these messages into the groundwork of her very person, and in doing so, creates a script, or blueprint, for living out life.

The early messages that you received from your parents are relevant to your present situation. You may find that not only did these messages get you where you are today—in a marriage that isn't working—but that they are keeping you stuck in a marriage that you do not want. Without some insight into the nature of your belief system and the way it was formed, you are likely to be controlled by it, not only in the present but throughout your future.

The concept of life scripts can only be given the briefest summary here. Eric Berne, and others in the school of Transactional Analysis, developed the theory at length, but perhaps some idea of it can be had from the thoughts of Claude M. Steiner, in his book *Scripts People Live*. He feels that Greek tragedy holds a never-ending fascination because it plays out deep-rooted truths about human nature. Typically, the leading characters in these plays act out their lives with behavior based on their personal ethical codes. The heroes and heroines of Greek drama are thoroughly consistent throughout the story; in fact, they seem almost predestined. From the early moments of the play, we can almost predict how they will act in any set of circumstances. So, too, with us.

We are influenced, and in some ways controlled, by the messages we received about ourselves when we were young. Often we are not even aware where our learning came from or what it's about. In a direct form, it came by way of explicit praise, criticism, demands, and expectations. You created your response to the world by overhearing your parents' comments about what they saw on the television news, by what your father said after a piano recital, with your mother's reaction to a wet bed, in why they wanted the door to their bedroom closed, and so on. But the messages also came in even more subtle ways: how your parents looked at you when you cried, the fact that your mother was always in the kitchen, the silence when Dad would come home late from work, the attention your baby sister always got from everyone who walked in the house. Some were messages of acceptance, others were messages of disapproval, neglect, coldness, or warmth. Some negative, some positive. Some messages were as intense as a father's burst of anger when you spilled ice cream in the car, or as mild as when he picked you up after you fell off your bike.

The way in which these early messages became structured into a belief system is unique to each person. It is not simply what came in but also the way that you decided to play it out. That became the ongoing drama of your everyday life.

If you feel blocked by a set of beliefs that are deeply ingrained but somehow don't make sense any longer, think of them as messages given to you by others when you had no way of resisting them. They are imprinted deeply but they can be changed. If a message cannot be completely unlearned, at least new learning can challenge it. Dorothy Jongeward and Dru Scott, in their excellent book *Women as Winners*, put it this way:

> When a woman becomes aware of the negative or destructive elements in the messages she has been programmed to follow, she realizes that she has options. If she chooses, she begins to examine these messages for what they are: ideas recorded in her brain most likely before her eighth year. She no longer limits her growth to bend to the boundaries set by collective pressures. Instead, she recognizes that *many of life's miseries are optional.*
>
> Just as a little girl can make early decisions that affect the blueprint of her life, a woman can make a *redecision* to change her life's direction in a positive way. She can help the little girl inside her choose to be a winner. Women with insight can learn to write their own "happy ending"—happy endings that in reality might actually come true.

It is useful to know the early messages you received and are still carrying around in your head. These may be influencing and prolonging your state of indecision. As you respond to the words and ideas in this exercise, don't be concerned if you are feeling right or wrong, or childlike.

- Write down your first reactions to the following:
  Women living alone
  Marriage
  Doing what I want
  Being a mother
  My ability to make decisions
  Divorce

Children
A mom who works
Women who never got married
Husbands
Divorcées
My ability to take care of myself

Do you get a better feel for your belief system? In what way is it a help to you? In what way is it a hindrance right now? Consider discarding the old messages that do not help you, and replace them with ones that make sense.

You Do Have Options

There is nothing worse than feeling trapped, whether it is being trapped in a marriage, or locked into the state of indecision. An inner terror builds as the world becomes an either/or conflict.

Many people have conditioned themselves to seeing life in terms of an either/or dilemma. In this kind of thinking, existence splits itself neatly into two parts—good and bad, right and wrong, them and us, black and white, beautiful and ugly. It is a seemingly simple approach to life. The problem is thinking exclusively in these terms. There is a built-in tension in the conflict of opposites. There may be occasions when you have only two choices, but they are rare.

The pressure we put on ourselves—and it is *our own* creation—can be eased if we think in terms of options. By that I mean we have more than two alternatives. As Paul Simon says, "There are fifty ways to leave your lover." It's true. There are many ways to respond to any given problem. Not every answer is desirable, some will work better than others, but we often have more choices than we allow ourselves to admit.

In the process of your divorce, your car breaks down. You need it for the new job that you are hoping to get. The immediate reaction is to spend $400 which you don't have, or go without it. But you could consider *all* the options. You could borrow a car from a friend for a few days to see about the job; or you could go to a bank and check on a loan; trade it in as is on a less expensive, older car; rent a car for a day; buy a repair manual and see if you can fix it yourself; take it to a high school or college where they teach car repair and see if they'll work on it; or barter some services with a friend who works on cars. The list of options can go on and on. Some are not always feasible, but the fact is you may have more choices than you first believed.

Many of the situations that come up in divorce present themselves as either/or dilemmas. Even the act of leaving seems to be that—either I stay or I go. But there are many ways to go and a variety of ways to envision your relationship for the future. Some of them might be idealistic, some unworkable, but there is a range of human behavior that falls between "this way or that way."

The very act of figuring out your options will help you define what you want. A client I recently saw complained of not being able to decide what to do about her marriage situation, but as I enumerated a number of solutions, she immediately rejected each one. It soon became clear: She wasn't looking for a solution.

The options you accept and the ones you reject can tell you something about what you want or are willing to accept.

A friend and former therapist/teacher of mine, Lucie King, used to require all of her clients and students to list at least three options to any problem we had. After, in a group, we would discuss what we had written and others would add to the list. The number of options was sometimes astonishing.

- State a problem of yours that calls for a solution. List all the options you can think of, even the ones you don't like. Check with some friends to see if they can come up with others. Brainstorming is a productive activity. Give this exercise some time.
- Divide a piece of paper into five columns. Title the columns with the following headings:
  Options
  Advantages
  Disadvantages
  Possible Outcome
  Payoffs

Choose a particular problem and list all the options you can come up with. Fill in the other columns. (Payoffs are not necessarily positive.)

PLEASURE

. . . the foundation of a joyful life is the pleasure we feel in our bodies, and that without this bodily pleasure of aliveness, living becomes the grim necessity of survival from which the threat of tragedy is never absent.

—Alexander Lowen

The nature of pleasure and what it means to you may be a key in helping you decide about your present relationship. An understanding of pleasure—how you seek it out and how you experience it—is a way of determining the state of your marriage. Of course, if you are looking for some kind of official certification of the rightness of your decision, it will never come. However, this much can be said: Good relationships are created by people who seek pleasure in the same ways.

Although it is commonly said that human beings desire pleasure and avoid pain, our daily experiences do not seem to bear it out. In the lives of so many of us, pain is the prevailing force. In fact, the very word "pleasure" makes some people shrink away. It conjures up ideas of unbridled excess, wild hedonism, irresponsibility, gross self-indulgence, and worse. It is hard to explain the uneasiness with which people handle pleasure. For some, pleasure can be tasted only on occasion, like a very rich dessert.

We are not nearly so cautious with pain. Not only do we manage to find ways to administer it to others and bring it on ourselves, we call the suffering "noble." We must have learned such lessons very early in life. The place to begin, as always, is with yourself. Perhaps you are out of touch with a natural attraction to pleasure because you are out of touch with your body. If your marriage hasn't been working, chances are that you have buried many of your pleasure needs. When you are keenly tuned to the wants and needs of your body, pleasure is its natural and legitimate goal.

There is no more reason to justify your desire for pleasure than there is your wish to avoid pain. A harmony exists.

But many people have only a dim awareness of their needs regarding pleasure. They join in marriage with the blind hope that the confusion will disappear or be resolved. For some it does, but for others the struggle is compounded. They hope the difficulties and differences will take care of themselves later. But often the novelty wears thin, and even though friends may be complimenting them on what a wonderful couple they are, they do not find satisfaction in each other.

The question can be asked simply: Is your relationship giving you pleasure?

Avra Kaufman, sex therapist and marriage counselor, suggests that you look for the answer in a special way.

> It's really intuitive. Talk openly with your partner about what gives both of you pleasure, and while you're doing that, check out what your body is telling you. How do you feel about what he is saying? Are you in harmony with it? Are you saying, "I think I can make myself adapt. He likes tennis. OK. Tennis doesn't turn me on, but I can make myself do it." It may work for tennis but it won't for your more basic pleasure needs.
>
> Listen to yourself. Either you get a feeling of delight, either you start to get turned on when he talks about his pleasure, or you don't. You may get it in a moderate amount, but the degree that two people get excited in a deeply felt way as they talk is the degree they connect. They act as a kind of tuning fork for each other, responding almost physically.
>
> Pleasure is like a fingerprint. Your pleasure propensity, or inclination, doesn't really change much in life. The degree that you may need pleasure to be comfortable, to feel adequate, is different from other people. Some people can get a little bit of pleasure from their work and find that's enough. Others need much more to think life is worth living.

Marriages that aren't working take their toll physically and spiritually. Ones that do work are wonderful. Stephanie spoke of her current relationship.

We take pleasure in the same kind of things. Not just physical things—a movie for instance—but in the way we *see* things. You know, if we sit down in a park and watch people go by, we'll pick out the same kind of things we enjoy about someone. "God, look at that person, look at the tilt of his hat." It's like we have a similar kind of lens we see the world with, and that *is* pleasure, because we are truly enjoying. It's so wonderful to know you are enjoying the same thing—you're not isolated. There are a lot of differences, too; we're not identical.

But we look for pleasure in the same way. We have similar tastes in music. I can put on something that I'm turned on to and, although Michael has a very trained ear in music, he'll love it. And he'll do the same for me.

It's wonderful. I never had this in a relationship before. I don't have to give up anything for the relationship. To have someone who is all of a sudden by my side while I'm doing something, and really seeing what I'm doing—that's really neat. I think that's probably the greatest thing in our relationship.

You don't have to live a life of self-denial. There is no reward for it. If you are not and have not been happy, look hard at your life and ask yourself if you truly believe that a joyous physical and spiritual communion is now possible in your present relationship. And freely use the concept of pleasure as a guide. A great teacher, Stanley Keleman, says of it in *Sexuality, Self and Survival*:

> Pleasure is not only gratification, it is not only satisfaction. Pleasure is also peaceable, the establishment of complementary aspects in life. . . . It is more a *unitary* movement toward contact, self-expression, toward becoming who we are. Being who we are is pleasurable; self-evaluation is pleasurable. It is the root of joy.

WHAT IF YOU DECIDE TO STAY?

If options are to mean anything, then the option of staying in your present relationship is real and should be considered. But the purpose of this book is not to study ways of reestablishing a relationship that is in trouble, as worthy as that effort may be. In fact, the following chapters assume that the woman reading them has chosen to be free of her present relationship. However, some thoughts about staying in your marriage are appropriate here.

If you decide to stay, it will take more than a sigh of relief and saying to yourself, "OK, let's get on with it." Problems usually don't just disappear. If your relationship has not been working, it has suffered from neglect in some way. Now you both must be ready to take radical steps to change it. Just as you *do* a job, both of you have to *do* your relationship. It will not take care of itself; it hasn't in the past. Whereas your intention may be good, the question remains if you have the renewed and sustaining energy to stay with it.

The changes that are called for have to be mutually agreed upon. One problem for some women who have gained a new consciousness is they begin to think and act differently, changing their attitudes and roles without ever discussing with their husbands what has gone on. In defense of the husband, he is bewildered and dismisses it as a phase she is passing through. The woman then resents him for being insensitive to her new but unspoken desires and goals.

I would suggest that if you decide to stay, you address directly the future of your marriage, saying something like, "I am no longer willing to continue our marriage the way it has been." The idea of renegotiating your marriage contract should be considered. After all, the old agreement doesn't seem to be doing it anymore. Your marriage started with certain stated ideas and agreements, as well as a list of assumptions about roles and responsibilities. Somewhere along the line you didn't find it satisfying. Rather than have your new relationship be your idea, to which your mate must agree or disagree, a more workable approach is to suggest he has choices, too. Ask him if he will think about what he wants. Be sure to know what you want.

A renegotiated marriage contract may sound attractive but it is not easy. You have a history with a man in which the patterns of behavior together are well established. Although your husband may accept the idea of change, and actually have some enthusiasm for it, watch out. Real change demands an ongoing commitment.

That means that next month and next year you will be acting differently toward each other. And surprisingly, you might find that *your* resistance to change is as great as his.

William Glasser observes:

> No husband can change a wife's behavior without altering his own; no wife can change a husband's behavior by disregarding her own. Each must change their own behavior. . . . Even in a case in which a husband is all wrong and his wife is behaving responsibly, she probably must change her behavior in some way to break the ice and motivate her husband to change his behavior.

You may find this difficult to do. If you have been used to seeing the cause of your unhappiness as being your husband's behavior, the idea of changing yours may seem unfair.

The process needs a neutral third person, preferably a marriage counselor. It is necessary to come to agreements in a frank, dispassionate way. Beyond coming together in this new understanding, the couple must bury old resentments. Letting go of the past, when it has to be done mutually, is very hard and often impossible for many people.

INDECISION AS AN OPPORTUNITY

Sometimes it is good to stand a thing on its head. You see it differently. The indecision you feel may be frightening, maddening, or wearisome. But if you turn it upside down, it can be seen as a tremendous opportunity. When everything that once made you secure is now in suspension, you have a unique chance to approach life in an innovative way. Literally, *anything* is possible.

I know that as you read this, one reaction is, "Yes, but . . ." Wait. Give yourself permission to let the idea play on your mind. You have the rare opportunity to take charge of your life and go in one of a hundred directions. It may be the first time in a long while you have had that chance. Certainly we are all earthbound and our daily lives won't let us forget it for long. But during this period, open yourself up to the excitement of life and know that there is the very real possibility of a truly fresh existence.

CHAPTER 3

Emotional Problems

Coming to grips with your emotional response to everything that is happening in your life right now is the first step toward freedom. The reason for devoting a chapter to the subject is not to wallow in the thick melodrama that is apt to be affecting your existence lately. An exaggerated focus on guilt, anger, fears, and depression could do nothing more than make them the dark reward for suffering. That's not it. The reason for dealing with emotions is that they are *there*, and they will continually control you unless you face them squarely.

Alan Watts used to say that whatever you are fearing is like a huge brush fire that whips across a field. It is terrifying to face the wall of flames, and one's first reaction is to run from it. That's a mistake. By doing so, the flames will quickly envelop you in their rage. What firefighters have learned is that when you are confronted with such a fire, run straight toward it, through it, into the burned-out area behind. So, too, with our fears. They seem formidable, a wall whose thickness we imagine is unending. But it is all a front, so to speak. Don't run from them; face them. And go right through. Most of what we fear is an illusion, the work of our minds. The substance is quite thin.

In the divorce process, confronting and dealing with the emotional turmoil you are experiencing is a very practical matter. It is not something done out of a matter of principle. The fact is that if you don't work through the deep and conflicting feelings that you are having, the whole divorce process will be unnecessarily difficult. Guilt, anger, fear, and sadness affect the outcome of each stage of your marriage breakup in real and concrete ways. When your feelings and emotions come to the point of being a heavy burden, you will handle yourself differently. It's like running a six-mile race with a twenty-pound backpack.

An attorney told me of a client who came into her office one day wanting to start proceedings for a divorce. When the client sat down and began the interview, she was overwhelmed by the unresolved anger she felt toward her husband, crying uncontrollably for the first half hour. The lawyer finally suggested that she not see her again until the client first saw a therapist. In a very practical sense, the woman's inability to cope emotionally wasted her money and her time—not an unnecessary concern given the hourly rates lawyers charge. It is not hard to imagine other situations in which a woman's inability to work through her conflicting feelings might cause more permanent hardship.

For instance, you might have strong and recurring guilt feelings about the rightness of your decision to leave your marriage. These in turn influence the way in which you approach your husband when it comes time to divide up the financial resources. The tendency might be to take a defensive, self-deprecating stance. In doing this, you are setting yourself up to be taken advantage of.

Nancy experienced this when she broke up with Larry. They lived in a fine old home in the Ontario countryside. To everyone who knew them, they were the ideal couple. In fact, Larry was adored by most of his friends. Although Nancy said later that he had no outstanding fault, she found the marriage stifling. But strong unresolved feelings caused her lasting problems.

> I felt tremendously guilty. It came from my knowing that everybody wondered how I could do this to someone so loving and adoring. When he realized we had to separate, he decided he was going to

make it as impossible for me as he could. "If you want to leave, I'm not budging. I'm not giving up the house—nothing in the house is leaving." He played on my guilt because he believed I was going to look like such a shit.

I left with virtually nothing—I had no money and I didn't have a job. I was also convinced, at that point, that we could work out the perfect separation and we would never get divorced. It would sort of be like Clark Gable and Jean Harlow—we could still meet for dinner. I was really deceiving myself. I struggled for a long, long time after that.

Her feelings of guilt blocked her from judging her future needs and actively pursuing a fair settlement in her divorce. In addition, her attempt to relieve her guilt by giving in to the demands of the situation only created more anger and resentment.

A variation might go like this: You have a deep fear that the children will disapprove of your leaving their father, and will resent you for it. In an attempt to smooth things over, you become the super-nice mom, letting up on the discipline, allowing things to slide. The kids now stay up way past their normal bedtime. As the weeks pass, your normally free evening hours are cut into, and you start taking it out on the kids with anger and sour moods, but you still can't get up the energy to enforce the regular schedule. The children in turn become more unruly, picking up on your wavering attitudes, and you react with even more frustration. The situation continues to escalate.

The point is this: Know yourself. It is essential that you examine the emerging feelings that accompany the breakup of your marriage, and work on them. Not doing so carries consequences for you that will filter into every situation that you face and you will be at a disadvantage. You cannot think or act with good judgment when your emotions are unconsciously ruling everything you do. Whether it is working with your lawyer, looking for a job, checking with the bank on refinancing a loan, explaining your decision to your children, or deciding whether to say yes to a date with another man after your divorce, if you haven't examined the part your emotions play in all of this, the results will be haphazard and self-defeating. You might well end up in some kind of personal disaster.

It is important at this time to regularly deal with your feelings and emotions—not so that you can hold them down, but so that you know them better. If you can understand your fears, for instance, you have already taken the first and most essential step in dispelling them. What follows is not a lesson in psychology, but a pathway toward effectively getting free from a way of life that is not doing you any good.

THE FEELINGS OF GUILT

My stronger guilt defeats my strong intent.
William Shakespeare, *Hamlet*

Sometimes guilt seems like a tired old companion—it has been around so long. Some women are affected by it more than others, but no one is free of it. It is usually instilled very early in life and gets into our systems of thinking and behaving.

When we were six years old and learned about the adult world, the ideas given to us were by their nature overly simple. In that sense, they were incomplete and inaccurate. It has always amazed me how permanently those first impressions stuck, and how seldom we requestion them. It is most graphically brought out in terms of our religious imagery. Children's books on religion often represent God as a wise old man with a flowing white beard sitting on a kingly throne. He was always taking stock and you wouldn't want to test him. Although as an adult I might totally reject this as ridiculous—God is not old, He doesn't have a human form, He doesn't wear white togas, sit in chairs, look at me all the time, and is not a "He." I am often surprised to think how long it takes people to fight off the recurring imagery that saturated early childhood: Is He *still* watching?

The last chapter investigated some of the early messages we receive. Guilt is a by-product of them. Most of the messages established criteria of perfection for anything they described. A good girl was, among other things, one who was always clean and neat, didn't cry, was good to her little brother, loved her parents completely and obediently, ate all her food, and went to bed without a fuss. When you fell short of that, you were scolded and encouraged to feel guilty. Because it was both unrealistic and impossible to be all the things demanded of us, especially when half of them didn't make any sense and went against basic human biology, we became self-condemning.

The ideal message of what a mother should be—totally self-sacrificing—may not have matched your experience with *your* mother, but somehow the messages were bent in such a way as to make them apply. The ideal mother haunts us all.

I remember the message I got about divorcées when I was young. In my neighborhood in Chicago, a divorced woman lived a few houses away. She was a frequent topic of conversation in our home. If my mother spotted her going off to work in the morning, there would be comments on how she was dressed or attempts to fathom what she was really like. Invariably there were laments for her children whom she was probably neglecting since she had done this thing. As seen through my mother's eyes, the divorcée became another species of woman, tainted by blind fate perhaps, but probably of her own doing.

The story seems dated now, but the attitudes still exist. Certainly for those brought up in conservative family traditions, the power of such messages lingers on. In my own case, when I first thought about divorce, the idea that I was joining in league with the divorcée set influenced my feelings. It was, for the most part, a negative feeling and my response was to feel guilty. I later learned that they were women just like me.

Guilt is a process most women go through when they initiate ending a relationship. It swirls around almost every idea connected with divorce and is reflected in their thoughts. If you don't already have enough things to feel guilty about, here is a list of the most common sources from which to choose:

● In breaking up the marriage, I'm hurting my husband a lot. He won't be able to take care of himself. What if he falls apart?

He might start drinking or damage his career. It's true we haven't gotten along but he doesn't deserve this. I am deserting him in a time of trial and I'm responsible for his unhappiness.

- When I leave I'll be damaging the kids. He might not have been a good husband but he's the only father the kids have. Who's going to play with them? They will be lost without him and it's my fault. Who knows what will happen now? Whatever does, I'm to blame.

- Good wives and good mothers don't do this. It may be OK in some extreme cases, but I'm not one of them. Maybe I could have done better, been more caring and unselfish. What's wrong with me? Why can't I just accept my life? It really is not all that bad.

- I'm messing things up again. But this is really it. I can't ever get my life straight. Things he's done are bad but maybe I'm exaggerating them. I've done that before. What makes me think I won't mess up this?

- I never was that good in bed. How can I expect anything from him? I have strong sexual feelings, but I haven't been able to really get it together and feel consistently sexy with him. Everybody else seems so seductive all the time. Why don't I feel that way? Sometimes I think there's something wrong with me.

- The truth is, the reason I've stayed in this relationship so long is for financial security. I haven't loved him for a long time, but what else can I do? I feel like I've cheated him or something. Money isn't everything, so why do I stay? When I was younger, I never thought something like this would happen to me.

- I've kept secrets from him and now I'm blaming *him*. I have been attracted to other men but I never admitted it to him. There have been other things too. How can I have a relationship with such dishonesty? The whole thing has been my fault.

- I had my doubts about the marriage right from the beginning. Even before we got married I wasn't sure. I don't know why I went through with it. It's been a lie. Deep down I knew it but never told him. Now I'm in deep trouble for something I should have stopped. I never did do what I wanted.

Feelings of guilt are common to everyone. Guilt plagues people through life, altering and limiting their response to the world around them. It is interesting that it is a completely human response, not found in any other animals. In that sense, it both distinguishes us as creatures with the capacity for moral judgment, and it damns us to a life of worry and hesitation.

Guilt does have a function in life. It acts as a cue to let us know when we may have acted unjustly. A person who is incapable of guilt or who has such distorted values as to make guilt senseless is seen as dangerous. This is a person with no conscience. We witnessed it in the leaders of Germany in the thirties and in the little Nazis of every nationality around the world ever since. It is frightening when you meet one. Guilt reminds us of guidelines, and in that way, it is a learning tool, prompting us to look closely at a problem, clueing us in to the value of an action, giving us reason for change, or determining what kind of restitution should be made. That's the good side.

The bad side is that women are usually too hard on themselves. Often we indiscriminately blanket ourselves with guilt in situations that we're not sure of, that are uncomfortable, or that just concern us. We become our own judge and jury, and the verdict is always the same—guilty.

Divorce magnifies guilt. It brings together all that you ever learned about the concept of "mother," "children," "adultery," "good wife," "everlasting love," and a hundred other words and phrases, and enlarges them into signposts that dominate your consciousness. You may have thought about these things before and even updated their definitions from the simplistic meanings you first gave them. But now with divorce imminent, the struggle is with trying to match the real needs of your present life with concepts that you stored away long ago and may never have seriously evaluated since.

What makes it especially hard is that, because of the extreme intensity of the divorce process, old messages, which usually reflect the wisdom of the status quo, are repeated with ever-increasing emphasis. And they have their special power. It matters little if they make sense anymore. Who can resist the aura of reverence surrounding the 50's image of a contented woman in her chintz apron cooking soup in a cozy kitchen surrounded by a brood of attentive children and a deserving and loving husband? And who listens when you say, "But it never really *was* that way!"

In the heightened drama of separation, the old messages take on a renewed impact. They usually come from two sources—your husband and your own internalized guilt. What Peggy experienced is quite common.

> He said the same thing over and over. He said it so many times: I was destroying the family because I was trying to find myself. His mother even wrote this to my mother. I was sacrificing four lives for one life. I was emotionally damaging the children. He comes down pretty heavy sometimes and lays out pretty much guilt, like, "Hey, you're taking everything and leaving me nothing. How can you destroy a family? How can you do this?" I was responsible that the marriage failed. I did a real trip on myself for a long time about that.

In the final analysis, it is the woman who is seen as responsible for holding the marriage together. The culture says that a woman is successful if she has a good marriage. If it fails, she did something wrong; she didn't "keep the home fires burning."

The situation is rarely reversed. The way in which we have interpreted the sex roles is probably the cause. Lenore Walker in *The Battered Woman* observes that when children are raised in homes where these roles are stereotyped, sexist attitudes teach little girls to be nurturers. "The not-so-hidden message contained in female nurturing behavior is that little girls must expend their energy in supporting boys to achieve success." The obvious way in which a wife fulfills this destiny is in keeping the home together and aligning all her personal desires to fit her husband's career aspirations. The whole concept of sacrifice is one that our culture charges women to accept and embrace.

Therefore, when you are not only involved in a divorce (an

admission of the failure of your mission) but are actually *initiating* leaving, you open yourself to the full brunt of whatever potential guilt is lurking in your life. As enlightened and advanced as you may think you are, you may find yourself reverting back to unthinking and apologetic behavior in the crisis of divorce.

The especially hazardous thing about guilt is that it can be triggered so easily. At a time when you are highly sensitive and your feelings are on the surface, the smallest thing can set off a whole chain of guilt responses. Seeing a boy playing catch with his dad in the park, watching a television commercial of a family in a new car, a song that once meant something, a dream—any such thing can conjure up nostalgic feelings that quickly metamorphose into guilt.

The most obvious place for guilt to be triggered is in the verbal hassles with your husband. People who live together in a combative state quickly learn how to play on the other's guilt to get what they want.

In your leaving the marriage, your husband has a huge repertoire of categories and subjects from which to choose. Sometimes the only problem is deciding which key to play first. When people get good at it, whole concertos can be performed. Or sometimes it happens in a series—Monday, play on your shortcomings as a mother; Tuesday, work on the fact that you never showed any interest in his job which was the source of your food and lodging; Wednesday, compare your selfish behavior to the woman with the no-good husband down the block and see who's got it harder. Variations on the theme are endless.

"It is hard to fight an enemy who has outposts in your head," notes American writer Sally Kempton. One outcome of the barrage with which a husband assails his wife is that she might retreat again into the safety zone of the relationship. Although it was miserable before, she was not prepared for the storm that her decision to leave created. She began the process with the best of intentions, but her guilt so muddled things that it seemed impossible to go on. And so she finds herself back where she started—wiser but not one bit happier. It is no wonder that many unhappily married women mention a similar recurring wish: They wish their husbands would die. In saying this, I don't mean to be lurid. It simply shows the depth of frustration for many of them. The desire may be a carryover from the simple storybook fantasy of childhood when dilemmas were solved by the painless death of the bad guy. Death in this situation would take away all the responsibility for leaving, give it over to fate, and relieve her guilt. Nobody would be to blame.

When a person tosses a stone into a quiet pond, the circles of ripples from the splash spread to the farthest shores. A woman immersed in guilt by her decision to divorce may feel that her act is similarly disruptive. The breakup sends out waves of change into the lives of those who surround her. Guilt builds as she imagines the consequences of the permanent disruption she has caused others. All of the turmoil is a direct result of her action.

But this analogy, and others like it, does not accurately reflect the situation. *Every* action causes some ripples. Movement, however, does not imply damage; it is simply a sign of change. Moreover, the waters were probably never very calm. A woman must remember that a marriage in trouble has been rough on all those involved with it for a long period of time. And she must believe that the unsettled surface will gradually subside; the disquiet is not lasting.

Each human act, positive or negative, alters life around it and the ultimate effect of any act is never known. You are not the only one throwing stones; everybody else is too. Life is a co-mingling of action and response that is unending. If you were to trace the ripples of influence in your life in a single day, the results would be awesome. Also rather useless.

Stop thinking that you are responsible (and therefore guilty) for everything. It is not only grandiose thinking, it is a go-nowhere place to be.

Turn your attention instead to solving your problems, and stop finding new ways to internally complicate your life. Guilt is not productive and it is energy draining. It also misses the point.

The late Hedges Capers, Sr., a therapist in transactional analysis, commented:

> Of all the hundreds of people I've seen in therapy who have felt guilty, after I've worked with them it turns out that *none* of them have ever been guilty of the things they felt guilty about.

Guilt stems from many sources, most of it translated from our past. If you wish to deal with your history of emotional responses, see a therapist and do so. But *don't use guilt as the payment you owe to get out of your marriage.* The cost is too great.

Guilt is not a feeling like happiness, sadness, or even fear. Those things come and go—guilt stays on to haunt a person. It can be consuming. Did you ever meet a parent who did not have some guilt about not having done enough, or enough of the *right* things, for her kids? The potential for guilt is enormous in a mother. Because she sees herself as the protector of her offspring, initiating a divorce brings guilt that tells her she is deliberately putting them in jeopardy.

But guilt won't solve this problem. It simply gets you down on yourself, immobilizing you. Feeling guilty will not mean that your kids will be better fed, clothed, or adjusted. It will also not resolve the problems you have with your husband. Continuing to nourish your guilt over these issues only inflicts punishment on yourself. It is as damaging as hiring someone to beat you up, or sticking needles under your fingernails. But at least then you might get it out of your system.

Seriously, this is your life and it's the only one you've got for now. You don't have to apologize—even to yourself—for taking care of it. This is not a selfish position; it is a survival position. In the end, no one else is going to give you the concern you give yourself. This doesn't have to be exclusionary. You don't have to forget your children's feelings or your husband's sensibility. But for once, *put yourself first.* Just reading that simple statement will make some women shudder with guilt. In a very real sense, it is truly revolutionary. Everything in our culture conditions wives and mothers to reject it. I am not encouraging wild egomania or a thoughtless reflowering of the Me Culture. What I am saying is that if your marriage is intolerable and you are not happy with it, don't feel guilty about following your natural survival needs— they point the way toward a healthy existence. Although it is not going to be easy, the difficulty you face doesn't have to be associated with guilt, as if each minor setback were just punishment.

Exercises to Help with Guilt

Let's face it. Guilt is not going to disappear overnight; it is more persistent than that. But you can put some limits on it so that you can control it, instead of it controlling you.

Some of us think that we must *pay* for our past and present transgressions. It is unlikely that we will just give up guilt. No matter what logical arguments are made, the mind and the emotions are not in sync. Here are healthy ways to pay:

1. Make an agreement with a friend (or with yourself) that you will set aside twenty minutes a day for the next four weeks and use that time to feel guilty. Pack it into that time frame and let yourself feel it all. But for the rest of the day (and this is the key to this exercise) agree *not* to feel guilty about any part of your life. If you find yourself doing that outside your "guilty time," tell yourself to STOP. You've paid your dues for now. You have to put your energies elsewhere.

At the end of four weeks, think about what you have learned from your experience. Talk it over with a friend.

2. Write down what you feel guilty about. You can do this during your twenty-minute "guilty time." Define your thoughts well. List in writing if you are: a) feeling guilty in order to punish yourself, b) allowing guilt to motivate or shape your behavior, c) letting guilt lock you into your past, d) taking on the blame for the actions and feelings of others over which you have no control. Read this list out loud. Use these questions as a daily checklist to assist you in limiting and diminishing the impact of guilt.

* * *

If those two exercises don't work, consider this one:

One day I took three women who were members of a support group down to the beach. All of them had been having a hard time emotionally, especially with guilt, and I wanted to not only get outside to break up the mood, but also to do an exercise with them. I had told each to bring a laundry bag with her.

After sitting in the sand and enjoying the ocean air for a while, I explained what I had in mind. They should walk down the beach to an area about a half mile away where the sea had swept many rocks and scattered them thickly on the sand. After getting there, they would begin to collect rocks for their bags. Each rock should represent a particular guilt they have. If it is a small guilt—not preparing breakfast for the kids a couple of days last week so that they had to make their own—you might put a good size stone in the bag. If the guilt was stronger—no longer being committed to your husband—throw in a larger rock. Everything they felt guilty about should be represented by an appropriate size rock: inadequacy about being a proper mother, abandoning their role as wife, feelings stemming from childhood experiences, and so on. The three women looked perplexed but seemed to accept the game in good spirit. They headed down the beach.

An hour later, I saw two of them coming back. They were struggling. Bobbie, a large, strong woman, was attempting to carry the bag over her shoulder but was stumbling and every few yards had to set it down to rest and regrip it. Leslie was not as big as Bobbie and trailed behind, having to drag the bag in the sand. I watched them for a long time and as they got close, Bobbie yelled out, "I can't believe how heavy this goddamn thing is!"

"I bet," I said impassively.

Bobbie looked put off. "Why did you have us do this?" I didn't answer and just looked at the ocean. She was perspiring and getting a little angry.

"This is crazy, stupid," she bristled.

"You're right," I answered. "Why are you doing it?" She was shocked and just stared at me.

"Because you told us to!"

"Yes—but why are you doing it?" I asked again.

Bobbie looked at her bag as if for the first time. "It's so heavy," she said, sadly this time.

"Why don't you get rid of some of it?"

"How?" she asked, but in saying it she had an almost embarrassing revelation. She immediately put her hand into the bag, picked out a large rock, and threw it as far as she could into the ocean. It disappeared in the surf. Bobbie looked ecstatic, then deliberately started throwing her stones into the water. Her form was beautiful to watch, becoming more fluid and free.

Leslie had been pulling her bag along the shore but now stood and watched in surprise. I went over to her, took a large, shining black rock out of her bag and threw it into the water.

"Hey! What are you doing?" she complained as if I had stolen something precious.

"I'm helping you. Do you want to keep dragging around this guilt?"

She looked down at the sack, her hands on her hips, and breathed heavily. "I don't know. It's mine."

"Right. It's weird, isn't it, how we get attached to our burden." I kept throwing her rocks. "In what way does hanging on to your guilt help you? Does it make you a better person, a better mother? Can't you act in ways that are caring and human without dragging along the negative weight of your past?"

Leslie just looked at me for a moment, then smiled and joined in throwing the rocks.

We went down the beach to find Mary Ann. She was sitting in the sand with tears in her eyes staring at a large boulder. The lesson had come home to her in silence. She had tried to put the huge rock into her bag but realized the futility of it. Then she tried to roll it into the ocean. It was at the edge of the water and was gradually becoming embedded in the sand washing around it.

"It's going to take some time," I said.

"I guess so," she said.

ANGER

Anger isn't nice. Most women not only are uncomfortable expressing it, they don't even allow themselves to feel it. And so they feel guilty instead. In my experience, when a woman comes to me with strong guilt issues, what is underneath is a great deal of unexpressed anger. Guilt is the lid. Guilt is an acceptable "feeling" for a woman, in that it doesn't disturb anyone else in an overt way. Explicit anger is confrontive, aggressive, and often loud. It takes an offensive position. Guilt works silently, undermining the person feeling it. Both have the potential for destroying. Anger attacks others; guilt eats away the self.

There seems to be a cultural block that stops women from getting in touch with and expressing deep-seated anger. Instead, they transform it. The women I see during the divorce process have been through years of marriage that have produced, for most of them, a storehouse of unacknowledged anger. Because it is seldom dealt with directly, it doesn't go away. It recurs the same way a physical sickness does if you have not reached the source of the problem. And the stronger the unexpressed anger, the heavier the guilt.

It is important to bring your anger to full consciousness so that you can experience some of the forces at work in your life. See if you can recognize yourself in a few of the following examples:

- I feel guilty about not being a good sexual partner. It's true that I haven't been very responsive. He keeps telling me that. *I'm really angry about him not giving me enough attention outside of the bedroom. He is generally insensitive to me during dinner and through the evening, then expects me to be responsive in the delicate balance of getting together sexually. I just don't get turned on automatically. I'm mad because he's not a good lover. There was a time when he had it together, but it's really his lack of interest. Yet I get blamed.*

- I feel guilty about the way our house looks. There is a lot of stuff that I'm not doing, and can't seem to find the time to get to.

I'm really angry that he has only one job and I've got nine. Besides working myself, I'm a taxi service for the kids, I shop, cook, and clean. What's worse, the house is really seen as my *responsibility; and even if I get others to help out, I have to be the manager. I'm mad because I'm left to take care of it all, and if things are not right—I'm the one who gets hassled.*

- I feel guilty about his being the primary wage earner. It's his paycheck that I'm living off of. He tells me I have no right to complain, that I'm getting a free ride.
  I'm really angry that what I do isn't recognized as work. This is supposed to be a partnership, and I'm more than keeping up my end of it. But I don't get paid for it, or even get recognition from him for it. I'm mad because nobody *gives me credit.*

- I feel guilty about not being a good mother. I holler and am impatient with the children sometimes. In fact, there are times I don't even want to see them.
  I'm really angry that I'm never free. There are no days off, and I'm never *not responsible. He plays with the kids when it suits his mood, but I get them the rest of the time, which is most all the time. I'm mad because I'm not getting enough help and I don't have a choice.*

- I feel guilty about not being smart. He keeps reminding me that I'm not up with things, that I'm not a good conversationalist.
  I'm really angry that he thinks what interests him should interest me. We're two different people, yet it's his *world that gets all the attention. Besides, I'm in the house a lot and feel isolated from others. I'm mad that I get stuck in the house and don't have more contact with the outside world.*

- I feel guilty about not looking as good as I used to. Sometimes I think my physical appearance is distasteful to him and others.
  I'm really angry that I must compete with the image of some perfect "10" in his fantasy. My breasts slope and my body shows that I've had kids—but that's life. They're his kids, too, but they cost me something he never had to pay. Besides, I don't have the time or money to play the

fashion model. I'm mad because his idea of beauty is so damn adolescent, yet I get pulled into it.

The events that have led to your divorce, and the process itself, have given you many opportunities for anger. Situations come up every day, and there is a constant question of what to do with these strong, infuriating feelings. Most women's guilt and anger about divorce can be summed up like this:

● I feel guilty because I'm the bad guy. I'm the one breaking up the marriage, ruining the family, wanting something else. A lot of my friends think I should be glad for what I've got. My parents think I'm terrible; they don't know what to make of me. My husband is bewildered and upset. He keeps asking me, "Why?"
I'm really angry that I catch all the blame. Nobody knows what I've gone through. He has been impossible to live with; but if I complain about it, he really doesn't listen. And if I had told my parents, then they would have had to take sides, and I didn't want to cause a problem there. I'm mad that it's not all right for me to want a better life. Just because I want a reasonable degree of happiness, people label me the bad guy.

Your feelings of anger are real ones, and they are in need of your attention. Your anger is genuine. This is not to say that you were always totally right in every position you held. We all distort reality, especially in times of stress. More important is that you may have diverted that anger into guilt, into feelings of inadequacy, because it seemed to be the safer course of action. But such situations are self-destructive in that you let guilt motivate your behavior where anger is the response called for.

If you did not see a way to vent your anger over the issues that came up in your life and if you transformed those natural feelings into guilt, then it's no wonder you may be plagued at this crucial time with self-deprecating attitudes, hesitancy, low self-esteem, poor health, and bad judgment They are the visible signs of guilt and they subvert your ability to be assertive, feel good about yourself, and make sound decisions.

The Way We Were

It is useful for you to know the real sources of your conflicts. In regard to anger, for instance, the average woman's upbringing works against her. Traditionally, young girls have not been encouraged or even allowed to freely express their anger. In the hundreds of small crises that a child faces—"Jimmy pushed me off my bike and won't let me ride it"—young girls got the message early that it was not nice to show real anger, especially in public. If the situation was reversed, a boy might yell, have a small tantrum, and grab his bike back. A girl typically would whine, complain, and end up crying. She was taught that it was OK to cry or be afraid because this is acceptable feminine behavior. Doing it even encouraged boys to protect her, thus complimenting *their* role. Parents' and teachers' stress on girls being "sugar and spice and everything nice" shaped young women into patterns of behavior that frustrated the spontaneous expression of anger.

Anger is an emergency response. But a young girl learns a whole repertoire of behavior that substitutes for anger. If she is unhappy about something, she might pout, be passive, run away, or even seemingly ignore the issue. She might also swallow her anger and smile sweetly. What begins as an adaptive response, however, can soon become a survival tactic. A girl who is frustrated and angry about her life often resorts to the opposite pole—being charming—to express herself. But as George Bach and Herb Goldberg explain in *Creative Aggression*, "The charm hides underlying feelings of resentment, rejection, and rage. . . ."

One of the most common ways that women displace anger is by crying. In situations that call for a strong or angry response, some women regularly cry. Crying is certainly a valid way to show emotion. It is a letting down and giving in to feelings of frustration or sadness. It is soft and vulnerable. But it can also make you feel helpless. And when crying becomes a fixed style of relating to imminent problems or threats which would naturally generate anger, it is a cover-up. You learn to express through tears what you are afraid to express directly in anger. Crying used in this way is never fully satisfying because the feelings are turned inward when the real object of your frustration is "out there."

Early role models are influential in forming young girls' attitudes toward themselves. Sandra, a forty-five-year-old woman only now facing her past, tells how she learned from her mother how to deal with anger.

> My mother never openly showed her anger to my father or other adults. If she got mad, she would bang some dishes around or throw magazines down in a pile or slam a door. Or she just yelled at us kids when she was mad. But when she was mad at my dad, she'd sulk or act cold. If she said anything it was in a whining, apologetic voice—almost a plea. My father ruled the house and my mother taught us never to question that. When I grew older she'd complain to me about all the things she didn't like about my dad, but I don't ever remember her saying anything to his face. She never said no to him.

Her mother created a whole scheme of substitute behavior for the straightforward emotion of anger which sprang from her inability to confront her husband directly. Sandra learned from her mother ways to handle her anger which were not open and spontaneous. Sandra, herself, is now at a time in her life when *she* needs to speak up and do something other than being evasive, frustrated, and depressed. The continual translation of legitimate anger into acceptable "nice" behavior warps her entire personality. It makes dealing with the world an overly complicated ordeal based on questionable coping skills.

Models for assertive female behavior in the media are not encouraging, yet they continually reinforce our learning on a day-to-day basis. When was the last time you saw a woman on television express pure anger about a serious or deeply felt subject and not be portrayed as a hard bitch? Men are allowed to express anger regularly. The frustrated male detective slams around department headquarters, venting his anger at his superiors for blocking his private investigation of a criminal. In his tone of voice and facial expression, it is clear that he is incensed. Women are seldom given that kind of emotional expression in a drama. It is easier to pout for what you want. I'm still waiting for one of the women in the coffee commercials, after the husband gives her a sour glance while tasting the less than perfect coffee, to drop a hot cup in his lap. But instead of responding in anger, she scurries off to her neighbor for advice—worried and very guilty.

When you internalize anger, you become the victim. The only one you get even with is yourself. Internalized, bottled-up feelings of anger will take their toll physically. If the hurts and frustrations cannot be discharged by the normal means of venting anger, the results will turn up in the form of nervous disorders, depression, ulcers, or worse. You must beware of this self-destruction. When your anger is strongly felt but not given natural release, it may turn up in ways and in situations that are unwanted. You end up being your own worst enemy.

What's Stopping You Now?

What is blocking you from expressing your anger? Certainly the lessons you learned as a young girl and the reinforcement they receive through the culture are strong influences. But there is more. As those attitudes are translated into the problems a woman confronts in leaving her husband, they take on a special force. Consider the following statements and see if some apply.

- When I get angry I don't feel comfortable with it. I feel exposed. There's something masculine about it; it doesn't feel right. It is as hard for me as crying is for most men.
- I'm not sure that I'm right. Maybe I'm all wet. I've never been able to hold my own in an argument, and I'm not sure that if I express my feelings he won't just put me down. I don't need that again.
- I don't like to show my anger because I don't want to be labeled

a bitch. I hear men call women that all the time and it's the final put-down. Who wants to be seen as ugly?
- I'm really afraid to get angry. When I do, he comes back at me in a vicious manner. He might beat me up next time. It's all too heavy. Why take a chance?
- I'm even more afraid of letting go of my anger. I'm mad about a lot of things. More than I'm aware of. If I ever really got angry, I'm scared of what I would do. I don't know how far it would go, or where. I don't know if I want to find out.

Such statements are typical of the anxiety some women feel in letting themselves fully experience their anger. But when any natural emotion is suppressed, it will resurface masked as another feeling. The problem is that the new manifestation of it may be harder to deal with than the original anger.

I have also suggested that anger is the underside of guilt. It goes beyond that, however. You may feel angry over the way your husband handles money, treats the kids, spends Saturdays, or makes love—and it may not have anything to do with guilt. It is important, if you have not been in the habit, to see anger as simply a normal, if intense, human emotion. Sadness, fear, and happiness are others. A very young baby expresses these emotions appropriately. A hungry infant left unattended and unfed will escalate a hunger cry into one of anger at not having these needs met. As we grow up, we don't lose these authentic needs and feelings. Dr. Harold Bloomfield and Robert Kory in their book *Inner Joy* say it plainly:

> Anger is a perfectly normal response to emotional injury. You have absorbed negative energy that has been projected at you with varying degrees of intensity. To balance your emotional scales and create an opportunity for resolution of the hurt, anger is important and healthy. If you suppress your anger, you add insult to injury by denying your own feelings and your right to stand up for yourself.

When you internalize your anger, you become doubly enmeshed. You absorb what would be directed at the other. As a stage of grief, anger is a predictable and natural emotion in the divorce process. To suppress it is to first run the risk of it resurfacing as another emotion. Second, burying your anger does not allow you to stay in touch with your integrity, and your right to stand up for yourself. I am not suggesting that you enter into an all-out battle, or even get into a contest of wits. But stay connected to your feelings, and especially the reasons for ending your marriage. Continue to stand up for yourself.

RESENTMENT

Resentment is anger remembered. If a woman is not comfortable expressing direct anger, she will often store it away, building a stockpile of unspoken negative thoughts. The women that I come in contact with during the divorce process will tell detailed stories of their relationship with their husbands and by the content and tone of what they are saying, it is clear that they have deep-seated resentments. But when I ask them if they are angry, they often deny it. It seems that it is all right to *talk* about what distresses them, but they have not allowed themselves to fully express it. Telling their resentments is one safe step away from feeling them.

But resentment *is* anger. The accumulation of angers. Whereas anger usually occurs in response to specific events, resentments encompass whole backgrounds of unresolved hurts, conflicts, and neglect. In your resentment, you have created a long agenda of past injustices which in turn gnaw at your memories and feelings. The virtue of anger is that it affords an immediate, spontaneous discharge of feelings. Such a release can be healthy when it occurs appropriately. In resentment, a steady hum of negative intensity remains.

In this way resentment is rather like a time bomb. Often an insignificant thing—your husband forgets to put away his shaving gear—can trigger an explosive argument in which his personal habits of the last two years are brought into it. All of the times that you swallowed your dislike or anger in the past never did go away and were silently added to your growing list of resentments. In a way, these things represent your whole history together.

During your divorce, get to know the nature and depth of your resentment, and watch out for it. Resentments need not be expressed now to your husband. Doing so can set off unneeded and painful fights that get into ugly accusations and name-calling. Resentments eat up your energy. There is no value in being mad all day, thinking what a yoyo he is, when your time can be better spent getting your life in order. It is easy to slip into vindictive behavior over resentments you have long harbored. It usually starts with something that is annoying and descends into trench warfare. Resist the temptation.

One reason to avoid engaging your husband with the full brunt of your resentments is that you may not be aware of the fury that they hold for you. Anger that has been bound up for years, when suddenly released, becomes rage—a blind and indiscriminate striking out at everything perceived as threatening. Because the rage may be uncontrolled, it is dangerous, especially when you cannot be sure what it sets off in the other person. Beware of the power your resentments contain and begin to give them up.

At this stage your resentments do you no good whatsoever, except as a reminder as to why you are leaving. Paying him back for a catalog of past hurts that you didn't allow yourself to fully respond to at the time they were happening is asking for trouble. Granted, it is very hard to let go of chronic resentments. They may control many areas of your relationship with your husband. But if you can't let go from a position of forgiveness, at least do it out of practicality. The feelings are old ones and don't have much to do with your life right now, or in the future. If your resentments are triggered thoughtlessly, you will find yourself acting out old patterns, getting into arguments, and messing up your chances for a relatively smooth parting.

Letting Go

So what *is* appropriate? You can effectively reduce your anger by *discharging*. Discharging is the release of the physical and emotional reservoir stored up when your anger or other emotions are not expressed. Because some people are in the habit of never letting go of the control they hold on themselves, some of the anger is very old. Unexpressed feelings dating from childhood build into powerful internal pressures. When the anger that grows out of the conflict in a marriage is added to this, the concentration of negative energy can be awesome. You need an outlet.

One way would be to just have it out with your husband. Couples engage in this all the time, but at this period of your relationship it is not productive and will most likely have disastrous consequences. You also open yourself up to being labeled as "hysterical woman." As tempting as they are, let the arguments pass and find other ways to vent your anger.

A way to begin discharging is to write down, in a letter, everything you are mad about. Address it to your husband. Say it all— be articulate, eloquent, vulgar—whatever gets it out best. Read it aloud; then tear it up, burn it, stomp on it, get rid of it.

But the best way to get rid of feelings of anger is through *physical* release. This kind of discharge not only flushes out your mental imagery but also the negative physical memories of anger that you store in your body in the form of muscle tension and restricted breathing.

Find a place where you can be free to yell. Such privacy is not easily found nowadays, but when you have pent-up anger you need to let it out vocally. Many women find that a car is the best place to do it. Go for a drive, and park someplace safe and fairly deserted. Roll up the windows and let go—scream. Tell the person off; say everything you ever wanted to him; call him names. If you feel it wasn't enough, go out the next day. Do it regularly. Take as long as it takes to get it all out. If you don't have a car and live in close quarters, lie on a bed and scream into a pillow.

A classic way to discharge is to take a tennis racquet or baseball bat to your bedroom and kneel next to the bed. Begin to beat the bed in strong, rhythmic strokes. As you do, focus your attention on the issues of your anger, and as the intensity builds, don't hold back your sounds and breathing. You may find yourself crying, screaming, or both. That's OK. It is valuable because you will find that it is an intense, fully expressed act that reflects your deep frustration.

Get into aerobic exercise. Whatever your style, begin a regular schedule of vigorous physical exercise. This may mean joining a health or exercise club and working out on an indoor track, doing laps in a swimming pool, playing racquetball, going to Jazzercise classes, or jogging. The idea here is to push yourself physically, At some point you will begin to release the physical tensions caused by anger.

With any release, there is a period of peace afterward. Enjoy it. It is also a time to learn something about yourself. Feel what you are feeling. Later you might want to be held by someone if that is possible. Take a warm shower and a nap.

Don't let the intensity of your discharge scare you. You have taken in a lot of abuse in your life; you can't expect the release of feelings about that to be easy or gentle. Anger is anger. There is a fury behind it. The problem is not with trying to stop it, but letting yourself feel it and blow it out.

At the risk of being repetitive, if you can also get into therapy to deal with your anger, it will help you to process in a safe environment all of the feelings that are coming up now.

Dealing Straight

Perhaps because men seem to have a corner on expressing anger, we assume that it must reflect an aggressive male style— one that is hurtful, physically threatening, and dangerous. After all, that's the way we have experienced anger much of the time, personally and through the media. But it can also be the healthy release described in this section. In the best sense, anger is a positive expression of how you feel—*in forceful terms*. It does not have to be hateful, and at this point in your relationship you should be especially wary of this.

Anger can simply be a strong and honest way of giving needed information, communicating the special importance that the issue holds for you. An example could be: "John, I'm really feeling mad about your not picking up the kids when you said you would! I had other plans today; now they can't be worked out. Give some thought to my needs, too. If we are going to have to do this often, we will have to be able to count on each other."

Such a statement deals with the present and doesn't call up past issues. During this time there will be many instances which can turn into endless rehashing of past arguments. Avoid them by cleaning up the way you communicate your feelings.

One final thought: Don't be afraid that by letting go of your anger you will make yourself susceptible to reconciliation, which in turn will simply lead to a new round of interpersonal madness. Some women think that if they get rid of their anger, they won't be mad enough to leave—that their anger is their strength. But if you have come this far, the reality of your life should say it all. And letting go of anger does not mean that you cannot act with resolution. It simply means that you are going to start taking better care of yourself.

FEARS

Fear is a human alarm system signaling a threat. It serves a good purpose in this regard. With advance warning, you can prepare to take proper action.

If it were only that, fear would be no problem. The confusion comes in two ways: When the object of the fear is in some way distorted, or when your ability to handle the thing feared is misjudged or underrated. In divorce, it is easy to exaggerate both ends of the problem. A woman may feel that her problem is overwhelming. Or she may think that she doesn't have the means to cope with it. Neither is probably true.

The most powerful fears tend to be nonspecific. This may have something to do with the way we first experienced them. The emotion of fear is primitive and goes back to the very birth process. The phrase "unspeakable fears" is appropriate because many of our basic fearful responses come from a period when we didn't have a language to articulate them. Without going into a long study of the nature of human fear, a few things are important to point out in how women deal with fear.

Apart from prenatal and early postnatal influences, women have been acculturated to view fear as part of their life experience. Consider what the popular culture does with it. There is a whole classification of motion pictures, for instance, which bases its story line on women's fears. Just as there are "War Films" or "Detective Stories," there is a category called "Women in Jeopardy" films. You have seen a lot of these: A woman is pursued through dark city streets by a mad knifer; a woman is left alone at her summer cottage only to be attacked by a gang of crazy bikers; a woman is hounded by a mysterious midnight telephone caller. Women are stalked by rapists, caught in subways, pushed off ledges, tied to railroad tracks—and all of them are screaming, screaming, screaming. Women face increasing physical danger in this society. One has only to read the daily paper to be reminded. But movies and television have played on women's fears (and perhaps triggered some deranged male imaginations) by constantly setting up dramatic conflicts in which we are automatically portrayed as victims.

As a result, we have the common reaction of being overly protective toward girls growing up. This is often done out of genuine concern, but the result is that women are subtly taught helplessness and encouraged to be dependent on others, most often one man. When there is the danger of being left alone, as in the case of divorce, some women panic in fear of every unnamed threat that can be imagined. Once fear becomes the dominant force in someone's life, it colors everything. For a woman, it can explain why many are even hesitant to enter a restaurant alone, are afraid to approach a bank officer for a loan, or are shy about calling the plumber to dispute an overcharge.

Physical strength is one antidote to fear. When you feel your power, you begin to take command of situations in your life. It begins with the body. This is not to suggest that you immediately join a weight-training class. But when you see yourself as physically inferior, it affects the way you approach the world. You

imagine yourself vulnerable to anything that wanders through
life. Women have for so long been classified as the weaker sex
that it is hard to resist the label.

However, women's physical weakness is a myth which has been
created and reinforced by standards drawn exclusively from male
needs and the male consciousness. Women *are* strong. If you have
given birth to a child, or witnessed it, you know the physical
strength of a woman. The entire female system is taxed to the
extreme, and a woman draws on tremendous physical stamina to
endure and carry through the birth process. This kind of strength
has no easy measurement. Unlike the feats of men trained for
brute violence on Monday night football, the records of women's
achievements are commonly shut in and internalized beyond the
closed doors of hospital maternity rooms. In this respect, we seldom see women as often in their physical triumphs.

But even in competitive sports, women are closing the gap. At
one time, serious sports programs for women at universities were
almost nonexistent, presumably because women were not interested. Today that has changed. In the marathon, after a seventy-
five-year head start, men are only fifteen minutes ahead of
women. Many sports observers believe that within our lifetime,
we will see women matching men stride for stride in this event,
and eventually beating them. And you don't have to be young to
find your strength. Laurie Binder was twenty-nine when she
started running, and four years later was the sixth fastest mara-
thoner in the world. Gertrude Ederle, in 1926, swam the English
Channel two hours faster than any man had done, and women
have dominated the sport of long-distance swimming ever since.
Men have physical advantages in some areas, but in less publicized
ways, women are superior, especially ways in which the spiritual
and physical merge.

With a renewed sense of physical adequacy, the world is less
likely to feel overwhelming. When you believe that you can literally take care of yourself, your fears will be greatly reduced. And
when physical fears are alleviated, emotional fears begin to take
on their proper perspective.

Yet there are common and significant fears that many women

report during their divorce. Some of them are normal responses to a new and confusing situation. But many fears, because they thrive on generalized or imagined conditions, don't hold up well under close scrutiny. When you look at them closely, they lose their mystery, and hence their power. The following are a number of fears that women have concerning divorce.

Fear of Being Alone

The fear in divorce of being alone is best summed up in the plain words of a woman that I interviewed: "I don't want to grow old by myself." You know what she is talking about. In those words is the fear that, after the split-up, she will slip into a life of dull routine marked by isolation and loneliness. Even in the horrible fights that failing marriages produce, there is a strange kind of caring. He cared enough at least to fight. The prospect of life without the nourishment of another person's attention can be frightening. George Bach and Peter Wyden in *The Intimate Enemy* state:

> Most people abhor loneliness; some are even terrorized to the point where their fears can be called solophobia. Except for a few diehard loners, men and women yearn to share, to belong, to be intimate. It makes their lives meaningful.

But it is important at the outset to get the terms straight. Are you afraid of being *alone*? Or do you fear being *lonely*? The two are quite different, although we tend to interchange the concepts. Nobody wants to be lonely. You may well want to be alone for a while.

Living alone needn't be associated with loneliness or any other negative state. It may simply be choosing to live for a period of time in a situation that is radically different from your former life. What is most scary is that it's new. Obviously, after you have lived with another person for some time, you get used to a certain shared environment. It may seem unimportant at the time, but just being able to exchange comments about the weather, the kids, or the neighborhood gossip in the casual flow of household conversation creates small emotional dependencies that form the background of daily existence. Arlene felt the difference after her divorce.

> It was really scary at first. Being alone at night. For the first time in my life, nobody was there. Nobody was around. I didn't realize how just having someone in the next room was comforting. It was strange not having that.

But being alone has certain rewards if you work through the initial fears. Most women report that, when they finally begin their new lives, the experience of being alone is actually an exhilarating feeling. It is the first expression of freedom. Janice was married for ten years and since her divorce has become close to another man. But for the present she has chosen to live alone.

> As far as living with somebody right now, I wouldn't want to live with him or anybody else. I've got the best of both worlds. I come and I go. I don't have to answer to anyone. I don't have to cook dinners. I can cook for the kids by my own schedule. I'm getting by financially, not great but I'm getting by. I like it.

Much of your fear of being alone may be imagined. Your stress about it is real, however. But be honest with yourself. How many interests do you actually share with your husband? Are you really involved in each other's conversations, friends, dreams? How much support do you get from him regarding your thinking? Do you have affectionate physical contact often? How much time do you really spend together in a day? Frequently two people are alone in marriage much more than they think. If your responses to the questions were negative, you are not only *alone* right now, but probably *lonely*. High on the list of complaints by women getting divorced is the feeling of loneliness. It's no wonder that women fear it after divorce—they don't want *more of the same*.

The truth is that many women will live alone for a period of time after their divorce. If it happens to you, it does not mean that you are not lovable, are not popular, or must permanently settle into that slot in life. You have made a free choice. Be prepared to live with it for a while. Arlene had this thought:

Culturally we're not brought up to be alone. You go from family to school surrounded by a lot of people, then to a marriage situation where you are sharing a place and always dealing with someone. You never had an opportunity to really live on your own. Anyone who has a chance to go live in a cave, or out in the desert, or up in the mountains, I'd say go. Just experience what it's like to be on your own where you can't really fall back on anyone for anything. Have that taken away for a while and see what it's like.

Although the idea is unrealistic for most women, the point is well made. Being alone can be seen as a great opportunity.

On the other hand, living alone does not mean that you don't have a need for regular contact with other people. In that regard there are some things that you can do right now to ensure a support system of other people you can count on for help and friendship.

A *support system* is simply a group of individuals whom you feel free to go to for caring, attention, counsel, even holding. This may be happening in the normal activity of your life right now, but it is good to take a second look. You will be in a different position after your divorce and you will find that support from others will, at times, be essential.

These persons can be drawn from your family, friends, neighbors, and coworkers. Decide which ones you trust to be there when you need them. It is not just a matter of surveying the people close to you now. You can develop new friends at this time to provide companionship. Obviously, I'm not talking about simply exploiting friends for what they have to give. If you are going to be close to anyone, you must give something of yourself. But don't hesitate because of pride or some other personality twitch to go out to others. There will be times when you need a shoulder to cry on, someone who will listen to a problem, help you in finding a job or apartment or used car. And it may be that you can help the other person in similar ways.

Even if you have just one good friend, it can be like gold. Most people can recall a time in their life when the advice and friendship of just one person got them through a difficult period. It may seem like an imposition, but it is really an honor of sorts. I feel very special when a friend in trouble relies on me during a temporarily stressful time in her life. Don't be afraid to ask for help. It is not a sign of weakness. It means that you know your limits. If you ask directly and for some reason the other person is not able to help, you have lost nothing. You may find that even that much shared honesty has deepened your friendship.

There are a number of other ways to get support in the face of loneliness. If you have children, the opportunities for establishing a new relationship with them are many. This is discussed at length in a later chapter. At this time, you might also think about getting a dog or cat. They are not only good companions, but in the case of dogs, good protection. Any new interest, whether it be a hobby, a class, or a good book, is a welcome change when you are alone. At first, sleeping by yourself may be a problem. Buy a stuffed animal or special pillow to cuddle with in bed at night. Pile the pillows on one side of the bed and sleep against them. Whatever works, use it!

Remember that some women choose to live alone and do so unafraid. In fact, many like it. It is important to refrain from equating living alone with timidity.

Fear of Taking Care of Yourself

The basic fear for some women is in the question, "Can I survive without him?" For a portion of the women in an unhappy marriage, the answer is a quick "no," and they continue to stay in their sad relationship. For others it is answered quite differently. "Of course; I've been doing it for years." These women have often worked at jobs outside the home throughout their marriage and although they will have to adjust their financial and emotional priorities, they feel quite capable of surviving in their future lives.

But I think for most women, there is still an underlying suspicion or fear that if they were really all alone, they might not make it. It was an issue when first leaving their parents' home, and it continues. Some women have never been on their own, moving from the parents' home to marriage. Dependency has become a way of life.

Because of this rather sheltered progression, a myth grows that it's a "Big, Bad World" out there, unfit for man or beast, and certainly not for women. It's a jungle, and only persons (men) with cunning instincts can survive successfully. It may be true that women fill in on jobs that give aid, but it's the big hunters who own the land and take the big chances. Women venture out at their own risk.

During the natural insecurity of the divorce process, the world outside the confines of marriage may seem formidable, survival being a life or death matter. A woman might question her ability to take care of herself. The many things that keep a household together can be bewildering and the thought of doing it alone is scary. What if I get sick? Who will fix the lawnmower? How can I get to the movies? Who will deal with the auto mechanic? A hundred detailed questions run through the mind.

What makes it worse is that during divorce, many husbands often foster and exploit these fears. The groundwork has been laid by years of subtle or direct remarks about the woman's shortcomings in regard to taking care of herself: "Don't go out at night alone; it's too dangerous for a woman"; "I'll handle the kids' argument; they'll listen to me"; "Next time the repairman comes, be sure I'm here. I know what to say to him"; "You better let me handle the checkbook; you just don't know how." Variations on such statements may have occurred for years, eroding a woman's confidence in her self-reliance. But at the time of divorce, they are restated with such emphasis that they undermine any confidence that remains. Because now is the time to pull out all the stops, husbands often come down on every point they know to be sensitive.

It's hard to resist these fears, but stop and think for a minute. For one thing, he may be able to do a number of things well, but *is* he doing them? Men often talk a good game, yet when you look at the action, it's disappointing. Gloria was married for nine years and became very close to her six-year-old daughter during the divorce. Her daughter was worried for a while about what would happen.

> My big concern was with Maggie. Maggie was a worrier. You know, she wondered how I was going to do this and that; how we were going to manage when she didn't have two parents. Well, she has discovered that Mommy can do all these things. (I always did anyway; Daddy never did them.) A friend asked if it wasn't hard adjusting to Allen not being around and I said, "No, he never did anything anyway."

This may be an overstatement when applied to your husband, but the fact is you probably *are* doing a number of things already. You are probably working a full- or part-time job, are probably paying the bills, doing the shopping, cooking, cleaning, doing the laundry, taking care of the kids, running a taxi service, gardening, dealing with doctors, dentists, and other bill collectors. You know the list; it goes on and on. In doing all these things, you are not only taking care of yourself but others as well, including your husband. Indeed, you might find your work load considerably lighter without him. You do have many skills and you could develop more as you go along.

Judith, a woman of thirty-five, exuded humor and strength when she talked about this.

> Maybe the purpose of this whole relationship was for me to prove to myself that I could take care of myself. Maybe that was the karmic purpose of it all—to find out I could do *ANYTHING*. You can move me into a house and stick three kids on me, and I'll still keep the hours I work now—and I'll bet I can handle it. I don't have any fear of handling *anything*—money, cars, anything.

Many women discount the tasks they do. They either think they're not doing that much or that what they're doing is unimportant.

The following exercises are helpful in clarifying that you *can* manage on your own:

1. Keep a daily record of what you do for two weeks. Include in it everything from going to work, to entertaining, to cleaning the hair out of the shower drain. At the end, look at the list. Hang it up somewhere. Pat yourself on the back for all you have done.

2. Start learning something related to your survival needs. If you can't change a tire, learn how and do it. Read the instruction manual for your water heater. Talk to other women about how they manage their house and accomplish what they do. You might pick up some shortcuts. Especially check in with women who are doing it on their own.

Finally, dispel the myth of the Big, Bad World. It's not all that fearsome. When you get into it, you will find that it's just another system. It is made up of people like you, each trying to make his or her own way. Some of it is hype, some of it is hustle, but none of it is beyond your reach. Whether it is during your divorce or in any future relationship, you will want to establish your independence. There is no feeling more precious and no need more imperative.

Fear of Being Responsible

It's not easy to admit that some of your fears about leaving might have to do with the fact that from now on you will have to take full responsibility for the results of your actions. In a marriage that has been in trouble for a long time, the partners get into the habit of blaming each other for all the awful things that are happening. The next step is that this crutch becomes a permanent and necessary support, and the responsibility for every misfortune is automatically placed on the other person. However justified some of your complaints are, it is easy to grow fearful in the area of making decisions and carrying them through when you realize you no longer have someone else to blame if they don't work out.

Eric Berne once described the situation as one which couples commonly play. He called it the game of "If It Weren't for You." In this psychological interaction, a woman unconsciously chooses a man who is domineering or unreliable so that she will be the victim, and thus not be responsible for either her actions or the outcome of them. When things predictably go wrong, she then can blame him and avoid confronting her own decisions. We don't often set out to play these roles, but in the complicated games of relating that take place in the intensity of failing marriages, you may find yourself caught up in them.

Much of the problem of fearing responsibility has to do with performance anxiety. When leaving a relationship you find that you are at a point in your life where you can do whatever you want. You may feel that the spotlight is on you, that after having made strong claims about independence and personal growth you had better come through. What if in six months you are just as miserable as before—whom do you blame then? And how will you face the knowing looks of others whose smiles are saying, "I told you so." The questions that you ask yourself can be agonizing ones: What if I fail? What if I find out that I have some hidden personality flaw? What if I have been wrong?

When you are finally divorced, there is no ready scapegoat for the random ills that befall you. There will no longer be anyone to point a finger at or complain about. If your life isn't working, *you* are going to have to do something about it. You may have always had the luxury of blaming someone else for things—Mom or Dad, a sister, your boss, your husband. But there comes a time—and now is that time—to stand alone and face the fear that you may make mistakes. Accept that responsibility.

But also remember, a mistake is not a disaster. It is a *mis*-take. When a movie is being made, the people involved in filming it expect to shoot a particular scene over several times. It is rarely done in one "take." This is an accepted procedure.

You are not being kind to yourself if you expect to do everything right the first time. You are lucky if you succeed the first time.

There are going to be *mis*-takes, and they are simply that. You can learn and gain experience from your mistakes. They can be valuable learning tools.

Look at the other side of responsibility. You can be responsible—solely—for the *good* things that happen to you. This sense of personal achievement can be wonderful. If you find a job that proves successful, *you* can take credit. If, by yourself, you decorate your living quarters in a warm and pleasant way, *you* have created this. If the children seem more secure and less agitated, *your* actions have produced this environment. It feels great to be able to take credit for accomplishments, large or small.

Being responsible means being in control. This does not have to be a tight, ever present scrutinizing of everything that goes on around you. It can mean being in charge of both initiating actions that are needed and seeing them through to rewarding conclusions.

Fear of Disapproval

> One of the first things Bobby said when I told him I wanted a divorce, and had filed for it, was, "It's going to be published in the paper!" and I'm thinking, "Yes it is and the world's going to know." He was hoping I could do something less public. He was worried about what people would think.

In this case Susan's husband was more concerned about disapproval than she was, but men certainly have no corner on that fear. In fact, when a woman initiates a divorce, there is often a very strong negative reaction toward her by both friends and family. It has to do with the still uncommon practice of a woman putting her needs first, and the courage it takes to express that. Women can expect this disapproval, though the fear of it can inhibit even the most committed person.

For instance, many women dread the day when they will have to tell their parents that they are getting a divorce. There is always a long, careful explanation to be given, and at this time the woman herself may be struggling to make sense of it all. It is hard to face parental judgment; they were the first and still may represent the final authority. In some ways, you are becoming a "loose woman" in that you are entering those uncharted areas where any liaison could be struck up. Your minister, relatives, coworkers, and "friends" may respond in similar ways. Add to that the fear of disapproval when you tell your children, and it is not surprising that many women are tentative and worried.

It would take another chapter to study the subtleties of why some people might respond strongly to your action. Some disapproval is disguised envy. There is more than one person you know who secretly wishes she had your nerve. Others might be outraged, threatened, or genuinely saddened. But there will be some who will say, "Great!" and others who will think it but never tell you.

A friend of mine refused to tell her mother that she had separated from her husband because of her family's strong Catholic background. Her parents lived thousands of miles away, so for six months she was able to carry on the illusion that she was still living with her husband. When she finally visited them, she took her mother for a long drive in the car, at last getting the nerve up to announce the "tragedy." Afterward, there was a short silence. Then her mother matter-of-factly responded, "I *thought* something was the matter. I think it's good that you're taking care of yourself." And that was all.

If you are hoping to get everybody's approval, give up. It's not going to happen. It is not realistic, even from the majority of those you care about—at least not at first. And it's not necessary that they *do* approve wholeheartedly. In this regard, you have to get a little tough with your feelings. A frank and realistic approach is needed here. Cynthia Poole, a psychologist who counsels reentry women, remarks, "Usually the people who disapprove the most about your breakup didn't approve of your marriage either!" You might check this out, especially in relation to your parents.

It is not essential that you please others. In a year from now, they will care less. In the meantime, it is your life and these are your decisions. Stop looking for that list of reasons for leaving that will be good enough to suit everybody. Naturally you want to explain yourself; but after you do, you can't control their reactions.

Be good to yourself in this matter. Seek out other women in similar situations and share your feelings with them. There are small accomplishments you make during this time that can only be appreciated by another person who has gone through it. Look for that kind of help.

Don't spend time with disapproving people. You may be stuck with them at times, but avoid the pressure and don't seek them out! You don't need that kind of punishment.

That doesn't mean that you shouldn't listen to a genuinely concerned friend or professional. Good advice may not mean that they rubber stamp every idea you have. But you can tell who these people are by the way they relate to you. They come to you because they care for you and not to quietly condemn.

Fear of the Unknown

This fear relates not only to divorce, but to life in general. Many women and men tend to be afraid of what they don't know. Fortune tellers and astrologers live on people's insecurity about the future. We want to know what it will be like tomorrow, next month, next year. What's the weather going to be? If I take out that car loan, can I count on my job? Should I trust my health?

During divorce, the issue of the future takes on an urgency. The unknown future moves from being the subject of curious conversation to a pending emergency. It seems impossible to pierce its opaque nature and determine what shape your life will take. Factors that you have no way of predicting may enter your life and your reaction to them will determine the course of your future actions. Money matters, housing, new friends, old relationships—all of these have a vagueness about them. And in their shifting possibilities, you can hardly guess what the outcome will be.

It gets into the very question of who you are. For years a woman may have had the name Mrs. Gabrielle Smith. She not only had the name, she *was* that person. It was her identity, and it represented a complete social system. Built into it was her role of wife, mother, and a whole fabric of ways that she connected with the world around her. When faced with divorce, it was as though she was plucked out of her environment and set down in another town. Should she now, for instance, give up her married name and go back to her maiden name, Gabrielle Paxton? And what does that signify?

Sylvia is a thirty-five-year-old professional in her field, and at the time of her divorce was as confused as anybody about her identity.

> My major fear was, "Who am I? Who the hell am I?" I knew who I was as defined by the world I'd been a part of, who I was as defined by my role as his wife. I knew who I was as my parents' daughter—but I had no idea who *I* was. I had lived alone before, but those periods were so brief, erratic, and crazy that it was no basis for comparison. Actually, one of the reasons I thought marriage would be wonderful was that I'd have structure.

What makes the fear of the unknown so hard is that there seems to be no way to prepare for it. Since you don't know what is involved, you feel vulnerable. You are also drawn to think the worst. It's not hard to imagine some pretty disastrous scenarios for what will happen to you after you leave. It is a normal human reaction when faced with an obscure future.

When you were young, the fear of the unknown might have been that dark closet with its half-opened door in your bedroom. At night, *anything* could have been in there, and your imagination made the worst of it. But when you called your mother and she turned on the light, you saw that it was just filled with clothes and shoes. The outcome of what you are experiencing now may be as ordinary as that. The future will reveal itself in its own time; and when it does, it will be manageable.

The unknown is also an adventure, and you can react to this situation from that perspective. It is a rare chance to explore parts of yourself and the world that you have never known. Fear can also be excitement, the kind of thrill that any scientist or explorer feels when he or she is on the verge of discovery. The mystery of the unknown is seen as a challenge.

Audrey has been divorced for two years now, and spoke to me about her experience with this.

> Since my divorce I discovered that I am all right, that the universe does support me if I put out the legwork. My friends are there for me, too. I didn't fall into some abyss—it just wasn't my experience. But I had to find out for myself.

Here's a practical way to start to work on your fears.

1. Ask yourself, "What's the worst thing that could happen?" When you know it, say that fear out loud. Write it down. Now, begin a process that I call "buying insurance." Write down all the things you could do to get through that fear should it become a reality. For example, you may be afraid that your husband will get custody of the kids by proving you are an unfit mother because of an affair you have had. An option you could list to deal with that fear is to go see a lawyer and get specific information on the issue. Your fears can usually be dispelled when you become informed. At least the punch goes out of them.

2. Next, make a list of the rest of your fears, and go through the same process with each one. Allow yourself several sessions to do this. As you eliminate your fears, cross them off your list. Now, put the paper away, and go back to it in a month. See if any of the fears have lost their power. As you get through some of them, others will lose their potency.

Fear will stay around for as long as you want it to. It can literally determine every decision of your life, from who you talk to at the grocery checkout to what you wear to the beach. Now and forever you will live with some darkness. The world is composed of light and shadow, day and night. You cannot cancel out these elements. But consider that "dark" is not synonymous with bad. The same would be true if you chose to stay in your marriage. The security of it is an illusion. It changed in the last five years; it would have continued to change. However, if that change was a downward spiral, your new future holds real hope.

Liz put her whole experience in this perspective:

> I have only one fear—a dead mouse in the mousetrap. And I will have to find myself a mouse taker-outer of mousetraps. Someone I can call who will come over and do it.

DEPRESSION

Depression hardly needs definition. If you are in it, you know it; if you are not, be thankful. It is, as they say, the pits. At various points in this book already, depression has been described. It is a common and recurring state of being for women during divorce, something that counselors deal with regularly. It is especially hard for everyone because it is such a consuming state, affecting the person as much physically as mentally. You can *see* a depressed person. Her facial muscles, the slope of the shoulders, the way she carries herself, even the skin tone will reflect how she is feeling. A depressed person has little energy to do anything despite the fact that she might sleep more than usual. A suppressed appetite will add to this, although some women react by eating much more (of the wrong things) to fill up their needs. When a person is very depressed, it is always hard to know where to start first—helping her verbally or physically.

Depression for most women during the divorce process stems from feeling overwhelmed by problems that seem too large and too numerous for her to handle. It may be the first time she has even managed problems of this magnitude so directly. She responds by putting more pressure on herself but in the process does not allow for the natural release of her feelings of anger, fear, and sadness. The energy it takes to both hold down feelings and deal with current problems so drains a woman that she finally responds by giving it all up and shutting down. The result is that she becomes immobilized. Long days and longer nights are spent wondering if it will end, and how. One woman caught in the depression of divorce recently said to me with simple irony,

"I don't understand how people don't go crazy through all of this."

To be depressed is to feel powerless. Physically you have little energy. The events of life seem to be beyond your control. Strangely, although depression is based on past events and future anxieties, there is an overwhelming sense of the dead present. It makes coping even more difficult. It makes leaving a relationship an almost impossible effort.

There are ways out. Movement is a key. Because depression is such a static space, simple physical movement is the beginning. The very act of walking from one room to another is simple proof that you can change your state of being and your relationship to the things around you. Start by doing ordinary physical activities around the house, ones that call for going from place to place. Take a shower. Get outside. Walk to the store instead of driving. Jogging is highly recommended. This doesn't have to mean a huge training program; simply going to a park and running slowly is enough.

Make sure you include physical and sensual experiences every day, even though it seems to go against your instinct at this time, and pay attention to your diet. A later chapter is devoted to their importance.

One way to deal with depression is not to deny it. Feel it, accept it, but go *through* it. This also means an opening up to all of your feelings, expressed and suppressed. Even depression can have its ultimate rewards. Audrey went into depression after she left a twelve-year marriage with her husband. She was with another man when her low point was struck.

Hitting bottom was very dark. Extremely dark. A lot of crying, a lot of anger. When Mitchell came into my life, he was an expert on the dark side. Both in living it and accepting it in other people. So here was someone who kept pushing me to be angry or to be afraid, and to be upfront with that. And I would say. "No, no, I'm just fine." But that whole dark side started coming up and I gradually learned it was all right to be angry, even terrified. So all the terror came up and I was pretty much of a basket case for a while. I was angry, hateful, jealous—all the dark fears. It was pure terror. It was like going down to a real dark, dark, place; but it was where I needed to go.

And coming out of that, I'm much more human now. Much more accepting of other people, much less righteous. Having it all together was a facade.

I'm not opting for people getting stuck on the dark side. I simply recognize that's part of who I am, and it's OK to be afraid or angry. And it's all right to be joyous, too.

Her willingness to confront all sides of herself and accept them was a way out for her. It can be a harrowing experience. But the denial of your problems by holding them down turns out to be a holding down of *you*. You are depressing yourself.

Use the techniques suggested in the exercises dealing with "anger." Repressed fear, sadness, and anger cause depression. Release is what is needed here. For some, however, relief may be found in something as simple as what Dr. Gerald Jampolsky suggests:

It seems strange indeed that most people understand that they need to urinate and have a bowel movement regularly or else they would die from the toxins in their bodies. Yet most people do not on a daily basis rid themselves of the toxins they put into their minds, such as guilt, fears, and painful experiences.

A simple mental "imagery" you can do every night before going to sleep is to put all your guilty feelings, painful experiences, and fears into a garbage can or box and attach it to a balloon filled with helium and let it go.

By including this, I do not mean to treat depression lightly. It has become a prolonged and recurring theme in many women's lives. But sometimes changing your mental imagery helps. I find, for instance, that going to a good movie always helps me to change my moods. In a darkened theater, I can usually get out of my own problems and into the story of another person. The identification that goes on with the character allows me to be that person for a couple of hours. When I come out of it, I find that I'm free to choose a different state of mind from the one I entered with. Good drama is cleansing. So is good music, or a good conversation with a friend.

Despite what you have been telling yourself, this is not the end of the world. There is a solution. If you need professional help, don't hesitate to seek it out. If you have recurring thoughts about suicide, take it as a warning and see someone immediately or call the Suicide Hotline in your area. Depression has come from not taking good care of yourself at various points along the way. Start right now to change that. You will begin to move away from depression when you experience what you know to be true—that you have the power to change your life in ways that will give you more happiness.

SADNESS

Sadness is a soft emotion and one you don't have to be afraid of. It is a normal response to a loss. You can't expect to live with a person, sharing some of your deeper moments with him, as well as dreams for your life together, and not feel badly about breaking up. Whereas guilt is a personally damaging response to divorce, sadness is not. It is a simple admission of caring, and the feelings should not be confused with other emotions. Sadness is not depression. Depression locks you in, but sadness washes over you in waves.

There is really no purpose in suppressing sadness when it comes. Nostalgic feelings are a part of human nature. Blocking those feelings only hardens you and binds you up. Some women feel more potent when they are angry, and feel weak when sad. But sadness does not mean that you have changed your mind about your husband or that you can't be realistic about your present needs. This doesn't mean that you must communicate your feelings to him. Choose a close friend or a therapist to relate your sadness to. Don't cut yourself off from the full range of human emotions. Each has its place.

Barbara was married for twelve years, and as often happens when children are involved, has kept in close touch with her former husband. Although she is firmly convinced of the rightness of her decision and is happy in her new life, she still allows herself to have mixed feelings about it all.

> I still feel sad at times. I noticed that the other day when Frank came along to our son's soccer game. We all went there together and came back together. I had sadness about the family—not about me not being with him—but about this lack of family.

Barbara would find no advantage in not letting herself consciously feel that. The alternative would be to close off her feelings and take on a cool, unaffected exterior. The problem is that shutting off sadness completely can begin to influence other parts of your life that call for natural human emotions. Human beings are of one piece, and nothing happens to one part of us that does not show up throughout.

Liz was able to feel sadness yet continue in her resolve, putting it all into perspective and coming out feeling strong.

> I truly believe in my heart that I am glad we had these years. I am sorry that I continued it for so long when I started to be so unhappy. At that point I was unable to split. And there was the growing apart—the tension, the fights, and the things that shouldn't have happened. I'm sad about that. But I'm not sorry for what I've learned from the relationship. I'm not sorry that I was married.
>
> I also know there will be things that I will miss. And I'll hurt for those things. But you can't have the whole basket.

GETTING SOME HELP

As George Bach and Peter Wyden point out in this passage below, getting help in the form of some kind of professional therapy is not a luxury but almost a necessity. The act of divorcing yourself from another person is wrenching and the aftershocks touch every part of your existence. The effects cannot be ignored.

> Unless partners wean themselves away from each other, preferably in therapy groups that help reduce their feelings of fear and guilt, they are likely to emerge from divorce like battle casualties. They

may congratulate themselves on their freedom, but psychologically they resemble zombies. They find it difficult to accept their changed status in the community and become vulnerable to sexual and financial exploitation.

If you have had some experience in psychological counseling, you will probably recognize that your action in leaving and the events that surround it need some guidance. If you have not been in a program of therapy before, dispel the idea that such help implies that you have serious personal flaws. Just as with physical problems, there are times in life when the stress of things demands that you get some outside help. It should be neither controversial nor embarrassing.

Finding the right kind of counseling for you may take some time and investigation. Begin by asking some friends who have been involved in therapy. Your doctor may know a good psychologist, or check with the community mental health organization in your area. Women's organizations usually have ties with psychological counselors who are sensitive to the special issues of women in divorce.

It is important that you be comfortable with the person or persons with whom you are going to share your most intimate feelings. Before you commit yourself to therapy, see if you can find out how the therapist feels about divorce, a woman leaving a relationship, and working mothers. Ask about the fees and whether they are negotiable.

There are many forms of counseling, including private sessions, group therapy, weekend workshops, self-help groups, classes in self-awareness, and meditation retreats. Choose something that fits for you.

When the therapy begins, give yourself to it. Set some goals for yourself and make a commitment to stick with it for at least six to twelve months. Growth is change and change is both scary and exciting.

The point is that changing your life is not merely a matter of moving into a new house or living with someone different. That is a beginning. But the real change happens when you take on new attitudes and respond to the world as if you are discovering it for the first time. That is when life really gets exciting. Therapy can give you a boost in that direction.

SELF-ESTEEM

Throughout the chapter, we have seen a variety of ways in which unresolved or distorted emotions can undermine your determination, judgment, and hope. In the confusion of feelings there is a gradual erosion of a sense of well-being and confidence—in short, your *self-esteem*. Healthy self-esteem is the single most important key to sustaining your sense of validity in life, and it is especially crucial during this difficult period. If you have a high level of self-esteem, it will make your entire transition much easier and more productive. The problems won't go away, but the way in which you approach them will be much different.

So much of life is common sense. A truth: When you feel good about yourself you can better handle whatever comes along at any moment. Each day takes on a warm glow. This is not a Pollyanna approach to life, one in which the unpleasant is simply ignored or imagined not to exist. A person with strong self-esteem recognizes the complex nature of human activity, but also has the courage not to use that complexity as an excuse for apathy or self-pity. High self-esteem fosters trust in your ability to take charge of your life. This attitude filters down into everything that you do during the day—from the way you handle the children, to the attention you give to your financial future, to the manner in which you deal with your husband.

Dave Chittock, a counselor who regularly conducts self-esteem workshops in schools and for business groups, has thoughts on the subject as it relates to women and divorce.

> Your self-esteem is nothing more than the sum total of the thoughts you have about yourself. Low self-esteem is usually the total of all the negative judgments you have made about yourself, or that others have made about you that you have accepted. If you want to know

where your self-esteem is, take a look at how others treat you. Because you will get what you think you deserve.

In relationships, *that* can be a real stunner. Sometimes I say to a client, "Well, I hate to tell you this—but you're getting exactly what you *think* you deserve! Remember, I'm not saying that you *like* what you are getting. But the way it works is that you align yourself with the kind of people who reflect the way you feel about yourself."

In your marriage you may have gotten a lot of garbage. Perhaps you believed that you deserved it. In that sense you unwittingly invited it. Low self-esteem wants its own confirmation—its motto: "Tell me how rotten I am." We can usually find another person to provide it. If during your marriage this was the nature of your ongoing war game, it is likely to be intensified during divorce. It's not hard to feel guilty and believe that you are a crummy person for breaking up your marriage. And when your husband starts dumping on you during the struggles and arguments, your self-esteem can hit rock bottom. It is up to you to be aware of your vulnerability and the damage being done.

Begin building positive attitudes by blocking those negative messages, both from within and without. A major source of destructive self-imaging comes from the fruitless and unending fights that mark the end of a relationship. Both people are hurting and want to punish the other, so that arguments quickly degenerate into insult sessions. As much as you might want to ward off the impact of such name-calling, those negative messages have a way of sinking in, furthering your self-doubt. End this kind of harmful activity. You can feel it coming a long way off—don't be seduced. Have you ever felt better about yourself after one of those arguments?

In fact, don't book time with anyone, whether it be your husband, family, or friends, who attempts to chip away at your feelings of adequacy. You shouldn't regularly engage people who don't, as Dave Chittock puts it, "support your highest good." If your mother, for example, doesn't approve of your divorce and you cannot avoid contact with her, at least cut down on the time you spend together. And don't bring up subjects that you know will invite her criticism. If she, or anyone else, continues to put you down, be frank. Say that you want to be around her and need her support, but if the criticism continues you are going to have to stop seeing her for the present.

Seek out friends who like you. Perhaps this will be a friend that in the past was not terribly close but, because you are at a new stage in your life, could become a warm and affirming companion. Spend the effort to find and be with friends who are not threatened by your changing status and who will respond to your worth and integrity.

Sometimes the source of our low self-esteem comes from within. Many of us tell ourselves, a hundred times a day, that we are not worthwhile. This becomes an ongoing inner dialog, a background noise in our heads, composed of repeated negative thoughts:

"God, am I stupid!"
"I really did a rotten job on that."
"I should get organized. What's wrong with me?"
"I was really awful with the kids yesterday. I'm a terrible mother."
"I'm overweight again—just look at me."

Self-deprecation becomes a habit, then almost a philosophy of life. It's time to reverse the process. Begin by spending a day or two paying attention to what you tell yourself *about you*. Listen as you go through your daily routine. Be aware of your internal dialog. The next day when you criticize yourself, say out loud, "Stop that!" Say it again if you need to. Then give yourself a counter-message—one that is soft and nurturing:

- I don't deserve this. It's OK, everybody makes mistakes. Next time I'll do my best to do it differently.
- Maybe I *am* too fat but putting myself down is not going to make me thin.

● I know that it's not good to yell at the kids and I don't want to. Maybe I need some time off from them.

Give yourself the break that you give other people. And stop being the first one to invalidate the positive things others have to say about you, by either mentally canceling it out or by being embarrassed. Look for and accept compliments from others and incorporate those attitudes into your own feelings about yourself. Enjoy the good feeling that comes from knowing that you are appreciated.

SELF-ACCEPTANCE

"I, _____, am lovable and deserve love." This is one affirmation that we all should acclaim. The importance of loving one's self is not a new one and the late Erich Fromm has written brilliantly on it. But the ideas need repeating, especially when you are at a point at which your sense of personal self-worth is being tested. Unless you develop a strong respect and love for yourself, you will not act in ways that are healthy and productive.

Take a look at your life and pay attention to how you treat yourself. Is it in a loving way? Or do you always put yourself last? Do you take care of your body, eat the right food, not drink too much? Do you readily believe that person who says you are cold and uncaring? The questions could be multiplied but if you truly care about yourself, you will begin to prove it in your actions.

The claim that the act of desiring a divorce is heartless selfishness is probably the most common accusation made against a woman, and the one that haunts her. But self-love is not selfishness. The two should not be confused. To be selfish is to deal with the world in a misguided way, routinely ignoring needs of others. It is the four-year-old sitting in the corner with all her toys piled around her, refusing to let her playmate have any of them. The selfish person is self-centered, egocentric, convinced that the only way to get what he or she wants is to grab at life and things. In her fear and confusion, it's no wonder she doesn't like herself.

A person with an adequate sense of self-love moves in the world with an inner feeling of security, and although events in her life may be in some turmoil, there is no panic in terms of self-questioning. When a woman has this confidence, personal attacks that attempt to trigger automatic guilt responses are seen for what they are. It is true that you are acting in your best interest in seeking a divorce. That's as it should be. It does not mean that you have been thoughtless and unfeeling or that in the future you will be uncaring. Only when you love yourself can you begin to love others.

Self-love begins with accepting yourself in your frailty and in your glory. Accept your needs, your intuition, your accomplishments, your laziness, your desires, your body, your humor, your mistakes, your wantonness, your intelligence, your failures, your dreams, your limitations, your common sense, your contradictions. Start accepting the truth of your own worth.

A FINAL WORD

The end of a relationship is a kind of death. And just as in the death of someone close to you, strong, often irresistible feelings will come over you with the end of your marriage.

The same elements are at work. If a close friend of yours died, you might feel angry that the person died of a certain disease or by sudden accident; or guilty that you had not done more for her when she was alive; or fearful of the loneliness you expect when she is now no longer around; or depressed at the thought of life without such a friend; or afraid of the unknown element of death itself.

The reactions to divorce can be just as strong, even stronger. Your feelings and emotions are acutely sensitive at this time. There will be pain. There is no way to avoid it completely. The pain of leaving is a part of life that everyone must deal with at some time, in some way. The acceptance of this reality is the beginning of your peace of mind.

CHAPTER 4

Necessary Strategies

The very idea of having a strategy in the divorce process may be repellent to some women, going against everything they believe in and have practiced. The word *strategy* brings up images of a military commander studying maps of enemy territory in some underground bunker. What does that have to do with a broken marriage? For many, this is seen as a time to grieve, to think ahead some, but not in graphic detail. To do that would be cold-hearted. As marriage seemed to just happen for these women, so too would their divorce. If a relationship is to die, it should not be premeditated.

It is essential to make the point forcefully, and it will be repeated in several contexts in the next few chapters: *You must take time right now to think through the action you propose to take, and make specific plans to achieve your goal.* If you are going to come out of your divorce in good shape with respect to your finances, living arrangements, custody tangles, and emotional stability, you are going to have to develop some strategies.

You don't have to apologize for that. It is what every reasonable person does when faced with an important issue, and surely in a case of survival. You think ahead. This is not to say that you drop your present value system. Fair play and concern for others must be maintained, but in this matter, put your needs first. If you are going to survive your divorce in one piece, you are going to have to start thinking practically. This may be an alien concept, but you are asking for trouble to the degree that you are unprepared.

One day, for instance, you might find yourself looking around at your furniture and household goods thinking about how they will be divided. As you choose some special items, you feel guilty. You shouldn't be so materialistic and selfish. It's like picking over the possessions of a dying person. You tell yourself that you shouldn't be worried about who gets the toaster.

But the fact is that some months from now you will either have the toaster, or you will be at a discount store buying one, or you will not be eating toast. That may not seem to be the biggest issue in your life right now, but some February morning it will be. And although you may be able to handle *that* situation, you also might not have a refrigerator, a car, a home, adequate child support, and the rest because you were insufficiently prepared.

I challenge women who say that they don't believe in making decisions in advance and wouldn't get involved in specific preparations without first telling their husbands. It has been my experience that most women think about leaving, as I did, well in advance of doing so, and fantasize in precise terms what they might do, and how it will turn out. But because of their guilt, they often short-circuit these thoughts and refuse to actually carry them to a stage where they are fully acknowledged and accepted. Blocking yourself from making preparations that are in your best interests is another method of self-defeat. If you are going to do something—anything—do it in the most conscious and effective way.

When Christine was at this point of her divorce, she faced some criticism from women with whom she worked. But she stood up to it.

> Some of the girls I talked to thought I was very cold-blooded. At first I felt that I had to defend myself, but then I told them that it takes courage to act on what you believe. It's not cold. I thought it was kind of smart myself. If I had done it the way they wanted me

to do it, God knows where I would be living, what I would be doing. At least this way I'm comfortable. I took care of myself first and it gave me time to get my head together. It didn't hurt my husband anyway—he's doing just fine.

The other side of making preparations is doing nothing, just letting things happen as they might. This is not a morally superior stance. It is an avoidance of taking responsibility for your life. In this situation, no one is going to come and rescue you, so it's no time to play the victim. Taking care of yourself, however, sometimes means being willing to do unpleasant things.

STRATEGY AND YOUR HUSBAND

One of the most disagreeable parts of these plans is that it calls for you to begin them without telling your husband. This may seem like heresy. Nobody likes to be thought of as sneaky and the first response to the idea might be, "No, I can't—it's dishonest. That's going too far. I'm going to talk to him first." I would generally not recommend that.

Leaving a relationship calls for a delicate balance. The entire subject is a mine field. It should not be a kamikaze adventure in which one plunges ahead recklessly. If in the name of honesty you flatly tell your husband that you are going to leave, but have done nothing beforehand to prepare for some money, shelter, or job, who benefits from it? Is it good for you or the children? Your lack of preparation is not even good for your husband, because suddenly he has not only his emotions to contend with, but also the details of *your* life. Neither of you gain anything from the complete confusion created by this.

But remember this truth: At some time in the near future, your lives will be going in very different directions. In the past, you shared a common life. The purposes and goals of your marriage were jointly agreed upon. In that sense, you might have felt yourself committed or even duty bound to tell him everything. But that is no longer the case. Your relationship is well on the way to dissolving, and in a relatively short time you will be independent of him. Begin to feel that independence right now, and do it in good conscience. If you wait until the divorce papers are served before you begin to act on your own behalf, it will be too late. Many of the important decisions about your future will already be cast. Five years from now you will be in separate worlds. Take care to shape your own world well and trust that he will take care of his.

Do not hesitate to begin to give your life an autonomous structure. For instance, you might want to open a separate checking account at a bank under your own name in order to establish your own credit and prevent your husband from having access to it. It is important to do it now because building credit references takes time, and you may need good credit as soon as you are on your own. If you told your husband that you had done this, a confrontation would follow in which your full intentions would be revealed. Your whole timetable for leaving would be shattered. It is not that some abstract sense of order would be upset, but very practically you may be unprepared to take on all of the responsibilities that are demanded after your private desire for a divorce becomes an announced reality. There may be some satisfaction in saying that you were "open" with him, but the premature revelation of your plans could cause misery to everyone.

If you are bothered by the "fair play" argument, think about it for a moment. As a woman in this culture, you are at a disadvantage. There is no place where that is more clear than the job market. For every dollar a man makes, a woman will make seventy-two cents (1991 figures). According to a recent study by the U.S. Department of Education, women achieve higher grades than men in school, but that performance does not pay off in the workplace. After graduation, women earn as much as men in only seven of thirty-three major occupations. Without getting into futile discussions about who works harder, the situation is such that a man enjoys the monetary fruits of the economic system much more fully than a woman. In all practicality, you must compensate for this penalty with wise and prudent preparation, and without regret. In many ways, your marriage has been your occupation. It is what occupied your time and energy. Especially if you worked in the home, the value of your efforts were probably never computed or properly rewarded.

When a smart man is planning to change occupations, he doesn't announce it to his company beforehand and then go look for something else. He writes a résumé and sends it out to several places. He checks with employment agencies. When he has something, he gives notice to the people at the office. That is the accepted practice. It is not considered disloyal, and he would be considered foolish to do otherwise.

Do the same with your preparations. Almost every attorney interviewed suggests that women adopt this course of action. Take your time and act with deliberation. I know that to some this may sound harsh. But I have seen too many women, in the name of sensitivity and nostalgia, stuck in a swamp of half-realized intentions and broken dreams.

In none of this should your actions be mean-spirited or vindictive. You may or may not think that your husband deserves it; that's not the point. At this stage you are working to get free of the relationship, and you can do that while still acting with civility, and even caring. That means he does not need to *know* everything. What we are talking about here are your survival needs.

TIME

A primary concern for a woman is *when* she should leave. As her marriage deteriorates and as the idea of divorce comes closer and closer to being real, there is often an urgency about when and how to do it. It is natural. You don't want to spend your life just putting in time when you know that the relationship is at an end and has nothing more to offer.

I should, however, advise you to slow down your inner time clock and consider the many points brought up in this chapter. You have been in your marriage for years. Don't panic and hurry the process unnecessarily. The extra time that you take now getting your life in order is well spent. If you try to pack too much into a short period, you will find that the overload will only bring on confusion and turmoil.

It is very hard to generalize here. Each marriage has its own set of problems, tensions, living arrangements, and economics. A few common characteristics can be noted that affect the time span needed for preparation and leaving.

If, for example, a woman has a job that pays well enough to give her a sense of economic independence, and if she is childless and lives with her husband in a rented apartment, the time spent in the leaving process can be very short. It is primarily a matter of becoming emotionally secure. This doesn't mean there aren't going to be problems, however. Even when the primary issues are who gets the stereo and the television set, arguments resulting from this can trigger tremendous hostility. It is not the value of the property, but what it represents in letting the other take it.

But most marriages are not so fortunate. When two persons are intimately joined for a number of years, their lives become so intertwined that separating the threads is not a thing that can be readily done. The more stuff that is accumulated, the greater the difficulty. Who *does* own the house, the car, the washing machine, the couch, that piece of property you bought? Who will get the children? When a woman enters into a marriage, she gives little thought to the complex ways that she has bound herself to her husband. The husband often brings in the primary income for the family, and it is understood that the money is to be equally shared between them. The woman receives these benefits for her contribution to the family structure.

But with divorce, what about her rights to the retirement fund that her husband has paid into all those years at work? How hard should she push for her share? Her future security is as important as her husband's, more so if she will be the primary caretaker of the children. These are problems that need her careful consideration. There are many others. When you leave, weigh the relative importance of your future safekeeping and support against your urge to be rid of your present married relationship. Don't be impatient.

The preparation time necessary to leave varies according to your state of readiness. For a woman who has continually stayed on top of the details of life, this could mean that she could be ready in a matter of a month or two. Most women, however, should think in terms of six months to two years. The idea of spending that much time in an unhappy marriage gets a lot of resistance from women at first—until they seriously consider it. During a workshop that I taught, the question came up about how much time I thought a woman needs to prepare to leave. I said that it was not unusual for a woman to take at least a year to get ready. Many of the women agonized over this estimate, one giving out the complaint that others were thinking, "My God, a year! I don't think I can stand it that long!"

Looking back on the members of that group, and what they did, is instructive. Some of the group left their relationships in a matter of months, and things seem to have worked out well for them. But what most of them had in common was either a good job, some specialized training or skill, or a comfortable financial arrangement. Their preparation consisted of readying themselves emotionally and getting support from other women in the group.

For the women who took longer, the problem of dependency was a more serious issue. Their economic prospects looked grim and as that became more apparent to them, they realized that they needed to solidify their future.

Roberta came into the group in October. She was a woman of thirty-five with two girls in grammar school. It was clear that she had a very strong desire to get out of her relationship right away, but it was also evident that she was neither emotionally nor financially prepared. She soon realized this, and in the next few months the group helped her break through one barrier at a time. By January, she had narrowed down her needs to money. At that time she studied her problem and began lining up some finances—borrowing money from her mother to see a lawyer. The lawyer gave her the factual information on what she could expect to get from her husband. Finally Roberta settled on a date: She would wait until the income tax return came. That would give her a solid amount to start off with, and it also fixed a definite goal to point to. The check came in early April and she left.

This may seem too systematic for some women, but don't discount it. Life can be very uncompromising, and unless you take time to protect your interests, you are simply hoping for things to work out by the fortune of good luck. It may or may not happen. Gretchen was another member of that group. She was very unhappy in her marriage, and although she admitted to being unprepared, within two weeks she told her husband that she wanted a divorce. The roof fell in on her. Because of incredible fights that became increasingly violent, she was forced to scramble to keep even a semblance of sanity for herself and her two children. Finally in the midst of a very bad situation, she left. But the cost in terms of wear and tear was excessive. When she came back to the group for help, she was the first to admit that she had made a big mistake, but the damage was done.

I don't mean to minimize your understandable need to get through this time and get on with a life that is more joyful. The point is if you take a little extra time, that goal will be more surely achieved.

Charting Your Way

How do you begin to get your finances together now? Before you start thinking about it, dispel the echoes of male complaints about women as gold diggers. Men can afford to make such statements, but only you know what your intentions are.

What follows is a guide to practical ways of starting to take care of yourself financially, even before you have left your husband. An intensive study of money matters is a subject unto itself; there are some fine, readable books on the subject, notably those of Sylvia Porter. The Recommended Reading section lists several important titles. But a woman at this point in her life can use some simple and direct help in finding her way out. Give each step your serious consideration. The chart on page 121 is an overview of the steps you will want to take:

MONEY: THE *SHORT* RANGE

Many references have already been made to your need for financial security. It is clear that money is a fundamental concern

● **Short-Term Goals**

    1-Start saving money.

    2-Pay off as many of your bills as possible.

    3-Get a post office box.

    4-Open a bank account in your name.

    5-Establish credit in your own name.

    6-Do some detective work. Find and make copies of all important documents and tax records.

    7-To get direction, make a one-hour appointment with an attorney for information and evaluation on your specific case. Bring your documents.

    8-Investigate all your assets. Get professional help if you suspect you must research hidden assets.

    9-If you own property, consult attorney and financial advisor regarding real estate value, sale, and tax consequences.

    10-Evaluate where you will live. If you will be moving, check out the housing market and rentals to determine costs.

    11-Arrange for the car to be in top working order.

    12-Schedule your dental work and medical checkups before leaving, for both you and the children.

    13-Renovate and renew your wardrobe for work.

● **Long-Term Goals: Creating a financial picture of your future**

    1-Evaluate your present financial condition and job situation.

    2-Draw up a mock budget of what it will cost you to live separately.

    3-With input from an attorney, figure out approximate income from spousal support and child support.

    4-Calculate your separate income.

    5-Set goals for your career future, and start taking steps toward that end.

for a woman setting out on her own. This is the reality for women "out there" alone. The fact is that to survive in the world you will need some money now. Traditionally, women working in their home have not been rewarded with any kind of salary, and women in the work force are greatly underpaid. Even families on two incomes are struggling, so this presents an obvious problem.

Start Saving Money

You will need some cash on hand for the small and large expenses that will come up as you leave. Your lawyer, for instance, will want some money up front. Again, how to get this and not let your husband know is a real problem. In many traditional marriages, the wife is treated like an overgrown child, slightly irresponsible and, therefore, supervised closely where money is involved. It is a dilemma. On the one hand you need some money to tide you over during your transition period, and on the other you may be reluctant to take money for your own private use out of the general pot.

Martha is forty-one and worked in her home all of her married life. She was caught at the juncture where her lack of finances was the only thing stopping her from leaving.

> Terry watched over money pretty closely. Besides, there really wasn't much money for me to play around with and certainly not enough for me to have some on my own. But I was able to save some out of the grocery bill. I shopped carefully and didn't buy the expensive brands. Then I'd write a check for five or ten dollars more than the bill. It didn't take long before I had $240 saved. It wasn't that much but it was a help and I wasn't so worried.

Some women may need several thousand dollars in order to leave. The amount of money that must be saved will differ based on your individual situation. If you know of a way to make enough money to get you through this difficult period, do it. But it is going to take planning and thought. The reality is that you can't leave with your purse empty. Money allows you to have choices.

Be sure to let your attorney know if you have any savings. He/she may want you to fill in that amount on the financial statement in the divorce papers. Check with your lawyer regarding the likelihood of your having to return any of the money.

With your attorney's guidance, transfer your share of joint funds into a separate bank account. Timing here is important.

Pay Off Your Bills

As much as possible, take it upon yourself to pay up existing bills, credit cards, doctors, dentists, etc., with joint funds before separation. Remember that you have one-half responsibility for all of the debts that you and your husband have incurred. If he has been a free spender (or charger), the debt for this after you leave could become partly yours.

Don't run up any new bills. Resist the temptation to buy and charge unneeded items. It doesn't make sense to create more debts.

With that idea in mind, be frugal with yourself. Begin to do without. Spend half as much as you normally do on birthday and Christmas presents. Shop at discount stores and go to thrift shops for clothes for the kids. Barter when you can. Find out if there isn't something you can exchange for what you want.

This stripping away to the essentials can be very healthful and freeing at this time in your life. Most of us carry around too much baggage. You may find that a simpler existence relieves you of a burden you forget you were carrying. Starting over sometimes simply means letting go of ways that we have grown used to.

Get a Post Office Box

A post office box costs very little and can be very handy. You will not want bank statements, loan applications, correspondence with your lawyer, and other mailings being sent to your home address. This is especially true if your husband is home a lot.

However, if you live in a small town, even a P.O. box might be a problem, depending on the gossip level of the community. In such cases, be sure to seek out banking services, a lawyer, and other arrangements in some place a safe distance away.

Establish Credit in Your Name

We live in a society built on credit, and prudent use of it can greatly assist you in meeting your immediate needs while at the same time give you breathing space. But credit is a problem for divorced women. Don't assume that if you had a good credit record as a married couple, you will automatically have it as a single person. It doesn't work that way. Unless you have had accounts in your own name and have established a record of payments, the credit for all the time payments made during your marriage will be assigned to your husband. It does not matter that you wrote the checks and paid everything regularly.

Take the time to establish credit in your own name. Do this before you are separated or divorced so that these accounts will be open to you when you need them. Apply for credit cards and accounts in your name alone, and never as Mrs. Somebody. Certain states have community property laws which will allow you to use the assets and property you own jointly, as well as your spouse's salary, when you apply for credit. Remember, you don't just want an extra card from your husband's account with your name on it. You want your own separate account.

If the creditors question you about this, tell them that you want to build a good credit history to establish your financial independence, that you are thinking about starting up a business, even that you are preparing for the day when you might be a widow. According to the Federal Equal Credit Opportunity Act, the creditor is not allowed to discriminate against a person on the basis of sex or marital status. But in practice, it still goes on. However, if your application is rejected, you have a right to be told the reason why. Press the issue.

Apply first at a local department store or local bank. They may approve your application even when you do not meet standards of a credit institution. After having established yourself locally, you can then move up to a national credit card. This can all be done during this interim period.

It is also possible to build a good credit rating with a bank or savings and loan institution if you start small. If you have a job and a good employment record, apply for an unsecured loan of say, $200. Pay it back in regular installments. If you don't have a job, try to get a couple hundred dollars together and put it in a savings account. Then go to the bank and ask for a loan of that amount. This "passbook" loan is relatively easy to obtain. It will begin to establish you as a good credit risk. Later you may want to apply for a loan on a car or some furniture, or use this as a reference for credit elsewhere.

Check into credit unions. These unions are usually organized to service groups of people with some common bond. Teachers' and state employees' credit unions are probably the best known. But in the past decade a number of feminist credit unions have sprung up around the country. They are sensitive to the needs of women who do not fit the traditional profiles demanded by banks.

Do Some Detective Work

In order to get yourself started on the right track, it is recommended that you consult an attorney in the early stages of the leaving process, preferably a specialist in matrimonial law. At first, retain the attorney for a one-hour consultation only. You will want to know the laws in your state, the amount of money you will need to start proceedings when you are ready to do so, and their evaluation regarding your divorce specifically. We take this up at length in the following chapter.

In addition, a financial consultant or accountant can help in wading through complex finances and documents. Obtaining preliminary estimates of the value of the property you own will help you get a clear picture of joint assets and liabilities. This helps set goals and future plans with the built-in likelihood that they will work.

Gather information about what you *own* and what you *owe*. Often these kinds of documents disappear or are hard to obtain once a divorce is announced. You will need copies of such items as tax returns, insurance policies, financial statements, statements from creditors, bank records, both savings and checking (preferably with copies of canceled checks), mortgage papers, brokerage statements, and retirement plan documents.

During the course of the divorce negotiations, women frequently express concerns that their spouse may be hiding the existence of certain money or property. This is especially true with regard to husbands who are self-employed entrepreneurs. If you suspect this is going on, discuss these concerns with an attorney or financial consultant at the start. Because of the complexity of such a situation, their expertise will help determine the location of these hidden assets, or whether in fact they do exist. A frequent way assets are hidden is if a person receives cash payments or in-kind compensation for work performed. A clue to this is if your spouse has a record of buying things of substantial value and pays cash. The list of ways to hide assets is a long one. Check and record the contents of any safety deposit boxes, and put away your keys. Your investigations will pay off.

Once again, these measures may seem "sneaky." But realize that in gathering information regarding your assets, you are collecting documentation to which you are entitled, and to which your husband also has access. If you do not take steps to protect your share of the joint assets now, it could cost you a great deal of money and grief later.

GENERAL STRATEGIES

There is more to leaving than just getting enough money to do it. Even when you have some, there are many questions to be answered. They may all crowd in on you at once, but don't get overwhelmed. If you take them one at a time, each accomplishment can be seen as a step toward your goal. Have faith in your capacity to work through it.

Housing

Concern about just where you are going to be living after your divorce may be a major source of anxiety. There are certainly advantages in staying where you are—it is simply less trouble physically. With all of the other changes in your life, you may not feel capable of handling this one. Moving can be costly and it is time-consuming. If you have children, it is somewhat disruptive. Given the change that is happening in their lives, you may not feel that you want to upset them more than is necessary. New schools and new friends are not a problem if you stay in your present situation, and it affords them a sense of continuity at a time when they will need it. The familiar surroundings could make things easier for everyone.

There are also financial advantages to staying. If you and your husband own the house, mortgage payments may be cheaper than rent. The payments that you would make on the house could be used in the future as a basis for loans, credit, and refinancing.

If you are presently renting an apartment or house with your husband, the issues may be of equal importance. In some cities it is nearly impossible to rent adequate housing, and couples wait for months and years to find the right place. Deciding who goes and who stays may be a point of major contention. If your present location is convenient to work, schools, shopping, and entertainment, giving it up may mean not only a drastic change of location but a radical alteration of life-style.

Very practically, however, you must decide whether you will be able to afford the monthly rent payments when you are without your husband. As comfortable as the place may be, if you are in over your head, the living situation won't last long. Take a realistic look at how much you will be bringing in and how much you'll be paying out. Remember, if you have to make a change, what you are moving to doesn't have to be permanent.

Know Your Tax Liability

It is important to understand the areas of your tax responsibility regarding income taxes or the sale of property. But for those who own the house, and plan to ask for it as part of the divorce settlement, be sure to consult a CPA about the capital gains tax liability and how that works into your overall financial settlement. According to Ginita Wall, CPA and divorce specialist, women who choose to accept the house as part of the divorce settlement and continue to live in it need to investigate that decision. For instance, if the house is the last in a string of homes purchased as family dwellings, and if capital gains were deferred, a woman could wind up with a heavy capital gains tax burden should she decide to sell that property somewhere down the road.

Ms. Wall contends that the home coveted now, at the onset of the breakup, may later turn out to be "The Marriage Museum," no longer desirable, in fact, an uncomfortable and burdensome reminder of a marriage you chose to leave behind.

Looking for Another Place to Live

You can make good use of your time right now by discreetly checking into the availability of other housing. The act of doing this can give positive reinforcement to the reality of your leaving.

However, be sure you consider the following items:

- Cost is a key factor. Ask if all of the extra charges are included: Utilities, water, maintenance, etc. Some lessors require credit references before they will accept a lease.
- Give some thought to the location. What would be ideal for you not only in terms of the area, but also in relation to your work and the proximity of public transportation? Will you be isolated from family and friends? Does it afford you the opportunity to meet new people?
- If you have children, are there other kids around for them to play with or is their recreation going to be your sole responsibility? Look into the availability of playgrounds, child care facili-

ties, boys' and girls' clubs, public swimming, and the like. What is the school system like?

- Is there good security? Will you feel safe being alone there? Could you leave the children alone and feel comfortable about it?

Your decision to move or stay is a major one and you don't have to decide right away. Ending the relationship does not always mean you have to leave the house, despite what your husband might say. You have options and are not powerless in this matter. This is taken up in the next chapter.

A Car

If you are like most people, you will need a car. Naturally it is more vital to some women than others, depending in part on where you live.

If there are two cars, try to get the one in the best condition, so that it will last as long as possible after you separate. In any case, have repairs done to the car while you are still in your relationship, using money from your joint earnings to pay for the costs. Pay the insurance so that it extends into the period after separation. You will need free time without extra expenses.

Learn how to do simple maintenance. The manual that accompanies the car can provide guidance. If you anticipate having to live on a very limited budget, find out how to drain the oil, change a filter, care for the battery, check for worn belts, change a tire. All this costs money at a gas station, to say nothing of the possibility of being overcharged or receiving inadequate service.

Medical and Dental Expenses

Your good health is your most important resource both before and after you leave.

Medical expenses today are outrageous, but if you neglect your own physical welfare or that of your children, the results will be even more costly. Take advantage of any medical insurance that you presently have. If you need corrective surgery, see your doctor about it and have it done. Reconsider your method of birth control and change it if you're not happy with it. Get physical examinations for the children.

Also check with your dentist. Have your teeth cleaned and any necessary dental work done. With the children, also see if they are in need of orthodontia. You may not want them to get braces at this time but if they need them, you will want that expense written into the divorce settlement.

You will be needing your own medical insurance after the divorce. Coverage will not automatically fall into your husband's area of responsibility. It is a settlement consideration which must be negotiated. Some states are considering a conversion privilege in health-insurance policies for the divorced spouse who cannot produce proof of insurability. Check into this with an attorney. If there are children, you and your husband must decide who will provide their medical coverage.

Personal Care

Take a look at what you have in the closet. In the future you may find that your need for certain kinds of clothes is rapidly changing. If you have spent most of your time working in the home during your marriage, the kinds of clothes you are probably wearing are not the type you will be needing when you go out to look for a job. If you are already working, it is a good time to reassess your wardrobe and add some things to it.

If you think that you will be working in an office or public place and won't be wearing a uniform, you will need several outfits that are interchangeable. Don't just buy impulsively. Give some thought to what you think you will need and gradually build a flexible wardrobe. Concentrate on buying a few basic and tasteful pieces that can easily combine with other things.

The way we feel about ourselves is often tied to how we look. Or how we *think* we look. Dressing in a way that boosts your self-confidence is an important consideration when starting out in a new life. Most of the women I interviewed began changing their image as they prepared to leave. The outer look began to more closely reflect the person inside that had been put aside for so many years.

MONEY: THE *LONG* RANGE

All of what has been said to this point about finances is good short-term advice, but you can't live for long on the dollars that you may have managed to save from grocery bills and birthday presents. In the long run, you will have to give some serious thought to what you want and are able to do in the years to come. If you haven't done it already, you should sit down sometime soon and actively plan for your future.

It may be tempting to avoid the issue of how you are going to support yourself by imagining that sometime shortly after your divorce you will meet an attractive, mature man with plenty of money, looking for someone just like you. You will both fall in love as he sweeps aside petty worries about things like car payments or hospital insurance. All of this may happen—but don't count on it. In fact, if it does happen, you should seriously consider whether you want to enter into another relationship in which you become so financially dependent on another person that the thought of losing such support might deter you from leaving, even if that relationship isn't working out.

If you have developed talent in some area and become confident in it, you have an invaluable advantage in life. A marketable skill gives a woman a sense of security that even the comfortable paycheck of a husband can't replace. It is a very good feeling when you realize that, despite whatever might happen to the person you are living with, you can go out and get a job that will fully support you and any dependents you may have.

The day of the kept woman is over. The Victorian tradition of the sheltered woman untainted by the crudities of real life in the business world lingered on through much of this century in one form or another, but it certainly has no meaning today. The number of women working full time has jumped from 22 million in 1970 to 40 million working women in 1990, with a projected 67

million women by the year 2000. In addition, over one half of all
new mothers were in the labor force by 1988.

What this means is that if you have not yet awakened to the
long-range economic facts of life, begin to prepare yourself. You
will soon be on your own, in one sense or another. There is no
way that this will be felt more acutely than in the economic realm.
You are going to be totally responsible for making ends meet. It
may be a role in which you feel confidence or whose prospect
excites you. Or it may frighten the daylights out of you. In either
case, certain realities have to be met.

Two Can't Live as Cheaply as Two

Probably the harshest truth of divorce comes with the revelation that when a couple splits up, both of them will immediately
feel the shock of reduced financial resources. Two persons living
apart do not live as cheaply as two persons living together. An
almost unavoidable duplication of space and services will simply cost more money. There is no real mystery to this, and yet
it is a reality that people divorcing are very reluctant to face.
Some women show a great readiness and maturity in handling
the emotional parts of leaving their marriage, but they are
woefully naive when it comes to the hard economic questions
of how they will financially survive afterward. They simply
trust that things will work out, that the money will come. Such
faith is admirable in some parts of one's life, but economics are
rather uncompromising.

Divorce brings changes and its impact will be quickly felt in your
budget. If you were relatively secure before your divorce, get
ready for some new thinking. If you were having a hard time
financially, be prepared to take some radical steps.

Your Financial Picture

It's time to take a candid look at just where you stand financially.
It may not be the most pleasant task, but you can't get away from

it for long. Although the picture may seem to be discouraging, it is better to have some reasonable estimate of your status beforehand, rather than be taken by surprise later. If you know your position in relation to money, you can intelligently plan for the future and weave your way around the pitfalls.

The assessment of your financial situation divides into two categories: An accounting of the *present* economic reality of your life, and a *projection* of what is likely after your divorce.

A reasonably accurate estimate of these two areas should give you sound information on which to base your decision for the future. Naturally, it is to your advantage to work within the monetary boundaries of what is possible. If you rush blindly into financial commitments in your haste to get out of your marriage, you will soon find yourself in over your head, compounding the potential for disaster. Take some time with this section and find out the answers to your financial condition.

TAKING ACCOUNT

The following charts serve two purposes. First, they are a handy way to get a handle on your present financial situation, and second, they can afford an educated guess at what the future may hold. Fill out and tabulate the columns twice, once for getting a clear estimate of where you stand moneywise *right now*; next, what you project as your fiscal status after you have divorced.

At the onset of your divorce plans, look through your records and statements to get the hard figures. This is more than an exercise in curiosity. Your lawyer will ask you for this information at some point, so you may as well get it together now. The data are the essential groundwork for your divorce settlement. For the time being, don't worry about what your share will be, simply get the figures down.

This is not "nosing around." These assets are partly yours. You have a right to know where they are and what they are worth. It may be true that in the past your attention to these matters was not great, but many things which happened in the past have changed.

Naturally, the necessities of your current life give focus to financial matters. You don't have to apologize for that.

When you have finished filling out the lists, study them. A comparison of the totals will give you a rough estimate of where you stand now and what you can expect. How does your income match with your expenses? Are your liabilities overwhelming or under control? Is there anything that you can do right now to strengthen your financial situation? Is there any way to get more income should you need it? Can you begin to cut expenses and put more money in the bank? Which loans could be paid off? Is it a good time to get the best market value for some property or a car that you own?

Looking ahead, what do you foresee as realistic economic possibilities for the future? Will you be able to generate enough money to live independently? Will you need help from others? How much? These questions may be hard to answer at present but they need your attention. While everything in the future is speculation, it is in your interest to weigh, as best you can, the probable circumstances of your life after leaving your husband.

PRESENT AND FUTURE *ASSETS*

$_____ CHECKING ACCOUNT

$_____ SAVINGS ACCOUNT

$_____ REAL ESTATE

$_____ STOCKS AND BONDS

$_____ VALUE OF BUSINESSES OWNED

$_____ RETIREMENT FUND/PROFIT SHARING

$_____ INSURANCE POLICIES (CASH VALUE)

$_____ PERSONAL PROPERTY (CARS, BOATS, TOOLS, JEWELRY, ART AND HOBBY COLLECTIONS, HOUSEHOLD FURNITURE, ETC.)

$_____ MONIES DUE (RECEIVABLES, ROYALTIES, PATENTS, ETC.)

$_____ MISCELLANEOUS

_____

$_____ TOTAL

Your present assets will give some clue as to what the future holds, but it is difficult to estimate how much you will receive as your share of the settlement. That will be determined by many factors: the cash value of your combined assets, whether you retain primary custody of the children, your ability to earn money, the negotiating skills of both you and your attorney, and if you go to trial, the decision of the judge.

Consult with your attorney, using the figures that outline your assets. Popular thinking grants one half of communally-owned property to each party. Often a lawyer give can you an educated guess as to what you might expect. Your plans for the future will be contingent on this amount. How you fare financially in the divorce can mean the difference, for instance, between having enough money to return to school, and simply scrambling to make ends meet.

PRESENT AND FUTURE *LIABILITIES*

LOANS:

$_____ HOME MORTGAGE

$_____ AUTO

$_____ FURNISHINGS

$_____ PERSONAL

$_____ MEDICAL BILLS

$_____ DENTAL BILLS

$_____ CREDIT CARDS

$_____ INCOME TAXES AND ASSESSMENTS DUE

$_____ MISCELLANEOUS

_____

$_____ TOTAL

After you leave, there may still be some debts from your marriage. Sometimes the principal wage earner, often the husband, is ordered to pay them by the court. You may, however, have to assume some responsibility if your income allows. This is certainly true in the case of income taxes owed. Should your settlement agreement specify that your husband pay off a set number of debts, you may still not be free of the ultimate responsibility for them after the divorce. Consult your attorney and get help in projecting the amount of money you might still owe. Be sure to discuss including a "hold harmless" clause in your divorce papers. This clause will not keep creditors from your doorstep should your husband not pay the bills, but it will leave you the legal means of recovering those monies from him later.

PRESENT AND FUTURE *MONTHLY EXPENSES*

$_____ RENT OR MORTGAGE PAYMENT

$_____ FOOD

$_____ AUTO (GAS, INSURANCE, REPAIRS, LICENSE)

$_____ UTILITIES (HEAT, WATER, ELECTRIC, GAS)

$_____ TELEPHONE

$_____ HOME MAINTENANCE (REPAIRS, PROFESSIONAL UPKEEP)

$_____ TAXES

$_____ INSURANCE (HEALTH AND LIFE)

$_____ CHARITY

PERSONAL:

$_____ CLOTHING

$_____ MEDICAL AND DENTAL

$_____ MAINTENANCE (HAIR, NAILS, ETC.)

$_____ RECREATION

CHILDREN:

$_____ MEDICAL AND DENTAL

$_____ EDUCATION (TUITION, BOOKS, LUNCHES, ETC.)

$_____ CHILD CARE EXPENSES

$_____ MISCELLANEOUS

_____

$_____ TOTAL

It is important to get a clear idea of what your new life will cost to maintain. For example, if you would like to stay in your present home and continue the payments, what do those figures look like in relation to the rest of your expenses? How does the house payment compare with an apartment rental? There may be some new expenses: if you get a different job, will your clothing budget and auto expenses go up? What about day care?

Investigate as many items as you can. Even a difficult financial picture loses some of its sting when you know exactly what to expect. It may become evident that some of your priorities will have to change for the time being. Many women tell me that they are quite willing to live in a one-room apartment (with a sleeping bag and packing crates for furniture) if they can have peace of mind and control over their lives.

PRESENT AND FUTURE *MONTHLY INCOME*

$_____ TAKE-HOME PAY (YOURS)

$_____ TAKE-HOME PAY (HIS)

$_____ INTEREST ON SAVINGS

$_____ OTHER INCOME (COMMISSIONS, DIVIDENDS, ETC.)

$_____ MISCELLANEOUS

This is a questionable area to project. It is hard to have complete control over how much money comes in. A woman in the process of divorce is usually looking at three income sources: her salary; spousal support (if it is awarded); and child support payments (if she has the primary or shared custody of them).

If you plan to continue in your present employment and see no advantage in changing jobs, then you have a pretty good idea of what your salary will be. If you are moving to a new job market for the first time, or hope to upgrade the nature and value of your work, the amount you will be taking home depends on several things: your preparation, your skills, the national economy, and some luck. It's not easy to predict.

The other areas—spousal and child support—can cause even greater confusion and, often, disappointment. In the past, divorcing women could frequently count on these two sources as a means of income. A woman might hinge a whole set of future plans on the imagined money she would be receiving. Such money is a reasonable and fair thing to expect. And occasionally the courts do make generous awards. But for many women the whole system is a cruel hoax. Sadly, your chances of receiving the money due you from your husband range from fair to nonexistent. For some women it is a matter of basic survival. The national record is abysmal and needs further comment.

Spousal Support

Women used to expect alimony as a reward for years of faithfully taking care of the duties and responsibilities of family and home. Divorced women were entitled to a just compensation in the form of monthly support payments. It was recognized that the woman's work was in the home, and once that came to an end she deserved recognition for it in terms of money. Whether it worked or not in practice, the notion was that a woman could rely on an unending financial connection with her husband. Granting alimony was akin to a kind of lifetime pension for women. Whatever the rationale was then, the fact is that few women nowadays actually receive such money with any consistency, and it is increasingly evident that to count on it is foolish. Only 15 percent of divorced women are even awarded alimony, and the average amount they are awarded is decreasing each year. Recent figures show that the amount is only one fifth of the divorced woman's average total money income for the year.

The whole philosophy of spousal support has changed in the recent past. Today it is considered to be, at best, a temporary award designed to continue only until the woman becomes self-sufficient. It is seen as a vehicle for rehabilitation, affording financial support for the transition and a short period of education or retraining afterward.

Even at that, less than half of the awarded payments are regularly made. One study shows that over one third of the divorced or separated women had not taken any action against ex-husbands who were not in compliance with the law. Women have meager recourse. Lawyer's fees for initiating lawsuits to recover the money are often expensive and time-consuming. If the husband is feeling strong animosity toward his ex-wife, the chance of his paying her in any way that can be relied upon is small.

A client of mine has chosen to put up with her husband coming over to her house each week and walking through it. He uses the time to complain and usually accuses her of being a total incompetent. If she argues with him he delays or reduces the amount he pays her that time—with a good excuse, of course. She is putting up with the situation until she can afford to do without his money.

Child Support

One would think a woman should be able to figure on getting help in the form of money from the father to feed, clothe, and shelter the children. If the woman has primary custody of them, she is, after all, spending an inordinate part of her week taking care of the children and getting no financial recognition for it. The father is free from that consuming responsibility and certainly should provide enough money to give his children the basic necessities of life. A great many don't.

To begin, a 1990 study of the U.S. Census Bureau reports that of the 5 million women who are *supposed* to receive child support, only half reported receiving the full payment for what was awarded. One fourth of the women got a partial payment, and one fourth received no payments whatsoever. Added to that is the sad reality that there were another 2.7 million women who said they wanted support but were never able to obtain an award.

A seven-year study of the child support system by David L. Chambers, a University of Michigan law professor, points out the prevailing psychology of divorced husbands' thinking:

> Unconsciously, many men, especially those least involved with their children, may regard marriage as a contractural arrangement in which the wife agrees to take care of the husband and the husband in return agrees to support her and the children. Upon separating, she stops caring for him. He may feel at some level that he is no longer obliged to support her or "her" children.

A major block is the court's inability to effectively enforce the law. Prior to 1984, local government agencies could only recover delinquent payments if you were on welfare. Thanks to Congress, legislation has been passed requiring local governments to help *any* custodial parent to collect child support. Each state varies in the methods it uses to collect money, but some of the measures include garnishing paychecks, seizing tax returns, or sentencing the errant parent to jail for non-payment of support. In spite of this, the 1990 figures from state agencies show that they were collecting money in only 17.9 percent of the 12 million cases they were managing.

How do fathers get away with not paying? The answer could ultimately be found in the statement of the director of a child support enforcement agency in Dade county, Florida, "Most men simply do not pay support until they are forced into it. . . . If they don't pay for electricity, it's cut off . . . if they don't make car payments, the car is taken away . . . but if they don't make child support payments, nothing happens."

As noted earlier, local agencies have a low rate of recovery— primarily because each caseworker is extremely overloaded. For a woman who must rely on securing a lawyer each time a monthly check doesn't arrive, the situation is dreary. The expense of recovering the money owed is often more than the value of the delinquent payment. The whole process becomes a strange ritual. In the end it is often abandoned.

If your child support payments do come regularly, nurture the situation. After the divorce, if things are not actively hostile between you and your former husband, encourage him to stay involved with the children. Arrange for him to have regular visitation with them and find opportunities to give him credit for his help. Include him in events such as birthday parties, school conferences, and discussions of the children's future welfare. Interviews with divorced men who regularly pay their child support show that they do so because they are actively involved with the lives of their children. They see the need for, as well as the results of, the money they contribute for the care of their children. The contact with your former husband may not always be terribly satisfying to *you*, but if it helps your children have the things they need, it will be worth it.

INTERMEDIATE NEEDS

There will be certain transition costs that will come up during and just after your leave-taking. The amount of money is significant and some plans for getting it must be made. The problem is that they all come within a short time of one another and could place obstacles in your path if you don't have the ready cash.

The lawyer. You will need a retainer, or down payment, as soon as you engage his or her services.

Moving expenses. An alternative to a moving company is doing it yourself with the help of some friends and a U-Haul.

The gas company. There are charges for turning on the utilities.

The telephone company. They will bill you for a new installation.

Apartment charges. Many landlords demand the first and last months' rent immediately. Though in the long run you are not losing anything, for the present it is a considerable investment. Added to this is a cleaning or security deposit, usually much harder to recover.

Stocking and outfitting new living quarters. This can be costly. The first grocery bill after moving in is usually staggering as you find yourself buying staples that fill the back shelves of cupboards and kitchen gadgetry for the drawers.

Most of these expenses are a one-shot ordeal, but when they all come at once, the impact is considerable.

THE CASE FOR MUDDLING THROUGH

It might be good to pause in the middle of all of this to say a word for the muddlers. In this and other chapters, the approach is to define the problems and outline a way to get through them.

But you may feel swamped by the multitude of details and feel that the advice is too exact and clean, as if it assumes that you are in perfect control.

Human nature as it is, that's seldom the case. You may be just hanging in there. And the truth is that thousands of women are unprepared and yet stumble through the divorce process, surviving it somehow. This certainly will continue to be the method for many women.

The suggestions given here and in other parts of the book are meant to be pointers—thoughtful direction during a confusing time. Nothing is meant to be a rigid formula. If there is, however, one piece of overriding advice to be given it is this: Whatever you do, don't dig yourself a hole that you can't get out of. Create as many options as you can, so that if one thing doesn't work, you won't be stuck.

JOBS

For women, a review of the employment situation and the politics that surround it is mixed.

- **The good news** is that the number of women working full-time has doubled since 1970.
  The bad news is that 70 percent of the females who are in vocational schools are enrolled in programs that will lead to traditionally female jobs, with accompanying traditional low pay.

- **The good news** is that the number of women entering traditionally male occupations is on the rise. For example, there was a 71 percent increase in the number of female certified public accountants between 1983 and 1990.
  The bad news is that when men come to work in a woman's world, they earn more money for the same job: A male cashier in 1990 earned $242.00 a week compared to $210.00 for a woman; a male information clerk earned $340.00 weekly, the female clerk, $283.00, a wage gap of 18 percent.

- **The good news** is that there are many innovative approaches to work scheduling that are advantageous to the working mother. The variations are interesting: *Flexible time off* allows employees to use a specific number of days each year for anything from caring for a sick child to taking a vacation; *job sharing* assigns two women separate responsibilities for the same job; *flex-time* allows women to work full-time but to arrange more flexible hours; *compressed work week* gives women the opportunity to squeeze their work into fewer days.
The bad news is that not enough companies have adopted such innovative practices, and many are in no great rush to do so.

- **The good news** is typified by a recent statement by a female executive of a computer company: "Things have never been better for women in industry. Excellent opportunities are opening up. It is much easier than when I started."
The bad news is that only 10 percent of the female work force is employed in managerial or administrative positions with only 3 percent holding top jobs at Fortune 500 companies.

- **The good news** is that the women's movement has made great and genuine progress in this last decade. It is evident in almost every phase of contemporary life. Things are changing.
The bad news is that the Equal Rights Amendment has failed to be ratified by the required number of states and the prospect for it looks poor in the future. Anti-feminist backlash is strong in some circles, and unfortunately they are the circles of political power.

Your Job Future

There was a time not long ago when neat and tidy recommendations could be made to a woman on her career choices. Certain jobs were traditionally set aside to be filled almost exclusively by women and any woman venturing outside those limits was considered, at best, rather odd. Today it is impossible to give general guidance that would fit the needs of a particular woman. Everyone is really in the process of discovering her uniqueness. But it is safe to say that most of us want both financial security and a sense of personal fulfillment in our work.

An artist friend of mine, Alisse Suess, tells the story of what an old Swedish woman friend, Tora, said to her one day: "I've lived for eighty-three years and I'll tell you, the most important thing in your life is not your husband and not your children—it's your work." That statement may not be true for every woman, but you might meditate on it for a moment. The words do not mean that the family is unimportant, but how many women were instilled with the belief that there was a gravity and magnitude in their choice of a job or career that was equal to the importance placed on it for a man? The insidious message given to us by our culture says that whatever a woman does outside of being a mother and homemaker is either just a temporary activity or a slightly abnormal overcompensation in an attempt to deny the secondary role of women in the marketplace.

The male culture's dominating prejudices surface every once in a while in unexpected ways. For instance, who could forget the incident in the Los Angeles, California, Ninth United States Circuit Court of Appeals, during a sex discrimination case brought by a fired woman employee of the county housing authority, where United States Judge A. Andrew Hauk described the woman as a "buttinsky, always writing memos, always complaining." Hauk raised the question: "But would they have let her go if she had been a man? I would say probably not, because a man wouldn't do these crazy things if he was an employee. But I suppose that's one of the prices we pay in this day of women's lib for hiring women in some of these jobs. They have different problems. They have their monthly problems, which upsets them emotionally, and we all know that, at least any of us who have wives and daughters." So spake the judge. If one wonders how the myths about women and work are given currency, it is only necessary to read the newspaper each day. It is that attitude, masked in a hundred ways, that a woman faces when getting a job.

But your work, whatever kind you might choose, can be experienced with pride and dignity. Surely as women, we should broaden our respect for the worth of a woman's daily activity. Work is a continuous act of human endeavor, and no matter what its nature, it can be done creatively.

Find out what your work is.

Jobs and Careers

There are jobs and there are jobs. And although ideally there is value in everything we do, the fact is that some jobs pay much better than others. Some jobs call upon human inventiveness; others are routine. Some offer the chance for mobility and growth while others go nowhere.

In some ways it is awkward to make definitive statements about the nature of a particular job. What is interesting and challenging for one person may not be for the next. The idea of being on the sales staff of a hospital supply company would be exciting for a certain woman. The sense of competition might be exhilarating and the opportunities seem to be unlimited. For another, it would be drudgery, a submersion into corporate high-pressure hustling. Every job is, in the end, what you make of it whether it be waitressing, construction work, secretarial service, social counseling, executive management, or driving a bus. It is possible to find genuine rewards in any kind of work.

Still, in recommending a career direction for a woman coming out of a marriage, there are certain helpful guidelines which can be followed. For instance, it is important to distinguish between the job you take—or that you continue to stay in just after your divorce—and the career you eventually want to pursue. After leaving a relationship, the primary concern is often just surviving from month to month, and to do that, almost any work that pays adequately is welcome. At that point, a woman does not have the luxury to ask herself a lot of important questions about the nature and long-range goals of the job. Those thoughts evolve later. For the present, if the job is paying the bills, it's OK.

But when the fear of survival subsides (and for some women it never does), a few important questions should be asked.

- Do my wages reflect the energy output of my work?
- When I am on my way to work each day, am I looking forward to it?
- Am I usually angry during and after work, and is it related to what I am doing there?
- Is the job I have routine, and do I like routine?
- Do I learn anything positive in the course of the work day about life? About myself?
- Do I like the type of people I come in contact with at work?
- Do I want to be doing this job or some variation of it five years from now? Ten years? Fifteen years?

If your answers are generally negative, then for you it is a dead-end job. It may be work that is temporarily useful during a transition point in your life. The amount of your paycheck may, in fact, be rather impressive. But you know if you are happy in your work and whether it has a future that is worthy of your time and energy.

Adrienne got into working ten years before her divorce. At first it was just a desire to get out of the house a couple nights a week and help out their financial situation. She took a part-time job in a good restaurant in Chicago. Her husband, Jerry, would stay at home on the nights she worked, taking care of their two small boys. She kept this particular job for seven years and the experience taught her about work, divorce, and life.

> It was a fancy steakhouse in Chicago, a family-type restaurant, and they prided themselves on good service. People would wait for hours for dinner, but when they got seated, the service was good, so the turnover of customers was pretty high, and we made really good money. It was a very attractive place to work for women who were in the single-parent role. You could make seventy to eighty dollars a night, and I found that working there was a good learning experience for me.

I learned about dealing with the public, first of all, but mainly what I learned was by watching. Probably seventy-five percent of the women who worked there were divorced. They had been in waitressing a long time; because it was such a good place to work they would stay for many, many years. Some of them were there fifteen years, twenty years. It was hard to get a job because it was such a well-known, popular place. The people that worked there stayed a long time.

A lot of women working there were stuck in their situation because of their children. They were unhappy. They had two, three, or four children, and couldn't do anything else with their life—felt they couldn't because they had the financial burden of raising these kids and it was bad—I felt it was *really* bad.

When I first started working, my kids were babies, and it was kind of nice for me to work two nights a week. But I saw, as my children grew older and were in school all day, that I was alone. At night I would go to work, and that's when they needed me to be there. The women I worked with were in the same situation. They had teenagers who got into a lot of trouble, and they were the single parent and had to be gone at night. That's when you made your money, at night. And that's when the kids needed them the most, and yet they were torn. The women couldn't find a job where they were making that much money and could still support the kids by working during the day. And they had no skills, beyond waitressing.

So they were working not two nights but four and five nights a week to make ends meet, and were totally physically fatigued, and mentally fatigued. They didn't have the energy to go on to school during the day, or to do anything else with their life. They were really stuck in a hopeless situation. Just miserable—just totally miserable.

Then with their family situation getting worse, it was even more of a drain. I saw a lot of them get into alcohol as a relief, sort of like the end of the night was a climax to their whole life—and they'd sit around after work at a booth, and have a few drinks, and sit and talk, and some of them would go out after work.

And that was self-defeating because the next day they were so tired—they'd sleep late, get up and get ready for work—and it was like a never-ending vicious circle. But where else, then, could you make sixty to seventy dollars a night—clear—which you *need* in order to support your children alone. Most of the women that were there were not getting child support—and of those that did, it was very little.

It was a real education for me—a real awakening to what's *really* out there in the real world, as far as divorces.

My advice is to definitely find some type of career that you're happy in. Maybe it *is* waitressing—maybe that'll be it. Just make sure you are happy in it—and decide whether or not, if it is waitressing, if you can physically continue doing it when you're fifty or fifty-five.

The dilemma faced by the women in the restaurant is a common one—better than average wages, but back-breaking work at odd hours. It was clearly a dead-end situation for many of them but their choice seemed limited because of their financial responsibilities toward their children. Most of them probably could have gotten into lower-paying jobs that were less physically taxing, but it is hard to let go of a decent paycheck so they stayed locked into a job that would eventually wear them out.

As Adrienne's future plans became more clear, she saw that waitressing was only interim work. She enrolled in school and studied dental hygiene, struggling to balance her homework with parenting and work. She made it. Now, after her divorce, she is a myofunctional therapist in a very progressive dental office.

Planning a Career

Don't let the word *career* put you off. It is not used here in an elitist way. Your chances of beginning medical school and spending the next ten years consumed in medical books are admittedly slim. (On the other hand, don't rule it out. *Don't rule anything out.*)

But more realistically, a career is simply a line of work that strongly interests you and which you think would be both personally rewarding and worth pursuing in the foreseeable future. This could be a career as a cross-country truck driver, working in a Montessori school, or being a police detective. It may mean going into apprenticeship training, a business school, or a major university. Or it may entail getting on the inside of some business and learning the ropes by practical experience. Whatever the nature of the occupation, it is essential that you know what the job is really about, have the ability to function in the work area, and be willing to carry through with your ambition.

Even though a career may not be the first thing on your mind at this time, don't simply get caught up with the short view of things. Temporary measures are important, but also survey the future. If, for instance, you are thirty-two years old, you may have another thirty-two years of work on the job ahead of you. You can slide into some work and ten years from now awake one morning wondering how you ever got trapped into the job you are facing that day.

Women do enter traditionally female jobs. In 1990, 60 percent of professional women worked in nursing and teaching. There is nothing wrong with these jobs, although most of them tend to be underpaid because the fields are so dominated by females. And it is understandable if your experience has presented you with these limited options.

But if you only go the conventional route, you are cutting yourself off from a whole range of possibilities. One of the signs of genius is a person's ability to "think the unthinkable." *Think* about the possibility of being a geologist, a computer programmer, a forester, an engineer, an insurance salesperson, a chemist, an accountant. Most of us unnecessarily limit ourselves. And isn't it interesting that these jobs pay much more than the "women's jobs."

Certainly every woman once caught in a marriage that didn't work should know the danger of letting life just take care of itself. Your future work will take up a major portion of your time and energy in life. You now can choose the course you want your life to take and make it happen over the years to come.

Think about the difference that can make in your life.

Thinking about Work

Cynthia Poole, a professional career counselor with a great deal of experience with reentry women, makes this observation about divorced women looking for work:

One of the biggest hurdles women need to get over when getting a divorce is to see themselves again as productive, competent, self-motivating people.

They need to look at themselves and see their skills, competencies, and strengths, then transfer those attributes into the marketplace to see what they can do to make some money. And not only make some money, because they can go down and get a minimum-wage job—but what they can do to support a family.

Women are very agile—someone called it multiphasic—whereas men in our culture are single-minded. Women take care of the very complex logistics of running a house and everything surrounding that. That's a skill. It's a management skill, it's a personnel relationship skill, and many times it's a financial skill.

Ask yourself some basic questions and, for the moment, set aside all of your preconceived notions about what you are "naturally" suited for. Forget your high school grades or what the math teacher told you. Instead, do something constructive.

For instance, if your long-term goal is to be an accountant, take a job as a clerk in a tax preparation office—they are very busy the first four months of every year and do quite a bit of hiring to handle the tax crunch. The job will give some experience in the area of numbers and taxes, allow you to meet people who are doing what you are interested in, and keep alive your ambition while you are going to school to receive accreditation.

Staying with your career decision is often not easy. It will probably take real sacrifice. But the sense of accomplishment you will feel when it is decided makes it all worthwhile.

THE DESPERATION FACTOR

The strategies outlined to this point are sound and workable. But there are many women caught in situations that need more immediate help. The kind of preparations described assume that a woman has sufficient time to plan a gradual restructuring of her life, and the emotional strength and security to carry it out. But some of the relationships are so bad that it is impossible as well as dangerous for women to stay in them any longer. Every marriage is individual and only the woman involved can be the final judge. However, if your situation is so desperate that you feel it is urgent that you do something *now*, then surely much of the previous advice must be telescoped or cut through.

The first priority is always your physical well-being and that of your children. If there is a danger of physical or deep emotional damage, then your need for basic survival breaks through the practicality of a slower transition.

A marriage threatened by a climate of emergency demands special measures. In general, these cases fall into two categories: First, those marriages that, because of their continuing interpersonal or economic problems, have a long history of being in a state of hopelessness; second, marriages that suddenly reach a crisis point and the volatility of it spells disaster. In either case, the woman may be convinced that she has to get out right away and that staying any longer would be foolish.

Long-Term Desperation

For many women, desperation has always been there knocking on the door. One in every five households in the United States is classified as living in poverty. The supposed affluence of the society is a sham to this group because the system offers little escape— especially for the woman in such a household. She is doubly bound—first in the tight ring of her marriage, then by the larger circle of her depressed economic class. Her condition may be weighted down even more if there is a history of physical abuse and neglect.

On the other hand, a woman who has lived in a marriage at this end of the economic ladder hasn't much to lose in leaving immediately. Realistically, her relationship offers little security or comfort that cannot be easily gained on her own. She probably knows the welfare system well enough to be able to survive with it, and the emotional factors in her life have long ago been tempered by the harsh reality of her existence.

Tina had been married for eight years. They had two children, ages three and five. Doug worked for Chrysler since his discharge from the Navy, but what with low seniority and the economic problems of the industry, he had been out of work most of the time for the last three years. At first he talked about moving away from Detroit but always hoped things would get better; then he sank into a routine of living that Tina couldn't stand.

He was around all the time. He'd get up in the morning pissed about something and stayed that way most of the day. It got so that he would hardly go out. We used to go places when we first got married, to a show or just drive around, but now we didn't. Besides, we didn't have any money. With his unemployment check we hardly had enough to eat. I'd complain to him that he should get a different kind of job, one with more security, but I knew he wouldn't. He didn't for the six years we were together. He looked for something one time at a furniture store, but when he didn't get the job he got discouraged.

He'd say, "Why the fuck don't *you* work?" I looked for one about a year ago and got one at this lunch place but the pay was so bad it wasn't worth it. Besides, he'd complain about having to take care of the kids. Mark was still too young, and I didn't really trust Doug to watch him. So I quit. At the end, things got really bad between us.

Tina felt locked into a life that didn't really offer any alternatives Finally, the negative intensity of their relationship built to a point that she felt the need to leave immediately.

It got crazy. He'd be at home all the time picking away at this or that. I'd be in the bathroom for fifteen minutes and he'd ask me what I was doing. Then he'd complain all the time about how stupid television is but he would never turn it off. Just bitch about it.

It got so that I had to leave or go nuts. I didn't know how I'd do it. We had a car but something was always the matter with it and anyway I couldn't just drive off with him sitting there.

Finally I talked to my mother in Flint. She was remarried but we talked and she said she would come down and pick me and the kids up some day. She said I could stay with her for a while but I'd have to get a place of my own.

The whole thing took a lot of timing. I had to call her right before Doug went out to the unemployment office one Friday. He usually stayed away most of the day that day. I had our stuff ready and split. I called him later.

In Tina's case the constant pressure of her marriage gave little time or space to maneuver. Although she was well aware that she was unhappy, her decision to leave was made quickly. To stay for three more months in such a relationship would achieve little more than what she was able to do by leaving immediately, and indeed by staying she was probably inviting more trouble. As it turned out, Tina went on welfare, then met a construction worker and the two of them eventually moved out west.

Sudden Desperation

The explosive nature of some marriages will often be the final determining factor when a woman leaves. You owe yourself basic self-protection because even though you are progressing on some kind of timetable in leaving your relationship, there are circumstances that might force you to abandon everything and leave quickly. This will create a certain amount of hardship, but you must judge this against all the consequences. Your safety and that of your children is the overriding consideration, and you must make the decision. For cases in which the home environment has become plainly frightening, getting out is the only answer. Often, however, the situation is not so clear-cut, and women stick around with mixed results.

For a while, Beth was confused about what to do. She had been married to B. J. for seven years and they had a two-year-old son named Tony. Katie, her eight-year-old daughter from a previous marriage, also lived with them. Their marriage had been fine for a while but B. J. always drank too much, and in the past two years it had started to seriously affect their relationship. They lived in Phoenix where B. J. worked at a machine shop and Beth cleaned rooms at a local Holiday Inn. Between their salaries, they managed fine.

He started taking off on Friday nights and I wouldn't see him again till Sunday. Once in a while he'd take off during the week but then

I could call him at work. At first I was really mad because I thought he was out with someone, some girl. After a while I didn't care as much. In fact I kind of liked it. I had my time alone and I'd fix my work schedule so I could get weekends off. There would be no fights and the kids and me would get out somewhere. But he always had the truck so that made it hard.

After a while I was sure my marriage was at a dead end, no place to go, so I started thinking about a divorce. I started doing some stuff. One weekend when he was gone I had my sister take the kids and I went out dancing. I had to take a bus for miles to this bar on the other side of town because I didn't want to run into B. J.

I met this guy in the place and we danced and had fun. He asked me back to his place, a really new apartment. The lovemaking wasn't great but it was the most fun I'd had in years and I thought a lot about it after. He drove me home and B. J. never knew about it.

Their relationship got worse as B. J. started drinking more. They had always had loud verbal arguments, but now he was becoming physically abusive to her. The issue was never clear or related to one thing except that it usually happened when he was drunk or hung over. Beth thought he might just be feeling guilty about his life.

He was feeling shitty most of the time. You could actually see it in his face. He started taking it out on me, and the kids sometimes, too. I got used to it in a way but one night we got into this violent fight that really scared me. It was so *ugly*. We were in the kitchen eating dinner with the kids and it starts up—I really don't know what it was about—but I had had it and told him so. He started pushing me and just kept pushing me. I was falling down and trying not to cry because I didn't want to freak out the kids, but they started screaming. Tony didn't know what was happening but Katie kept trying to stop him. He just went crazy with that bully crap that he'd pull. Then he started using his fist. He hit me right in the chest. I thought my ribs were broken and I could hardly breathe.

He stopped after that. It's the first time in my life that I was really scared for my life. It happened before, but not like this! Later that night he said he was sorry and I said it was all right but it wasn't. I didn't mean it. I was hurting all over and I knew I had to get away.

On Friday I knew he wouldn't come home so I talked to a girl friend at work who said I could stay with her. I don't know what I would have done without her. But I would have done something. I wasn't staying around there.

It is hard to plan for the future when the present demands so much. However, there are things that can be anticipated, even in emergency situations. Part of the strategy for leaving is to *be ready for anything*. There is always the possibility that what starts out to be a rather tranquil separation will become one in which your ultimate behavior directly relates to the threat of physical harm.

A Backup System

Every woman getting a divorce should develop a backup system; that is, friends or family who will support you with the basics—loving care, food, but especially shelter. The desperation factor is a reality of divorce that has to be considered not only by women whose married history indicates a strong need for this, but also women who, for the moment, feel safe. It doesn't take much time or effort to ask your friends for support so that in case of extreme need you can call on them for help.

If your family is within range of where you live, find out whether it would be all right if you moved back for a while. Sometimes things can get touchy with one's family and there are some disadvantages in moving back in with Mom and Dad, but it may also afford the nurturing that you will need. Ask them whether you could borrow some money, enough to carry you through the month if it became necessary. Check on the possibility of borrowing a car, and temporary child care.

Staying with parents can be good for several reasons. Although your husband would probably know where you were, he might be more reluctant to physically abuse you in your parents' home. Parental authority can still work its magic. It could also ease his mind that you are at a place where you are not likely to bring home other men, thereby avoiding an issue that can trigger a whole set of jealousies and retaliations. Depending on your relationship with your parents, this can be a time of cooling down and recovery when things are still mercurial.

But don't assume that you can automatically move back home. Your relationship with your parents may have gradually altered over the years, and they may be as protective of their independence as you once were. Some diplomacy is required. Stress that your stay would be temporary and specify the period of time that you think their help would be needed.

Creating a backup system of friends calls for more preparation. Explain your situation as frankly as you can. Tell your friends that although you don't think that you will need assistance, you want to be safe and sure. Ask if you could stay for a few weeks, enough time to recuperate and make some further plans. Find out if they would mind your calling at the spur of the moment, even if it is at night. If they are concerned about getting involved, indicate that in no way would you divulge your whereabouts to your husband and that, if you did find it necessary to speak to him during this time, you would do it by phone, and you would initiate the call. You don't want friends to worry about whether or not your marriage hassles will be transplanted into their living room. On the other hand, this is a most crucial time for you, and if friendship means anything, it means helping out when a person is in trouble.

Stay away from choosing a single man to stay with. Your husband will think you are romantically involved. If his male ego is already wounded because you left him, it is not smart to hurt it further, no matter how innocent you know your actions are. Choose a person who is "safe"; it is to your benefit.

Have a second or third backup system available if possible. It may be that your primary choice is away when you are in need. If you have to leave immediately and you have no other choice, you can always stay at a motel for the night. Again, have some handy cash stashed away for such an eventuality.

Assuming that this would be a true crisis, it is extremely unwise to let your husband know where you are staying. He might come after you. When you leave, write him a note to the effect that you will contact him shortly.

These strategies are practical safeguards in the event that an emergency should arise. I do not mean to exaggerate these situations, but neither do I want to underestimate the danger. Pick up the newspaper any morning and the proof is monotonously recorded. Nothing is so unpredictable as human behavior during the divorce process. The range of what some husbands will actually do is enormous.

Emergency Shelters

If you are unable to stay with family or friends on the day you must leave, there are a few options. Many communities have emergency shelters for women and children. They are often listed in the phone book under Battered Women's Services or Shelters. The sheriff's department in your city should also have the names of shelters for abused women. The Salvation Army operates in most cities. Their facilities and services vary from city to city but they may have a waiting list.

The primary purpose of a shelter for an abused woman is to protect her and the children from being harmed by her spouse. They normally offer food, beds, clothing, and if needed, diapers and formula. Counselors are available to help cope with the emotional stress of the crisis, as well as deal with applying for welfare assistance, legal aid, and finding a job or job training. The length of stay varies with each program, many of which are funded through grants and donations. The Salvation Army has many of the same services as a battered women's shelter, except they usually limit the time you can stay to about a week.

Another option is to call your church, or if you do not belong to one, the relief organizations affiliated with churches. Check with the local community resource center, or the women's center at the local junior college. They usually have listings of emergency help available in the area.

Welfare

Your public backup system is welfare. Many women are very familiar with it. One half of all families headed by a woman live at or below the poverty level and for most of them welfare-AFDC (Aid to Families with Dependent Children)—is a must.

For some women, welfare may be a very alien concept. Having listened to politically conservative male politicians over the years, welfare may seem like an unclean last resort, akin to the soup kitchens for downtown street people. Forget those images. Welfare is not a handout; it is a right. With your taxes through the years, you have paid into a system from which you may now want to receive benefits. In one way or another, most everyone in the United States lives off the taxes being continuously collected— from military contractors to highway construction crews to the bureaucrats at the welfare office itself. Don't be intimidated, embarrassed, or ashamed. The fact is, you are taking much less from the system than some doctors working the other end of the welfare system. However, if it makes you feel any better, think of it as a temporary measure, some assistance to tide you over.

If you don't have the need right now, don't assume that you won't need it in the near future. A woman in one of my support groups was going along quite comfortably toward her divorce when one night, during an argument that went on and on, she told her husband that she wanted to end the marriage and wished he would get out. He didn't come home the next night after work. She was not even too worried when she didn't see him for the next three days—it had happened before. Finally, the bank called and said some checks had come in against their "closed account." Her husband had cleaned out the savings and checking accounts, and just took off. She was stranded without a cent. She had no job, three children, and the rent was due shortly. Welfare, that foreign word, suddenly became a reality in her life; in fact, her savior.

AFDC is a program run by the state but partly financed by federal money and subject to federal guidelines. You can qualify if you are going through a divorce or separation and have little or no income, do not own a car or property, and have one or more children, or are pregnant. The father of the children must not be living with you. The distasteful part of this is that when you apply for welfare, you are submitting yourself to a complete investigation by the state and its representative, your service worker. The welfare service worker is responsible for much of what happens to you, although you have the right to appeal any finding or decision.

If you are eligible for welfare, you should also be able to receive some medical aid, as well. The coverage varies from state to state and in some places affords decent health care. If you aren't on welfare, you can still qualify for medical assistance if you are in need of it. Many women who are just making ends meet but can't afford their own health care use this system. Investigate it with your local welfare department.

If you are on welfare, be sure to ask for food stamps. This information is sometimes not offered and you have to seek it out. Every little bit helps.

Don't let the system put you off. Like most bureaucracies, welfare work seems to deaden those who work in it. Some of the office personnel look more worn out than those coming in for help. Don't let anyone intimidate you. Your purpose in getting on welfare is to get help for your immediate situation.

All of the strategies in this chapter may not be necessary. Then again, you may find that you need to do some things that aren't mentioned here. The ideas expressed often had an economic base, and for good reason. To be frank, money is a woman's ticket to freedom. You can't survive for long without some of it. The thrust of this chapter has been to impress upon you the need for preparation and planning. If you do it well, your chances of a secure life after divorce are greatly enhanced.

CHAPTER 5

The Legal Puzzle

Because as a culture we choose to have marriage recognized and approved by the state, the dissolution of the contract also must conform to the civil court. What started in a church ceremony with hearts and flowers and proclamations of undying love often ends up in a county courthouse with a stack of legal documents, lawyers, the divorcing couple, and a judge, all trying to work out a compromise. There is hardly a way to make it a pleasant experience.

Most of us are quite happy to pass through life with absolutely no contact with lawyers and the law. It is rarely a satisfying experience. Either we are giving up something that we want to keep, or we are not getting as much as we think we should. In divorce cases it is no different. But the legal system, although it is not perfect, is still the bottom line in working out disputes. Hopefully you will not have to explore and exhaust all of its possibilities; indeed, its complexity might motivate you and your husband to fully explore every chance to work out your differences.

Deciding to see a lawyer can be very traumatic. It's like finally saying, "OK, this is it—this is the end!" Many women find all kinds of reasons to put it off. It *is* a giant step. This act is a commitment of sorts, a statement not only to yourself but to a third party that your marriage is at an end. And you are giving that person the power to act on your behalf.

It is a step, however, that sooner or later must be taken. Whether you and your husband originally envisioned it in this way or not, your marriage contract was legally binding, and although you can spiritually dissolve bonds by an act of the will, it must also be done to the satisfaction of the courts.

I urge you to take the initiative to seek legal advice even if you are uncertain about wanting to end your marriage. Start early— do this even before you discuss your plans with your spouse. Interviews with attorneys confirm the wisdom of this action. First, it gives you the facts and necessary information needed regarding the laws in your state, and how they apply to your particular situation. You may be a long way from filing for divorce, but the information gathered will establish a realistic path. Second, a clear picture of the workings of the legal system will be a great help in your decision-making process. In a very practical sense, your plans for the future hinge on what you and your lawyer think will be the most likely outcome of the final judgment. For example, in order to realistically prepare for the future, you will want an educated estimate of whether or not support payments are forthcoming, and their approximate amount. In addition, you will want to know what to expect in terms of custody arrangements and how your shared assets might be divided. The sooner you can get some idea of your future rights and obligations, the faster you can move toward a final resolution.

In addition, by thinking about getting a lawyer in the early stages of the process, you have more time to shop around for one that suits your needs and personality. Cost is a factor. As with most things, the more money you have, the easier it is to find a good attorney. Remember, because you are the one leaving, you have an advantage. In most instances, it is your choice when to announce your intentions. Take the time you have now to find worthy representation. Guidelines for choosing an attorney are discussed later.

When you have found an attorney with whom you have good rapport, the confidence that this fosters in dealing with your divorce, as well as your husband, is invaluable. Having an advocate gives a sense of equality, a feeling of no longer being alone in the struggle.

> Women should protect themselves—emotionally, legally, financially. For the sake of the children and for their own sake, they need to be aggressive. That is, willing to step out of the traditional role of being passive and sweet and become willing to take care of themselves. And that doesn't imply being rotten or nasty or mean or vengeful. It means taking those steps that are necessary to ensure that you get what you are entitled to.
>
> —Sandra Morris, Attorney

This chapter does not pretend to be a complete and all-encompassing guide to the legal considerations that come up during divorce. Each state has its own set of laws in this area and, while there is a good deal of common ground, generalizations are difficult to make.

More significantly, individual locales, courts, and judges may have their special interpretation and application of the law, so that it is impossible to accurately predict the outcome on any given subject.

However, some general instruction can be given. There are things about which to be cautious and actions that are recommended. Most women getting divorced have similar concerns, and they continue to voice them in workshops and interviews. This chapter speaks to these concerns. This is not legal advice, simply *indications*. Only an attorney can provide legal counsel and interpret the law.

This legal information is based on interviews with attorneys having extensive background in divorce proceedings, many of whom are certified family law specialists. I have drawn on the knowledge and experience of two lawyers in particular and quote them frequently throughout the chapter: Sandra Morris has a private practice in San Diego, California, and over the past two decades has represented hundreds of women in divorce cases; Marshall Caskey is a well-known Los Angeles attorney with a strong background in marital litigation. The balance of their views in addition to others is the foundation for this section.

SOME WORDS TO LEARN

Law books do not make good recreational reading. They are filled with abstract words which define specific subjects. The result is rather boring to most people but vital to you and your divorce. Fortunately, you don't have to do much of it in your life but there comes a time—right now for instance—when you must take your medicine.

Listed below are some basic terms commonly used in the divorce proceedings. Being familiar with them before you meet with your lawyer will help. If you have any question about their application to your case, bring it up with your lawyer.

The terms are listed in the chronological steps that you will probably encounter them. This is the process of divorce—from a legal point of view.

Filing a Petition for Dissolution of Marriage, or *Complaint for Divorce or Legal Separation:* In order to get a divorce, you must first file a *petition* with the court. This document contains basic information about you, your husband, any children, your assets, and whether you are filing for a divorce or legal separation.

Most states have "no-fault" laws, which means it is not necessary to prove *fault* in order to file your petition. For the states requiring proof of "fault," you must be able to prove "grounds" for the divorce—the most common being adultery, cruelty, desertion, a felony conviction, and insanity. Your lawyer will advise you on this.

Summons. In addition to the *Petition* or *Complaint*, a *Summons* will be served on your husband by a marshal. This document is his notification that you have filed for divorce. It also tells how much time he has to prepare a *response*. Some women, in order to pacify their husband, elect to serve the summons by having the husband pick up the legal documents at the attorney's office. However it is accomplished, the *Summons* must be served in order for the court to have jurisdiction over the case, for example, the payment of support.

The response. The respondent, your husband, must file an answer within the time period stated in the papers, usually within thirty days of receiving service of the petition. Should your husband not file an answer within the stipulated time period, or if he cannot be found within your state, a *default* situation exists. The court can then grant a *default* divorce decree. In the case of a missing husband, the court can grant you custody of the children but the state cannot grant support payments until the missing spouse is located.

Restraining order. The petitions filed in most divorces contain *restraining orders* against both husband and wife that remain in effect until the petition is dismissed, a judgment is entered, or the court enters further orders. To begin, it is essential to have the restraining order contain a clause enjoining your husband from taking and spending any of the joint assets, i.e., bank accounts, stock certificates, life insurance policies, equity in jointly owned real estate.

A *restraining order* can also be designed to protect you from harm. To prevent physical or psychological abuse, your attorney may recommend to the court that your husband be kept from having contact with you, specifically forbidding his aggressive and threatening presence at your place of work, home, and in your neighborhood. Be sure to inform your attorney if your husband has had a track record of controlling and aggressive behavior. If he has a history of abusing you or the children, consider this: *As the marriage went, so goes the divorce.* And the level of abuse and threats is likely to increase as the divorce process continues. Follow your lawyer's recommendations to file a restraining order. This is discussed further in the chapter on "Husbands."

A note about restraining orders: A court order is *legally binding*, and if not followed, carries the threat of contempt charges. But it is only effective if your husband respects the law, and is capable of controlling his behavior. More often than not, a piece of paper—even a legal one—will not prevent an enraged spouse from forcing his way into your house or accosting you in a parking lot. If he were to do that, he could be held in contempt of court or jailed. But in practical terms, the damage is done.

Ex parte motion. This action takes place when you and your attorney are seeking emergency help from the court or when there are indications that injury of some kind (financial, physical, etc.) would occur to you if your husband was given advance notice of the paperwork being filed with the court. Basically, *ex parte* indicates an action and/or hearing without the other party being informed in advance or being present.

The hearing. This is a court appearance before a judge to obtain approval of documents related to your divorce. It is not a trial.

Temporary orders. This is not a legal term but a reference to the condition that exists after your petition or complaint has been ruled on. The "temporary" conditions ordered by the court are the stipulations with which both you and your husband will live until a final settlement agreement is negotiated or the case is tried and a judgment is handed down by the court.

The purpose of these initial rulings is to outline and establish, among other things, interim spousal support, child support, custody and visitation arrangements, occupancy of the family home, and restraining orders. The key word here is *temporary*. Statistically, however, many final judgments reflect what has been set up in these temporary orders. The court frequently deems the existing living and financial arrangements viable for a long-term settlement.

The Discovery process. As in all civil cases, during the time between the summons, and the final settlement agreement, a discovery process takes place to determine the facts of the case. During this process, it is essential that you supply your attorney with as accurate and detailed an accounting of your assets and liabilities as possible. Include in this a history of your marriage, the documentation of gifts, inheritances, money in the *community* that was yours previous to the marriage, and any assets that are exclusively those of the children. Expect your attorney to request this.

The goal of the discovery process is to identify all the aspects of what attorneys call the *community* (property, money, other assets). With this, they determine your separate property from what will be considered joint property. A settlement will be designed that divides the *community* between the spouses.

Let me warn that a settlement does not imply equal division. Nothing guarantees that things will be equal or fair. Therefore, it is important to supply solid and accurate records to your attorney. It is essential to be very clear about your priorities in the settlement.

Deposition. Should your attorney have difficulty discovering assets, or you suspect that your husband is hiding money, your attorney may elect to take a *deposition.* This means your husband is required to answer questions under oath. At this time, your attorney may suggest an appraisal of your husband's business (if he is self-employed), as well as an inventory of household goods, especially if there are valuable collections of furniture, art, coins, etc. This procedure is not necessary if you both could agree on the value of these assets.

Negotiation and settlement. After negotiation with both sides, a statement of terms is agreed upon which is called a *settlement.* When this document is presented to the court at the final hearing, the judge will rule on it. The judge may change or adjust some of the terms of the settlement if, for instance, it doesn't match with what the court feels is in the best interest of the children.

Settlements that are soundly and fairly negotiated outside of the courtroom are the ones that last. If you have both shared in the compromises, you are more likely to be able to live with the terms of the settlement.

If you and your husband are unable to agree on a settlement—or in "fault" states, on the divorce itself—then your attorney will put in a request for trial.

In many cases, you can expect to participate in a:

Pretrial hearing. There are two kinds of pretrial hearings. One is the settlement conference, an informal meeting probably in the judge's chambers. The judge will use his influence to help the parties reach compromises and agreement, offering an opinion on how the trial judge will rule on the case. Most pretrial judges do their best to discourage a trial, especially when they believe the case does not warrant it, or feel that a reasonable settlement is close.

The trial. When a settlement cannot be reached between the two spouses, they will proceed to the trial before a judge. The judge will hear the evidence presented, consider it, and render a judgment. There are disadvantages for both parties in going to trial. Costs escalate tremendously. Attorneys will spend many additional billable hours preparing your case for court (attorneys' fees for court appearances are approximately 1½ times higher than their normal rate). Some trials begin and end in the same day, others go on for days and weeks. On the other hand, this may be the *only* way a woman can obtain a fair settlement when her spouse is being unreasonable or vindictive, and she has a substantial amount of assets in community property.

The judgment. This is the final ruling of the court. It may have come through a court-approved negotiated settlement or the decision of the judge at a trial. Both sides must abide by it.

TEN QUESTIONS MOST ASKED BY WOMEN

In workshops I have given, certain questions come up again and again, reflecting the worries and anxieties of women caught up in an alien system.

This section is not to be taken as legally definitive. There could be any number of circumstances that give new shading to the nature of the problem. Again, each state and region may have a particular expression of the law. Discuss these questions in greater detail with your lawyer. This section is to give some reassurance and direction on items of common concern.

1. My husband refuses to move out of the house. He says I'm the one who wants a divorce so I should have to go—I must leave the house and the kids. I don't know what to do. Can he force me?

ANSWER: No, not for those reasons. And most courts are reluctant to order a spouse out of the house unless there is danger of extreme psychological or physical harm. As a result of the temporary orders, the spouse with the most need is usually allowed to reside in the house. During the negotiation of terms in the divorce, a decision is made as to who will live in the house permanently or whether the property will be sold. It is up to you and your lawyer to make a strong case for your needs.

You have an edge, especially if you have temporary custody of the children and will be caring for them. The tendency of the courts is to keep the children in a stable environment and familiar surroundings. For this reason, it is important to identify your needs when you file the request for temporary orders.

If you need him to move out because it is an emergency situation, have your attorney file a request for an order to have your husband move immediately. Again, you will have to establish that his presence creates some kind of danger, in which case an *ex parte* order can be issued. But even if it is not an emergency, other circumstances might allow your lawyer to file papers requiring your husband to move out.

Forcing your husband out without a court order—by the use of strong-arm tactics or changing the locks—is another way to remove a spouse from the home, but can result in broken windows, and violence.

However, if you are in immediate danger by remaining in the house, leave right away. Then work with your lawyer to regain access when it becomes safe.

If you don't have children or will not have custody of them, ask your attorney to help you determine your needs for staying in the house. For instance, you might be using the house for a business and losing it would disrupt your economic base. Or you might not be physically able to move at this time because of poor health.

You shouldn't be made to feel that, just because you want a divorce, the loss of the house is just punishment.

SANDRA MORRIS: *It is important that you not move out of the house. I don't mean you can't go out of the house—just don't move out. And if you want custody, then certainly don't move out and leave the children behind. The court will tend to give the house, at least temporarily, to the parent who is there with the children.*

2. If I file first, isn't that better?

ANSWER: Yes and no. In a no-fault state, because guilt is not an issue, there is no legal advantage to petitioning for a divorce first. It may afford an emotional edge in the sense that you are prepared for the events to come and can gear up for them. The more you are aware of what is happening, the better chance you have of surviving well.

If you live in a fault state, then it may be an advantage to file first, especially if you suspect that he will be resistant. It gives you a psychological advantage as well as a legal one, in that the spouse is left defending himself against the grounds that were filed.

MARSHALL CASKEY: *Normally the one who is going to be the custodial parent, usually the woman, is the one who files for temporary support. But the temporary support has nothing to do with who files first. If the woman's going to be the custodial parent in the family residence, and the husband will be the one to leave, then when the woman files, she asks for pretrial support and residency of the house with the children. If he filed first, that doesn't mean he will get the kids and the house.*

SANDRA MORRIS: *The only time filing first would make a difference in a no-fault state is if there is a custody battle and you're concerned about the other party getting an* ex parte *order giving him temporary custody. Sometimes the judge does not read the declarations that are attached thoroughly enough. An* ex parte *temporary order of custody is not supposed to be given to a person unless that person has been the custodian of the children. Even then, courts are not supposed to award custody on an* ex parte *basis. It is supposed to happen at a hearing with both parties present. But sometimes a client won't be truthful with an attorney and, therefore, the documents are not factual. On top of this, the judge has not read them carefully. So if there is a custody issue, there is some advantage in filing first, if only to make sure you are the one in a position to get an* ex parte *order.*

3. I want to be able to live in the house after we are divorced. That would be best for me, at least until I get myself established. How can I arrange that?

ANSWER: If you rent your house or apartment, attempt to negotiate for it. If you cannot reach an agreement in the bargaining for your settlement, then ask for it and demonstrate your need when you go into court. If you own your house, the same is true—negotiate or ask the court through your lawyer to rule in your favor. Again, if you have custody of the children you have the advantage on this issue.

However, retaining residence and/or ownership of the house as part of the divorce settlement has some financial considerations, as mentioned in Chapter Four. Be sure to consult with your attorney or a financial expert on the tax consequences of keeping the house as part of your settlement.

A complication arises if you are each poor and unable to work off your debts in a reasonable manner. If what is owed is very large and people are pressing for money, the court can order you to sell your house in order to meet those obligations. Anything left over would then be shared.

If there is plenty of cash and a fair amount of assets, the wife could get to keep the house as part of an equitable settlement and the husband would receive other assets.

4. He's threatening to take everything away from me and says he'll fight me all the way. He even threatened to quit his job so that I wouldn't get anything. What can I do?

ANSWER: Go see a lawyer, if you have not already done so, and get the facts about your situation, and hopefully some reassurances, as well. If your husband's reaction to your divorce is to come back with threats, the entire situation needs careful handling or things could go haywire. Refrain from endless discussions, which invariably lead to arguments with your husband. These will just feed into his temperament at this time. It's really not productive.

Take actions to protect yourself. In states that have community property laws, the understanding is that a spouse is entitled to one half of the joint assets. You have the option of going to your bank and withdrawing at least one half of all the money held in your joint accounts. Some women take more than half if they can demonstrate that it is necessary for their living expenses. Have your attorney guide you in this matter. This situation makes a backup plan even more important. If he does take a drastic step, you must have alternative strategies ready.

When the relationship is so deteriorated that you only confront each other with financial threats which in the end will damage you both, it may be the time to look into new means of negotiating, encompassing a different approach to communication. A later section of this chapter describes *mediation*. Look into this.

SANDRA MORRIS: *Don't panic. It does happen that a man sometimes quits his job—but not very often. It is more frequent that he threatens to quit. Or threatens to leave the country. They threaten all kinds of things. My experience is that women are often very overwhelmed by their husbands. Women and men assume certain roles with each other. The husband will say things like, "My attorney said blah, blah, blah," and she will believe it is true. It's the husband's attempt to bluff her down.*

5. I had an affair. If my husband finds out, can he use that against me? Will I lose my kids? Should I tell my lawyer?

ANSWER: If you live in a state with no-fault laws, this in itself should not be a legal problem. Many women fear that their husbands will attempt to prove them an unfit mother if extramarital relationships are discovered and they will lose custody of the children. Of the lawyers I have interviewed across the country, the consensus of their opinion is that the woman usually has to do something quite drastic, such as being convicted of a felony, in order to lose custody.

In any case, don't be frightened. Studies show that a growing number of women have affairs at some point in their marriage. If you are currently involved with a man, I would encourage you to suspend things for a while, at least until you get some legal advice. Tell your lawyer of your situation. This information is needed in case your husband should attempt to use it against you. Do not tell your husband. If you need to confide in someone, choose a close friend. At this stage, letting your husband know will only complicate your life, and could be very dangerous.

MARSHALL CASKEY: *Unless a woman has some gross peculiarity or is unstable, a heroin addict for instance, most of the time young children go to the mother. As the children get older, though, fathers have more of a voice in it. It varies from state to state and according to individual situations.*

In Los Angeles County, for instance, the offense has to be fairly specific—physical abuse, overt sexual behavior in front of the kids, a woman having lots of men in and out of the house. These could influence the court in favor of the husband. But I don't think a woman with a live-in boyfriend would affect a trial court negatively in Los Angeles insofar as custody is concerned. But it can affect child support.

6. How long can I collect spousal support (alimony) and how much would I get?

ANSWER: Spousal support is usually based on two factors: the relative financial means of the parties, and the duration of the marriage.

How much, if anything, you will get is hard to say. When no minor children are involved, spousal support depends on the special situations of both parties. Some issues considered are the age and health of the parties, whether the wife already has employment, the potential future earning capacities of both parties, and various other conditions. The trend seems to be that the more substantial support payments are going to older women who have been married for twenty years and have few job skills and have husbands who are fairly well established. It is not productive to ask for an unrealistic amount of support. The judge will not award you more than your husband is capable of paying. There is really no great mystery here. You usually know what your husband makes. If his income is $2,200 a month, you cannot expect to receive $1,700 in support payments.

Alternatives exist for making support arrangements. Often at the outset of her divorce, a woman will receive a larger amount of money in order for her to pursue training in some field and establish a career. As the years go by, this payment is reduced. Because of fluctuating human needs and financial conditions of either party, the amount of alimony can be readjusted by the courts. If the husband is unable to work or if he remarries and has children, he may petition the court for reduced payments. Remarriage of the wife cuts off payments.

Even if you are not in need of money, it is still a good idea to ask for a token amount of alimony—unless the concept of it goes against your principles. Doing this ensures that the subject can come up for review if in the future an unforeseen need arises on your part.

MARSHALL CASKEY: *The person receiving the spousal support will have to pay income tax on the money. The person paying it often gets the deduction. Women with children may want to go for a larger amount of child support and less spousal support to avoid paying as much income tax. Much of the money is directly or indirectly benefiting the children anyway. In addition, if you remarry, you are no longer entitled to spousal support, whereas child support usually goes on until the children reach eighteen.*

Food For Thought: I recently interviewed fifty men for this edition of the book. A uniform body of information showed up. When these men suspected that their marriage was in serious trouble, they stashed money away. If they were self-employed, they took steps to reduce profits or hide assets of the business, intending to come out of a divorce with a bigger share of the community assets. It was clear that many felt very possessive about their earnings and believed the fruits of their success were theirs alone. They did not feel that their wives deserved an equal share.

Agree or not, the situation exists. And this is where your self-esteem plays a big part in the settlement. It is important that you view your contributions to the marriage, to the rearing of the children, and to the advancement of your husband's career as having tangible worth. Get in touch with a sense of entitlement. And on a practical level, enlist the help of a financial advisor well acquainted with the task of discovering hidden assets.

7. He's going to fight for custody of the kids. I want them with me. Could he get them?

ANSWER: If you want to retain physical custody of your children, *keep them with you.*

When you file your papers and stipulate conditions for the temporary orders, state that the children will be living with you and that the father will have visitation rights. Although the courts are now recognizing that in many cases the father is equally capable of having primary custody of the children, a stronger consideration is still being given to the mother, especially when the children are under the age of eight.

The custody issue is legally complex and emotionally perilous. Because of its ramifications, the subject is taken up at length in a later chapter on children.

SANDRA MORRIS: *The person who has temporary custody of the children has the edge. The law favors a stable situation and as long as the person who actually has the custody is providing adequately, and the children are adjusting well under the circumstances, the courts will tend to leave the children where they are. There has been a trend for some time now toward more equal treatment of men and women. I think there is still a bias, partly because most of the judges are still of a previous generation.*

If you really want the children, no matter how great the pressures are or how awful it is, do not move out without them.

MARSHALL CASKEY: *Don't let your husband scare you with phony custody battles. Women are very vulnerable, I think, to threats about it. I find it very difficult sometimes to reassure women that the husband's requesting custody of the children is often specious.*

That's also an area where some lawyers can victimize women. When the husband requests custody in his papers, the wife will naturally be panicked about it. Some attorneys, instead of telling her that it's a bluff and that it is probably not going to happen, will indicate that this is really scary, really serious. They will scare the hell out of women. A woman is in a vulnerable position when a man raises the issue of taking her kids away, and if she is misadvised by counsel and led to believe that it is a real probability, she is twice a victim.

8. Who is going to pay our bills? Can I arrange it so that he has to pay them?

ANSWER: Generally speaking, the person with the bigger wage is ordered to pay the debts, but you are *both* actually liable for them. The court usually looks after the creditors.

MARSHALL CASKEY: *What happens is that the order to assume, pay, and hold the wife harmless action protects the wife in the sense that it gives her an action against the husband, whenever and whoever it is that comes after her. As between the wife and the creditors, it does not provide a shield. It does not say to the creditor that you can no longer sue the wife. For example, if the husband is supposed to pay off the debts and instead he takes off to Venezuela, the creditor still looks to the community (the wife and husband). The wife is still there. That doesn't stop the creditors. It just means that the husband is supposed to pay—if she can catch him. It's not a bankruptcy. There's nothing a divorce court can do to extinguish the debt. The IRS is like any other creditor, by the way. They'll go after the money wherever it is.*

9. Who has to pay the lawyers? Can I get my husband to pay if I don't have any money?

ANSWER: It is best for you to have enough money to pay for your own lawyer. Most lawyers prefer to work with a client who is paying them directly. Some attorneys will accept a number of cases in which the woman has no money. Others may accept a reduced fee. In both cases, lawyers will take action to collect their fees from the husband, or the assets in the *community* via the court system.

Psychologically, you are at an advantage if you are paying the lawyer yourself. It is a way of taking charge in a truly independent manner. You may at some point choose to have your attorney try to recover your legal fees as part of your final settlement, but your initial action is best taken freely of your husband.

MARSHALL CASKEY: *If you've got the cash to put down for a retainer, you are going to get better legal services. And you are going to get a better class of lawyer than you will if you go in with a lot of promises, or rely upon an award of attorney's fees by the court.*

10. In my settlement, is it better to go for a cash payment up front or larger monthly payments?

ANSWER: Divorce is a better deal for most men in community property states than it is for women. At first glance, it looks equal in that the couple divides everything fifty-fifty. But the husband usually has the built-in advantage of having a job with some specialized experience or seniority which makes his earning potential much greater than the wife's. If she is thirty-five years old and just starting out, her chances of matching his wage level are poor.

Even if she is awarded the house, it also means that she probably has the children and with them has inherited the emotional and much of the financial responsibility for them. This can be heavily restricting on the job market. In addition, the record of husbands' keeping up payments or rent or being faithful with support payments after the breakup is dismal.

Therefore, my recommendation is to push for a large cash and property settlement instead of larger monthly payments. If you have the money in your hand—even if it isn't as much as you would have gotten if you received *all* of the future installments—you know where you stand. You can take that money and invest it, or you can use it to immediately improve your position. But rather than taking my recommendation, check with your attorney on this point.

Also, don't forget that high inflation is a fact of life. The cost of living continues to rise. It would be to your advantage to have an adjustment clause written into your settlement that would allow for an increase in support payments. Your child support should especially reflect this increase. The court will not automatically order one, but you *should* try to get it. If the payment rate is a fixed one, it may seem fair at this time but five years from now you will be struggling unless you stipulate a cost of living increase. This is not just another angle to sap money from your husband. In the years to come, his wages will be adjusted to compensate for the inflation rate. Why should the support payments be fixed at a dollar value that is no longer realistic?

Rising prices are joining death and taxes as one of the inevitabilities in life.

Some considerations to follow when negotiating a settlement:

- Take your time. Every divorce is different, and has its own set of special circumstances. Give yourself time to think through each issue. Ask questions of your attorney, and listen to your inner self. Remember that divorce is an extremely emotional experience. It is a time when the judgment of both parties could be clouded; you may not be operating at the place of your highest functioning, and priorities are likely to be a little mixed up.
- Set *your* priorities but be prepared to make concessions and compromises on issues of less importance.
- Guilt makes the job of the attorney more difficult. As one lawyer said, "When I am dealing with someone who is feeling really guilty, I have to work like crazy to keep them from 'giving away the farm.' " The person being left will likely play on the guilt of the "leaving" spouse because they feel wronged, and self-righteous. Work with your therapist so that you keep from running up legal fees as well, and wind up in a stalemate over who gets the lamp grandmother gave as a wedding gift.
- Do not allow your husband to pressure you into settling when you are not yet ready.

The negotiations can often be compared to running a marathon. You need to be in good physical and emotional shape to run in the event, but remember that it's okay if you walk the last few miles. Most divorces take much longer to complete than people anticipate. Pace yourself and hold your position.

GETTING YOUR DIVORCE

The divorce process is never more a "process" than when you begin making contact with a lawyer and the whole machinery of the legal system is put into motion. Some of it is satisfying; some of it is confusing; some of it will make you uneasy.

Peggy was thirty years old with four children when she decided that she wanted a divorce from her husband who was a naval officer. Her response to the legal system is quite typical.

> I didn't have any idea of what it was all about. Even when I was there at the lawyer's office and he was trying to tell me. I wasn't quite sure what the procedure was going to be. I found out though. Women have a lot of rights they don't know they have. They don't have to *prove* anything.

The first step in clearing up some of the confusion is to recognize that you have several basic options in your approach to getting a divorce. You should seriously consider all of them before committing yourself to one of them. Each divorce has its own circumstances.

Do It Yourself

The simplest and cheapest method of divorce is to do it yourself. Several states have this option available and within them it is becoming more and more popular. In California, an annual edition of "How To Do Your Own Divorce" is available at bookstores. The legal forms appear simple, and the procedures for filing are clearly outlined. Check in your state to see if such a publication is available. I suggest reading it even if you intend to use an attorney. It will be part of your divorce education.

Do-it-yourself divorce agencies have sprung up, usually staffed by legal secretaries experienced in the paperwork and filing that most lawyers' services are actually about. The service is done at minimum cost.

Advantages. The simplicity of it is its beauty. Besides being inexpensive, it avoids the appointments, consultations, and telephone calls to lawyers. It requires a solid understanding on the part of the wife and husband as to the terms of the divorce. Negotiation is usually worked out privately between the two people. Because the compromises are mutually agreed to without resorting to lawyers and the court system, it is a way to establish a new relationship that recognizes a separateness but is based on understanding and civility.

Disadvantages. If the couple has complex financial holdings, even a home that they are paying off, the do-it-yourself approach can become very tricky. The more issues to be negotiated, the more need for outside help. If you share in a business, hold real estate, or have children and are concerned about custody, the issues need a perspective that may be hard for the persons involved to gain in the pressure of the situation.

Also, if the husband has been the dominant partner in the marriage, there is no reason to think that he won't want to take on that same role in the negotiations of a do-it-yourself divorce. You may be bullied into terms that are ultimately not agreeable.

In do-it-yourself, you have to be competent and aware.

Using One Lawyer

Some couples, in hopes of avoiding the adversary process and desiring to save money, might choose to use just one lawyer. Legal ethics dictate that the attorney can represent only one of the spouses in a divorce case. However, in this situation, the woman or man would contact a mutually agreed-upon attorney for an explanation of how the legal system works and what their rights are. If the lawyer is open to it, the process could become one in which all of the issues in contention were discussed and negotiated by the couple. When the papers are drawn up, the person not represented could take a copy of the settlement to another lawyer for a separate opinion to be sure that his or her interests were represented before signing them.

Advantages. One lawyer is cheaper than two. The method seems to put both clients on the same side of the table and defuses the adversarial nature of most divorces. In the informal and low pressure atmosphere of a mutually agreed-upon attorney, the nature of the negotiations stand a better chance of decreased hostility.

* * *

Disadvantages. Many lawyers feel uncomfortable with this situation. They feel that ultimately it is to the advantage of one party, that ethically one lawyer can't represent both sides. There is the contention that one person is hiring the lawyer and, therefore, the other is not actually being represented. In addition, when the one client goes to another lawyer to get the agreement verified, that lawyer could choose to raise all kinds of new issues, and the whole fabric of the agreement would come apart and all of the time spent would have been wasted.

Separate Lawyers

Having separate lawyers is certainly the most common method of proceeding in a divorce. The climate of divorce is regularly overheated with persons not thinking or acting clearly. Moreover, complex divorces with considerable *community* assets need expert handling. In this process, you go out and find an attorney who you think can best represent your legitimate interests. Your husband does the same. Hopefully, through the negotiating skills of the two attorneys, an agreement can be reached on the many issues involved in the breakup. A settlement is drawn up and signed, later to be presented to the court. In many states, if you and your husband cannot reach agreement on child custody, a referral is made to a court-appointed mediator who will work with both parents on negotiating custody. If that cannot be accomplished, recommendations will be made to the court based on interviews with the family and professional advisors.

Advantages. When you get a good attorney, you have someone in *your* corner, looking out for *your* rights. It may be the first time that you have felt that kind of security, and that assurance cannot be discounted. The confidence gained by it can affect your behavior in all aspects of your life and especially in situations involving your husband.

There is authentic satisfaction in knowing that a person is really listening to your side of the issues, and will act solely in your best interests. If you have chosen a lawyer well, it is a great relief to be able to trust in that person's skills to obtain what you think is fair in the divorce negotiations. A good lawyer also provides clarity and the sure direction you are in need of at this time.

In recent years, there has been a rapid increase in attorneys who have become specialists in family law. The additional training and accreditation allows them to specialize in matrimonial law, and to give solid and well-informed advice to their clients.

Another advantage is that your lawyer is not emotionally involved in your marriage and the disputes that grew out of it. Because of this, there is nothing to interfere with his bargaining for you. To the attorney, this is a business transaction.

Disadvantages. If one of the clients is feeling vindictive, that spouse, through the lawyer, can attempt to use the legal system to harass and frustrate the other spouse. Some persons use the system to vent their past hostilities and resentments in a most dramatic way. The process becomes a grand stage on which everything is again played out, but this time written into the records. Unfortunately, there exist lawyers who are only too happy to go along with it.

Some lawyers might even encourage this approach. Why not—it means more money for them. The longer and more complicated a divorce is, the greater amount of legal advice and representation is needed.

According to Marshall Caskey:

> Lawyers will sometimes take advantage of the fact that the parties are emotional. They let their clients dictate unreasonable stances and they litigate unnecessary matters, when the lawyers well know how the case is going to turn out. Unfortunately, a lot of lawyers get a classy reputation in the divorce area for putting up The Big Fight. Instead of sitting down with a client and honestly saying, "Look, that's not a reasonable expectation. You won't get that, so you might as well give it up in the negotiation stage," they take it to trial. Trials cost a lot of money. So do depositions.
>
> A good lawyer will tell a client that his or her position is untenable. Instead, many go down to the courthouse and make a big charade. Judges, as a general rule, play along. They won't say, "That's non-

sense." They used to be lawyers so they won't invalidate the position of a lawyer. They let the game go on.

A lot of times after the initial interview, a lawyer can with fair accuracy tell how the thing is going to turn out—within a few dollars. Much of the time it's pretty clear-cut. A lawyer can do a real service to the client by simply saying, "This isn't going to fly." On the other hand, if a lawyer does that, the client may go to someone else, feeling that the lawyer isn't willing to fight for her.

You may have been promised the moon by a lawyer but end up only paying for the trip.

MEDIATION

The word *mediation* seems almost like a foreign word when it is used in conjunction with a divorce settlement. It is hard to convince two persons locked in a contest of egos—for what seems at times to be survival—to become open to mutual understanding and compromise. Most couples are ready to do battle, and the adversarial nature of our court system is a natural place for it. The clients and lawyers traditionally stake out positions and dig in. As Robert Tigner, a staff attorney for HALT (an organization for legal reform) says, "If one or the other parties is absolutely determined to have a shoot-out, it's no problem finding a lawyer to do the shooting." So the husband and wife take on lawyers in the same spirit that the underworld uses a "hired gun" to do the dirty work.

The entire context of this process seems wrong. Robert Coulson, of the American Arbitration Association, says, "Divorce is one of the vital areas of dispute settlements in society and it is one of the worst handled." When no-fault divorce laws were rapidly being passed in many states during the seventies, there was real optimism expressed that much of the animosity in divorce proceedings would disappear. After all, there would no longer be a need for ugly accusations in the courtroom about sex habits, or claims of physical violence. Divorce would now be granted when—in effect—they were mutually desired.

But bad feelings and the fears that surround divorce don't go away so easily. Anger, vengeance, and insecurity seem to shift to the other issues that remain to be worked out: Child custody, visitation rights, spousal support, and the determination and sharing of financial assets. The bitterness that can grow out of these areas reflects their continuing importance, but it also indicates that people once bound together in a failing marriage have a tendency to want to even the score at the end.

Mediation is a process of negotiation which attempts to break away from the destructive adversarial system and search for alternate solutions. It brings the couple together with a third party, a mediator trained in working with marital settlement disputes. The process recognizes that both husband and wife have a legitimate position and from each perspective they are acting in their own best interest. But it also knows that just as marriage needs compromise if it is to work, so does divorce. As distasteful as it may sound to some at this time, you cannot get everything that you want. In the adversary battle of the courtroom, that realization may come after months spent in worry, hatred, and thousands of dollars in legal fees—but it *will come*. There will be a compromise, either by some kind of negotiated settlement finally worked out by the opposing lawyers or in a judgment handed down by the court. In the end you will both be bound to some agreement, even if you hate the conditions.

Jerry Murase, of the American Arbitration Association in Los Angeles, says of the mediation process:

> We try to impress upon the husband and wife that even though their relationship has broken down and they are not communicating, both have to come to the realization that, if they have kids, for instance, they are going to be seeing each other. It is like any other kind of continuing relationship, but the child is the common denominator. And unless you are satisfied with the agreement, even if it is a judgment by the court, you're going to find some way to make it difficult for the other person, either to see the child or find some roadblock for not paying support payments.

In mediation, the necessity of compromise is admitted from the start, and every effort is made to work for a conclusion that when reached is mutually accepted and agreed to. The chances of it working are greater, because the compromise was arrived at during face-to-face meetings in which the responsibility was understood by the people most affected—the husband and wife.

Kirsten and Neil got caught up in a legal fight at the end of their marriage. They had been together for fourteen years when she told him that she wanted a divorce. It was a shock to Neil despite the fact that they had not been getting along for years. Their life was relatively comfortable. He was a design engineer with a group in Cambridge, Massachusetts. Their two girls, Meg, age twelve, and Josie, age thirteen, were in junior high school.

At first they tried to talk about the divorce and the settlement, but it didn't go very far. Kirsten and Neil were at an impasse when they discovered mediation. Kristen was desperate at the time.

> We kept breaking down. Neil was hurt and angry. I would start talking about the fact that I thought I needed the house for the sake of the kids and we'd soon be arguing over some past problem—that he hated the way I fixed up the bedroom. But when we really did start talking about the actual sharing of the assets, he would really get uptight.
>
> He always thought, in the back of his mind, that he was building a little empire here with the house and all. But he really saw it as *his* empire. The thought that he might have to give it up, or even share it, was beyond him at first.
>
> Our lawyer fees were going up. We both had around $2,500 invested and still weren't close to a settlement and it had already gone on for thirteen months. It's strange but when you are wasting all that money, instead of stopping, the temptation is to keep going and see it through—like some kind of mutual suicide pact.

Divorce mediation works this way: When the couple comes together with the mediator, they are asked to read and sign an agreement emphasizing a commitment to good will in the negotiations. Mediation is not intended to substitute for legal representation. Although many mediators are attorneys, they will not represent either party individually. Also, mediation sessions may be done by a team consisting of a psychologist and an attorney.

The husband or wife may have their own lawyers present if they wish. Whatever is finally agreed upon is subject to court approval and must go through legal proceedings.

Mediation is *not* an attempt at reconciliation. It assumes that the parties simply want an equitable settlement of their differences so that they can get on with life. The mediator acts as a facilitator, but it is the couple who actually work out the agreements.

The mediator gets to know the couple through discussion and by observing the dynamics of the relationship. Mediators have been trained to isolate the central issues of conflict and present alternative ways of solving the problem. It is important for the couple to realize that the present reality of their dilemma of custody or maintenance is what must be encountered, and not to seek compensation for some past marital difficulty. Bringing up the history of the marriage only stimulates emotions and serves little purpose in the negotiations. The issues that each person sets as priority items become the agenda.

The mediator helps the couple see more clearly the common ground that they share. The focus is one of opening new ways to communicate and relate to the problems. Whatever the issue is, it is a mutual one and has to be worked out by the two of them.

Some lawyers may object to the process with the argument that you are not getting everything that you could. Jerry Murase comments from a mediator's viewpoint.

> We tell the couple that it is the job of their attorneys to represent you and they are doing their job when they tell you that you could be able to get more by going into litigation. The question *we* ask is if you would be able to accept something less than you might possibly be able to get in litigation when the consequences of that procedure are possibly hostility and additional costs.

When the couple agree on any single issue, the mediator formally recognizes it and both parties must state that fact. There is great leeway possible during the sessions in finding ways to resolve issues. If child custody is the problem, the mediator might call in a child psychologist to help out with advice. At another time, a tax expert might be consulted if that were needed. If one of the couple is having a particularly hard time emotionally or is unable to adequately express his or her needs, the mediator might hold a private session to get through the block. The primary goal is always to seek out as fair and workable an agreement as possible. Winning or losing is not the issue in mediation.

After their mediated settlement, Kirsten said:

> In mediation we settled our differences in four sessions. It cost about $600 and that was a bargain compared to what we were spending. I really can't remember what most of the original hassle was about. Splitting up is really hard when you get down to the nitty-gritty details of what is fair. There's less to go around than you think. But we found the thing a lot easier when we decided to do it by not hiding behind another person. I began to understand his side a little more and he understood mine. I think we worked out something that I can count on.

In order for mediation to work, the persons involved have to want to do it. If you are interested in mediation, check with a mediation association before choosing a lawyer. They have a list of attorneys that are open to working in this medium. The American Arbitration Association is a nonprofit organization which has worked in the area of labor disputes for over fifty years. They now offer mediation services for divorce in their regional offices around the country.

Why Mediation Is So Important

Your husband may set out to punish you through litigation and be determined at all costs to see it through. When that happens it is hard not to respond in kind. But don't overreact. His first action may be impulsive and, given time, it can change. Try to impress upon him the value and the need for compromise. It is the key to getting out of a marriage without ruining any future possibility of a relationship.

More and more lawyers are dissatisfied with the way the present system works and its results in human terms. Elenie Huszagh is a very successful Chicago-area attorney who used to handle many divorce cases but no longer does them because they were so personally taxing to her. She has strong feelings about it and some advice:

> The divorce process is so convoluted, so complex, and so crowded that very little can be tended to by the courts. So women probably have two things going for them: patience, because it will take a lot longer than they imagine; and a willingness to compromise. Unless you do, you'll spend your whole life dealing over who got the bedroom set, or whether it's thirty dollars or twenty-five dollars a week, or what weekends the husband is supposed to visit. It will all pass and you'll get into some routine whether you like it or not. There are twenty or thirty thousand divorces a year filed here in Cook County. There's no way a judge will walk out with some kind of magic wand and solve it all. Some people really believe that. Or they are so uncompromising and ungiving that the lawyer is forced into a position of being a brick wall.
>
> You may get everything you want, in the court order, but that doesn't mean it's going to happen. You may get everything wrapped up and the other person won't cooperate—won't sign a deed or a car title. And you know you can get a little crazy having to go back and do work over and over.

The importance of mediation is especially brought out when children are involved. Both parents usually have a large emotional investment in their feelings about the kids, and the court system has traditionally been a cruel battleground. Bleema Moss, a child custody mediator in San Diego for sixteen years, speaks from a wealth of experience.

> Be convinced that the court is not a place to decide what is best for your kids. Even if you can use the legal system to help with financial issues, when it comes to your kids, it's really important that parents work it out for themselves. You can get help. Fighting out a custody battle in court is very destructive. The system is designed to focus on your negatives. We all have liabilities, but that's all you hear in court. So it only makes you feel angry and victimized. Any judge in

town will tell you that he will be happy to make decisions on financial matters, but he strongly dislikes making decisions on children.

Divorcing parents need to learn negotiating skills. I always described the divorce relationship as a business partnership. Although you're not living together, you have to take care of this "business" you both started. You can't just walk away from it. Parents *have* to find ways to resolve their differences. There will be disagreements, but it is necessary to learn to resolve them. Interestingly, the emotional distance of being apart can allow them to build a structure for resolving their conflicts. Some basic negotiating skills are not mysterious. People need to learn to listen without interrupting. Timed, short-term discussions—perhaps ten minutes—are best. Only discuss one topic at a time. Both parties need to learn this: *They have to bite their tongue, and they're not doing it right unless their tongue is bleeding.*

HOW TO CHOOSE A LAWYER

Former Chief Justice Warren Burger once said that half the trial attorneys in this country are incompetent. Some lawyers might claim that same figure for the Supreme Court. In any case, when the profession itself levels such heavy criticism, it should be a warning. Take your time in choosing a lawyer. It will mean a commitment of money and personal trust that should not be taken lightly. Interview two or three before you choose. Your relationship with your lawyer will help establish a tone to your life at this point. If you are unhappy with your choice because of the way in which you get along together, the whole dissolution process can get rather crazy as you struggle with both your husband and your lawyer. So it is important to *begin* with an attorney with whom you are compatible. You can always change lawyers but that becomes expensive.

Unfortunately, it is also important to retain an attorney who you feel will have influence equal to your husband's attorney. If you know that your husband has hired a reknowned lawyer who carries a great deal of weight in the court where your case will be heard, then you will want to hire someone with equivalent impact. An attorney's reputation can often influence the consideration your side of the case receives.

And, watch out for this one: It is not uncommon to hear of a person interviewing some of the best attorneys in town. By the code of the profession, consulting about a case with a client prevents the lawyer from representing the other party on that same case at a future time.

So often with doctors and lawyers there is a tendency to blindly place ourselves in their hands—in effect handing over the power to them. It is always a problem when confronting a figure of authority. At the onset you must continually remind yourself that you are doing the hiring, that *you* are the boss. It is true that the lawyer knows more about the specific details of the law and the court system, but don't underestimate yourself. Trust in your own judgment and intuition and don't be drawn into any suggestion unless it feels right to you.

Finding a lawyer can seem like a gamble when you first begin. If you just pick a name out of the telephone book you are playing with rather poor odds. Here are some suggestions:

1. Talk to a friend or someone at work who has been through a divorce. Formulate a series of questions to ask them about the quality of the legal counsel they received, such as:

● Was the lawyer supportive of your position?
● Was the lawyer attentive to your needs?
● Did you feel ignored, just another case?
● Were you kept informed about the progress of your divorce?
● Were the fee arrangements clear and reasonable?
● Did your lawyer give you a reasonable perspective on the divorce?
● Did your lawyer unnecessarily make an enemy out of your husband?
● Did the attorney promptly return phone calls?
● Looking back, would you choose the same lawyer again?

2. Check with local organizations offering community service to women. Most of these groups have a list of lawyers available who are sensitive to women's issues. Contact your local NOW

chapter, consumer protection group, family planning organization, or woman's law group at a law college. The decision of whether to choose a female attorney or a male is a personal one. Some women who are feeling vulnerable only want to deal with the intimacies of divorce with another woman. Other women have a greater sense of security when represented by a male attorney, partly because they feel a man can stand up to their husband on his terms.

3. Ask an attorney you have used for some other legal business to give a recommendation. It may turn out that they handle divorces and if you have had a good experience with them in the past, you could decide to use them again. On the other hand, if divorce is not their specialty, and you believe your case to be complex, get a referral for one with more expertise in matrimonial law.

4. Check into legal clinics. Many of them offer a free initial interview, and divorce counseling at cheaper prices. This is because much of the detail work such as assistance in filling out standard forms is actually done by paralegals. If your divorce is not complicated, this may save you money.

Watch out, however. Just as with any discount store, unless you check the prices closely you may not be getting a bargain. The title "Legal Clinic" can be used by any group of lawyers wanting to create an economically prudent image. Ask to meet the attorney who will be handling any personal consultations with you. Inquire of the hourly fee for that attorney. Make sure there are no hidden costs and that you are aware of the price of all the "extras." Sometimes the final bill is no cheaper than that of a lawyer in private practice.

The Fees

Much of the fear of lawyers centers on the cost of their services. Everybody has heard horror stories about lawyers being the only winners in litigation.

At the outset, there are several things you should do. Most

lawyers require a retainer fee. You will need to pay this when you hire them. It is like a down payment against charges for which you will be billed, but is often not for the full amount needed for your divorce. If you are short of money, ask if your attorney will accept a credit card payment for the retainer. The amount may vary depending on the complexity of the case. Inquire as to the lawyer's billing procedure—how much for an office consultation, phone calls, letters, and courtroom appearances. Know that many attorneys charge portions of an hour with a fifteen minute minimum.

Getting Along with Your Lawyer

In some ways your relationship with your lawyer should be a refuge. You are paying him or her for a service, part of which is a sense of confidence and peace of mind. However, as in any relationship, it is a two-way street. If you want something, you are going to have to give something. Here are some points that will make your contact with the lawyer easier and more efficient.

1. *Bring all the information.* Be sure to ask your lawyer or the secretary what you should bring for your initial interview. Make copies of all your important documents so that there is no fear that they will be lost or misplaced. Write down any information about income and property that is not covered in the documents you will bring.

Be prepared to furnish information about your personal background: any health problems, previous marriages, the address to which they can send mail (if not to your home), telephone numbers at which you can be reached, the names and ages of any children, children from a prior marriage, and any special problems, emotional or physical, the children might have.

Be sure to go over any specific marital problems, in particular, any previous physical abuse or threatening situations. If you have already discussed divorce with your spouse, tell your lawyer of any agreements reached or discussed.

2. *Be on time.* The point hardly needs explanation. For a lawyer, time is money. If you are late for an appointment, you are putting the lawyer in a possibly antagonistic position. It is a good idea to leave the kids at home, even if it means spending money for a babysitter.

3. *Be honest with your attorney.* Don't hold things back from your lawyer, even though some of the information might be embarrassing. For instance, you may have had an affair that your husband doesn't know about, or you may have mishandled the finances. An experienced lawyer, like an old priest, has heard it all. He or she is not going to be shocked.

It is more detrimental if, in handling your case, the lawyer comes upon some surprising new information about you in negotiating with your husband's attorney. Lawyers like to be prepared; give all the help you can.

4. *Follow the advice.* Once you have settled on a lawyer, established some rapport, and gained trust in him or her, start listening attentively to the advice. Take notes if necessary, or use a tape recorder if the lawyer will allow it. Advice is what you are buying. If you are unclear about anything that has been said, stop the lawyer and ask that it be clarified.

Do what your lawyer recommends. It does no good to work at cross purposes with the person you have hired. If you have chosen a good lawyer, he or she has had experience in dealing with divorce cases not unlike yours and knows the course of action to take. Granted, if the advice seems ridiculous or if it goes against the grain of your belief system or code of ethics, you then have to rely on your own judgment and do something about it. Discuss your values and concerns with your lawyer and request another course of action. If all else fails, you may have to consider hiring another lawyer.

5. *Take full advantage of a lawyer's services.* If your husband has been threatening or seriously harassing you, tell your lawyer and let him or her deal with it. Your lawyer can do many things to help the situation, including directly contacting the husband and confronting him with your complaint, calling his attorney and

pressuring for changed behavior, or going directly to the court to obtain a restraining order. This is the value of an attorney—use it.

6. *Your attorney is not your therapist.* Neither is your lawyer a referee, a policeman, nor a patron saint. Establishing a relationship with a good lawyer may be a refuge, as I have described, but it is a *legal* refuge. Many women caught up in the emotion and vulnerability of their lives at this critical time try to use their lawyers in ways in which they were not trained to respond.

Gordon Sinning, an attorney friend, remarks:

> Many times women are so emotionally upset that they resort to calling the lawyer about every single argument. I can't help her if the guy dumps the garbage all over the kitchen floor. I can only listen and reassure. I'm willing to do that but it will cost her extra money for telephone conferences. I'd rather charge her for my time when I'm actually performing a service that I'm trained to do—legal advice and guidance.

Separate your legal and therapeutic needs if for no other reason than that psychological counseling is usually less expensive than legal conferences.

This entire area of your divorce can be a hazardous one. If the contact that you have with your husband is badly handled by you or your lawyer, the results of it will be reflected permanently in your divorce agreement and your life afterward. Naturally, it is hard to determine or control his response, but at least you can be aware of not unnecessarily provoking hateful attitudes. Marshall Caskey's advice is this:

> Both men and women should be reasonable. You know what's fair—don't carry your quarrels and struggles into the legal arena. Let the attorneys function and when something is right, do it. Don't try to overreach. Don't try to punish the other person. People do that, you know. They try to hurt the other side with litigation and it's all coming out of the same pie. The legal system is a piss-poor way to look for redress of emotional grievances. It just doesn't work—and it costs a lot of dough.

CHAPTER 6

Physical and Sexual Needs

For a woman preoccupied with all of the details that the divorce process brings—the legal hassles, emotional upsets, financial manipulation, and the changing living arrangements—any consideration of her physical and sexual needs is often put on the back burner. It is something that will get attention later. As she sees it, basic survival is what life is about right now and if her physical well-being must suffer for a while longer—well, so be it. Chances are that her sexual experience has not been satisfactory lately. It rarely is at the end of a relationship. When this energy diminishes, it often is experienced as a general malaise. Arguments and emotional distress further drain a woman so that she is at a loss on where to root herself.

A place to begin is with your body. There are many reasons to say this, but a simple truth might be a good starter: Your divorce will do nobody any good if you come out of it a physical wreck.

MIND/BODY: A UNITY

"But it's only my body . . ." is an unspoken statement that runs through our attitude when the importance of physical well-being is emphasized. Unless we are manifestly sick, the health of our bodies is given little attention. Most of us are not attuned to the nuances of the body, those messages that warn of imbalance and malfunction. It is no wonder. As a society, we block such sensitivity by eating bad food in quantity, letting our bodies become sluggish from neglect of regular exercise, clouding our lungs with smoke, artificially stimulating our circulatory systems with chemicals, and generally numbing ourselves to any serious questioning of our values in this regard. "But it's only my body . . ." is the underlying defense.

This chapter is not meant to be a righteous diatribe against the evils of modern-day culture, although that may be an unavoidable secondary conclusion. The first concern is that you—a woman caught in an extremely stressful period of your life—stay in touch with yourself physically and see yourself as a whole person.

I'm not sure who first presented the concept—it may have been Aristotle—but it is important to hear it and understand it: "I do not *have* a body; I *am* a body." It may seem like a subtle distinction, but the difference between the concepts is profound. When you say, "I *have* a body," the implication is that there is an "I" apart from the physical self. Our religions and culture have taught us to believe that the "I" is somehow independent from and superior to the body. After all, the body is continually changing, open to the chance happenings of the world, and will someday die. So the logical reaction is to downgrade the importance of the body and try to separate it from the "self." Sometimes we do this by placing outrageous demands on our body and then justify the abuse.

However, when you accept and integrate the concept that "I *am* my body," you begin to gain new insight and respect for what it is to be human. Your body is not of a lesser order than your mind, spirit, or soul, but in fact is the essential element in what makes you *you*. The way in which you experience and interpret the world is dependent on the acuteness of your sensory awareness. When that physical base is disturbed or nonfunctional, you are not only living a diminished existence, your very life is in some danger.

We artificially classify and separate existence. If, for instance, something is an emotional problem, it is assigned to the mind. That makes it a *mental* problem, and the cure for it is sought by using what the conscious mind seems to respond to best—words. So we try to talk our way out of emotional problems.

Broken arms, bad livers, and cancer are *body* problems and they, of course, require physical diagnosis and repair. It all seems to make sense. Everything fits into its distinct and proper category.

Outside of language, however, you cannot separate the mind and body. The two are one, and the interplay is so inherent to their nature that descriptions of their functions fail when they are considered mutually exclusive of each other. The human being is a *unity*, and each element blends in ways that are still not completely understood. For the convenience of communication, we say things like "I have a body," but if the result is that you see yourself separate from your body and therefore subtly disdainful of its needs and demands, you are then apt to cause damage.

The unity of a person is best shown, strangely, in the disorders of the body. Are bleeding ulcers a physical or mental disease? A woman may have been worried (a mental problem) about her marriage for many years, and under stress the acid secretions of her body increased to the point where they damaged the lining of her stomach (a physical problem). How do you treat it? Do you send her to a psychologist or a surgeon? At what point did the mental problem become a physical one, and how did it happen? Is a daily headache caused by the pressure of a woman's work a mental or physical problem? Or her constipation? Or her constant vaginal infections? Or her disfunctioning colon? Or her hypertension?

If your response is "What difference does it make?" you are on the right track. At some point, there is the realization that you are one living, breathing, spiritual, and physical being and if there is pain, you want relief. Everything that happens to you is reflected in your total person—your moods, sleeping habits, diet, sexual attitudes, and the hundred other ways that you relate to the world.

If you have split yourself into two beings, it may be time to personally come together. You are not two elements at odds with each other—Mind *versus* Body. In truth, what is good for one is good for the other. If you exercise regularly, you will be more emotionally alert; if you eat better food, you will find that you are more spiritually clear; if you give yourself full sexual release, you will smile more and be happier.

STRESS

Stress is a constant companion in life, but it is seldom felt more strongly than during divorce. Because it is with us so much, there is a tendency to underrate its effects. Indeed, the most elemental source of stress comes from a purely physical force—gravity. The very human act of standing is stressful in that it takes a continuous effort. We add to this by filling our days with things that must be done. Most people are well able to cope with a normal amount of stress that comes with daily activities. A certain degree seems, in fact, to have positive effects on life in that it triggers energy and excitement for living. But there is also a point at which it is overwhelming.

The leading authority on the subject is Hans Selye and he defines it this way:

> Stress is the nonspecific response of the body to any demand, whether it is caused by, or results in, pleasant or unpleasant conditions.

Almost anything, then, can create this stress. Naturally some things are more stressful than others. Your car breaking down on a freeway causes higher anxiety than missing a ride on a bus. But the real danger of stress is not in the result of a single event. We can gear ourselves to the impact and get through it. The real problem is when we let the tension of a succession of stressful events build for prolonged periods. Be alert to the cumulative effect of stress on your life.

A rather famous study was done a few years ago by Thomas H. Holmes and Richard H. Rahe, both of the University of Washington School of Medicine, and it clearly confirms the detrimental effects of stressful events on health. They developed the following chart of forty-three life happenings, and after studying the case histories of 5,000 persons, they observed that there is a direct correlation between the cumulative effect of stress and physical illness.

Evaluate your own stress level by listing the elements that are going on in your life at this time. Each factor on the list is given a numerical value—100 being the highest—depending on the weight of stress that it carries. You may notice that not everything listed is necessarily negative; in fact some are quite positive. As Selye pointed out, even those bring some amount of tension with them.

The most significant items for our purpose are divorce and the events that go with it. Divorce has the second highest stress value of anything that commonly happens during life. Study the list and look at your results.

The study suggests that if you have a cumulative point total of less than 150, your chances of serious health change in the next two years is one in three. When the total approaches 300, your chances are reduced to one in two. These researchers found that when scores were over 300, the chance of sickness ran to 90 percent.

Whatever the results of this study mean to you, it is not something to be recognized, then quickly dismissed. Although stress may seem to be a mental or emotional problem, it works more like an invisible toxin. It has a direct effect on your body and can make you sick. Dr. O. Carl Simonton, author of *Getting Well Again*, bases the approach of his Cancer Counseling and Research Center on "solid evidence that our psychological stance toward life plays a significant role in dealing with cancer and in dealing with the course of the disease." His research convinced him that persons under stress are more likely to suffer high blood pressure, ulcers, and other maladies, including cancer. Kenneth Pelletier in his book *Mind as Healer, Mind as Slayer* writes, "Most standard medical textbooks attribute anywhere from fifty to eighty percent of all diseases to psychosomatic or stress-related origins."

This information is not given to frighten you. Indeed, if that were the result, it would only increase your stress level. But a warning must be made. Certainly it cannot be denied that you are

Life Event	Mean Value
Death of spouse	100
Divorce	73
Marital Separation	65
Jail Term	63
Death of Close Family Member	63
Personal Injury or Illness	53
Marriage	50
Fired at Work	47
Marital Reconciliation	45
Retirement	45
Change in Health of Family Member	44
Pregnancy	40
Sex Difficulties	39
Gain of New Family Member	39
Business Readjustment	39
Change in Financial State	38
Death of Close Friend	37
Change to Different Line of Work	36
Change in Number of Arguments with Spouse	35
Mortgage Over $10,000	31
Foreclosure of Mortgage or Loan	30
Change in Responsibilities at Work	29
Son or Daughter Leaving Home	29
Trouble with In-Laws	29
Outstanding Personal Achievement	28
Beginning or End of School	26
Change in Living Conditions	25
Revision of Personal Habits	24
Trouble with Boss	23
Change in Work Hours or Conditions	20
Change in Residence	20
Change in Schools	20
Change in Recreation	19
Change in Church Activities	19
Change in Social Activities	18
Mortgage or Loan Less Than $10,000	17
Change in Sleeping Habits	16
Change in Number of Family Get-Togethers	15
Change in Eating Habits	15
Vacation	13
Christmas	12
Minor Violations of the Law	11

experiencing more than a normal share of stress in your life right now. Apart from the daily pressure, the reality of divorce has brought a raft of other things that must be faced. If you only had one or two items on the chart with which to deal, there would be little problem. But with your divorce may also come "more arguments with your spouse," "change in living conditions," "sex difficulties," "beginning a new job," and any number of other things. With so much happening simultaneously, the overload will take its toll. It is like putting coins in a slot machine. It takes them in—then suddenly dumps them all in your lap.

Clues

Because the consequences of stress are so serious, but the buildup is often gradual, it is important to continually take stock of your present physical and mental health. Sometimes the changes are not dramatic. But if you can get enough distance to be objective, or if you have friends who tell you the truth, you may find that the stress of your life has begun to show.

Some common signals include a general sense of fatigue and depression, muscle tension in the back, headaches, or irregular menstrual cycles. You may no longer feel capable of coping with even the small details of life, things that before were automatic. Tension causes the extremes of insomnia or excessive sleep, undereating or compulsive food habits. People in distress are more prone to accidents—they find they cut their fingers, bump their heads, and wreck automobiles.

In other words, when any of these behaviors or signals become regular, it is usually a clue that your body is in distress. Unfortunately, it is a malady more easily recognized in others than oneself. However, a most telling clue is crying. If you are crying much more than usual over matters that before were routine, you can be sure that things are getting to you. But even if nothing shows, damage may still be happening. What is necessary is first to get in touch with your feelings; then do something about reducing the anxiety.

What to Do

Begin by taking action. If you had broken your leg, you would give it immediate attention. There would be no doubt. As quickly as possible you would search for a hospital with an emergency room. Stress is not as visible, but it can be just as debilitating. Treat yourself as an emergency. I don't mean with panic. Simply give yourself the attentive care this situation deserves and recognize that it is as potentially serious as a more dramatic physical problem.

Many women do recognize the signs of stress and immediately seek out help from a doctor. Some of them wind up with a prescription for the latest anti-anxiety medication. We have written about this problem in earlier chapters, and it only needs a reminder here. A Mill Valley, California, physician, Dr. Michael Gerber, suggests: "Drug therapy does not relieve the cause of the problem. We are not nervous because of a lack of Valium in our blood." Or as Kenneth Pelletier sees it, "Millions of Americans are virtually on drug maintenance for alleviation of nervous tension and spend a great part of their waking activity in a sedated state."

Do get a checkup so that your family doctor can evaluate any effects your present stress may be causing. Listen to the recommendations of your physician. If you are concerned about taking medication, discuss it with the doctor, and if you feel it necessary, seek a second opinion. However, some people are so out of balance that medication is the only way to interrupt a downward spiral. But take precautions against abusing any substance. In addition, know that there are some very positive, growth-producing activities that effectively counter the negative effects that increased pressure brings on.

The remainder of this chapter recommends that you seriously consider three pathways toward better health: physical exercise, dietary awareness, and sexual release.

All three are solidly based in your normal body functions, and yet have tremendous impact on how you feel emotionally and spiritually. Giving attention to these areas is rewarding not only in your present life but your future. There is no better place to find harmony than in your body.

PHYSICAL EXERCISE

Not many years ago, strenuous or even mild physical exercise for women was considered to be the province of health nuts and overage tomboys. Passing and amused attention was given to programs that encouraged athletic activity for girls and women. There was a time when it would have been slightly embarrassing to be caught jogging in a park.

Today things are much different. More women have now awakened to the fact that good health and a vital appearance don't happen by chance. We were all seduced by the teen years when no matter how we abused our bodies with late hours, junk food, or plain laziness, we seemed to have an unlimited capacity to recover. But from the middle twenties onward, it is simply not the case. Inside and out, your body reflects the care you give it. If you are sedentary, your muscle tone will be slack and your coloring bland. Internally your body functions will be sluggish. And the less you do, the harder it is to do anything. Some women give up at this point and accept whatever happens as their fate. But many others have come to realize that feeling good is not an automatic reward for just being alive, but something to be achieved each day.

Make a program of regular physical exercise a part of your schedule. This is especially useful for a woman going through a divorce. The reasons are many and will be discussed. But know that you can do no better thing for yourself right now than to get into the best physical shape you reasonably can.

The beauty of it is that this part of your life is something you totally control. You may not be able to fathom your husband's attitude during the settlement, or foretell your children's response to the breakup, or be in charge of everything that passes through your life in the next few months, but you can decide what to do with your body. Nobody controls that but *you*. And if you haven't considered this idea before, then let this become the first step toward changing things. If the world out there is unpredictable, your private existence needn't come apart. On the contrary, this can be an opportunity to recharge yourself and develop new strength.

Benefits

The many rewards of physical exercise are readily evident. Very simply, it makes you look and feel better. Although clothes and cosmetics can do wonders, nothing can substitute for the healthy glow of a woman who feels fit. It is not a matter of an ideal figure or great facial features; when you feel good about yourself because your body is reaching its potential, that expression shows through in everything you do. It goes beyond vanity. When you respect yourself—your body—and feel at one with it, others recognize this and respond.

Kathy McDonald Peacock works with women daily as the director of Exermetrics, a fitness plan in the Detroit area. She is enthusiastic about the results of her growing program.

> In the physical area, you can *see* success. People move better, are more flexible. Women see a measure of success and it carries over into other areas of their lives. You not only see a body taking shape but you see that woman become more active in every part of her life.

When I asked if she could give a profile of women who dropped out of the program, she responded:

> You could say they haven't grown up. They still haven't come to realize that *they* are the ones responsible for themselves and their bodies. I guess they think that someone else is going to do it for them. Of course, no one is going to. They always have great reasons for not exercising, or for that matter, not doing anything that is enjoyable.

Much could be said about the value of exercise in terms of better health and increased stamina. It should be obvious that the body was designed to move and does very well when you give it a chance. But more interesting is how a flexible body correlates with a flexible mind. It is as if the ability to physically move freely— whether it is arching your back in calisthenics or swinging a tennis racquet—brings with it a capacity to see the world from different perspectives. Perhaps you remember standing on your head at some time and looking out at the world around you. It was different, yet the same. Your physical posture alters your mental response. The ability to see and choose options in your life may be closely tied to the degree of your physical flexibility.

Certainly it has a direct impact on your emotional state. Vigorous physical exercise clears the mind and transforms moods. The results are almost invariably positive. I asked Judy Missett, the creator and developer of Jazzercise, about her experience with this.

> I've had people come to me and say, "I was really depressed but I kept thinking, 'Well, I'm going to Judy's class tonight and I know she'll make me feel better.' " Well, as an instructor I think the same thing. I know when I go to teach . . . maybe I don't even want to. I'm that low. But I know in the back of my mind that when I go there and teach, afterwards I'm going to feel much better. Those worries, those troubles, and those things that have made me depressed aren't going to seem so great. And by gum, there has never been a time when that hasn't happened. It works every time, and I can talk with great conviction because my experience has taught me that it's true.

Responses from other women in other exercise programs are overwhelmingly similar. In a very practical way, exercise is a useful way to get through the negative feelings that divorce brings.

Begin with a Physical Exam

Before you start a program of exercise, see your doctor and get a physical examination. It is a good idea in any case, and it will give you reassurance that nothing is wrong. Seek out a doctor who seems to be in touch with his or her body. Getting advice on your physical health from a doctor who smokes or is in awful physical shape seems a bit ludicrous. Some doctors of the old school still do not emphasize the value of regular exercise. Find someone who reflects your general attitude and will give encouragement. Also, by establishing rapport with a doctor at this time, you may find it beneficial in other circumstances.

Starting Up

Much of the advice on how to get into a regular exercise program depends on your present physical condition, your history of physical activity, and your daily schedule. If you are in fairly good shape, enjoy sports, and have plenty of free time, the advice is rather easy. But if you have never been very interested in physical conditioning and your life is overcrowded, there is more to talk about.

A first general recommendation is to start slowly. Don't try to conquer the world in the first week; you will probably burn out quickly and then use the experience as proof that such programs are hopeless for you. Sometimes radical revolutions do work. Some women are able to simply change their behavior, totally plunge into a full agenda of exercise, and stay with it. For most, it is a more gradual process, as physical conditioning is not easily rushed. A Spartan schedule sounds impressive when you announce it to your friends, but instead make the nature of your exercise one that works with the flow of your life, and the extra demands you may be experiencing now.

Start with something that is relatively easy and complete it. It may be walking to the store instead of driving, swimming two laps in a pool, jogging around the block, or going to an exercise class and doing the first five minutes of the workout. In order to insure you will do it regularly, sign up and pay for a class. Don't leave it to your mood or chance.

Set aside a certain time each day. There are a hundred excuses why you just can't afford time for exercise, and they are all probably legitimate. And it is true that exercise does take time. After dressing, warming up, exercising, and showering, you may have spent an hour. But it is a necessary hour; give it to yourself. It could be the most personally rewarding thing that you do all day.

Get yourself in the mood. This may sound superficial, but dress for the sport when you can afford it. If you are jogging, get a good pair of shoes and some shorts and a top that look the part; if you are in a dance class, buy a new leotard. And don't forget to look at yourself in a mirror. You will be seeing changes.

Getting Into It

The nature of the exercise you choose is very individual. There is certainly no lack of things to get into. A few years ago it could have been claimed that programs of physical exercise were a fad designed to sell stylish warm-up suits or challenge the male domain. But today women are clearly serious about good health. New facilities and innovative programming have sprung up in every community. If you haven't been aware of them, start to take notice.

In most cities, the Department of Parks and Recreation offers a variety of group exercise classes and other sports programs for women in their neighborhood public facilities. There is usually no fee. Adult education classes in the physical education curriculum are given in many high schools and colleges. You might find such activities as hiking and camping being offered with field trips, as well as other fitness classes.

The YWCA and YMCA are very active in women's health and exercise programs. Most of the facilities put out calendars listing upcoming classes. They usually have a round robin of short courses available. Commercial health clubs and spas cost considerably more, but they usually have nicer facilities and give more personal attention. Check out cable TV for exercise programs, as well as the local video store for its collection of workout tapes.

If none of the above are handy, there is surely a park or some open space available. Naturally, the type of exercise you choose will be influenced by where you live. You can't snow ski in Louisiana and you may not find an aikido class offered in Hays, Kansas. But there is plenty to do right where you are.

Aerobics and Discharge

You have heard about the value of aerobic exercise. The dictionary defines it as "exercises that involve a workout of the lungs and heart as well as the muscles." Breathing is central to these exercises. Some workouts emphasize sustained deep breathing more than others, and the value of this kind of program is becoming widely recognized.

As elemental as it may sound, breathing is the key to life. It is the one activity that the body cannot do without for more than a few seconds. Oxygen intake is as essential to life as the food we eat. In fact, the body can be seen as an organism that takes energy, transforms energy, and discharges it. That is the nature of its ongoing cycle. We eat food, digest it, and discharge it—in the activity of our body and in waste matter. If a person is functioning in an optimal way, the flow of energy has a rhythm to it that is reflected in breathing.

But we also absorb energy from other parts of our environment. When a person is living in a period of intense feelings or stress, that energy must also be transformed and discharged. Problems arise when we don't give outlet to the energy. In the case of food consumption, the blockage is obvious when it takes the form of constipation. However, when emotional energy is taken in but not released, it is more subtle. There is a general muscle tension which restricts breathing and free movement. A person under stress and blocking energy release is literally "uptight." You can see it in the person's carriage.

Dr. Alexander Lowen, in his book *Bioenergetics*, explains.

> The living organism can only function if there is a balance between energy charge and discharge. It maintains a level of energy consistent with its needs and opportunities. A growing child will take in more energy than it discharges and use this extra energy for growth. The same is true of convalescence or even personality growth.

Growth takes energy. Apart from this, it is generally true that the amount of energy one will take in will correspond to the amount one can discharge through activity.

Physical exercise is a natural and easy way to discharge. Instead of holding it in, exercise allows for the flow of energy.

While it may seem silly to instruct a person on how to breathe, the fact is that many people don't do it well. Under continual stress, the tension of the body becomes chronic. This constriction reduces the ability and capacity for oxygen intake. Restricted, shallow breathing becomes a body habit and with it comes reduced energy. The blood is not being fed properly. We learn to get by with a little, but at a cost. There is an inherent anxiety in short, shallow breathing, as if the organism is continually on the verge of panic.

Aerobic exercises promote deep, full breathing. When we have done sustained and rhythmic exercises for thirty minutes or more, the breathing and increased heart rate that necessarily accompany them teaches our bodies what we could in no other way learn. It begins to free the chest and stomach muscles from rigidity so that oxygen is driven deeply into the organs and the increased blood flow gives us renewed vigor. Whereas depression was the result of depleted metabolism, now the body cells are flushed with life.

Get in touch with your breathing and feel it as the source of your life. Breathe deeply and feel the difference. Draw the energy right down to your pelvis. Regular exercise is a way to make this part of your daily life. The body cannot simply be a passive receptacle for everything that comes by. It must continually discharge energy so that the cycle of life may continue freely.

The most popular aerobic exercise started out as jogging. Recently, many orthopedic doctors and chiropractors have suggested that the heavy impact is not good for your spine or joints. If you decide this is not your sport, you might try swimming, bicycling, calisthenics, roller skating, yoga, or simply brisk walking. All of these can be done without the need of a partner.

For some women, exercising is easier in a social setting. It makes exercise an occasion, an event which regularly goes on three times

a week at the Y. The class becomes an enjoyable part of life as
your commitment grows. A special kind of camaraderie comes out
of such experiences. When you share your sweat and exhaustion
with others, you are also sharing common vulnerabilities and limits. Check into classes in dance or the art of self-defense. Tennis
and racquetball are fine workouts. Hiking and skiing are both
healthful and social.

You cannot do all of these exercises regularly. But try one or
two of them and stick with it. Give yourself time—ninety days—
to condition yourself to the activity. By then you should feel comfortable and be able to tell the difference between how you felt
before and after. Focus on the number of days you succeed in
doing something physical, not the days you miss. Trust in the fact
that you *will* improve. Nothing quite matches feeling proficient in
some area of physical endeavor.

YOUR DIET

There has never been a more challenging, thought-provoking,
or honest title for a book than one written many years ago—*You
Are What You Eat*. The truth of that statement rings on so many
levels. You hardly have to read the book to get the message. If
every one of us took it seriously, we would eat very differently.
Not many women would wish to be a Hostess Twinkie. If what is
printed in small type on the labels of the packaged food that I
buy actually becomes *me*, then it's no wonder I have a hard time
understanding myself sometimes.

Diet is a controversial subject to talk or write about. Some people
who are otherwise open and tolerant are often food fascists. They
are quite anxious to force their beliefs on everybody. The subject
of food and diet is as inflammatory in conversation as religion
used to be. The reason may be that what we eat keys so directly
into our anxiety about survival.

I would rather dodge the issue entirely except that it is important for a woman in a time of rapid change to *take care to eat
well*. In times of stress, a person's diet is usually the first area that
is upset. Food has traditionally been seen as either a form of

reward or punishment, and we often use it that way on ourselves, disregarding its basic function—a source of nutrition.

The direct line from stress to poor eating habits to physical illness is repeated by many authorities in the field of nutrition. While you may not be able to significantly reduce the stress in your life right now, look at what you are eating and ask whether you are doing yourself any good. Sometimes the whole process can become a rather vicious circle. Dr. Michael Gerber has seen this pattern in his patients.

> A lot of people who are under stress smoke a few cigarettes, have a cup of coffee, then head out the door in a rush with a white bread sandwich for lunch. They eat nothing in the afternoon, then have a gargantuan dinner with lots of fat and alcohol. Their physical appearance begins to change, they get bags under their eyes and their skin is puffy, their glands are not working and the adrenal goes down. Then they look in the mirror and say, "Oh, God, I'm getting old and nobody will ever look at me again."

Recommendations

The word *diet* has several meanings, but for the purpose of this book, I wish to focus on the value of what you eat in terms of your physical and mental health rather than the desirability of losing weight for appearance's sake. If weight loss winds up being a by-product of a healthier new you, consider it a bonus, not a requirement that will only add more stress. More important right now is that you maintain your strength and energy by eating properly balanced and nutritionally sound foods. If you are, in addition, exercising regularly, your food intake will find its proper level.

There are literally thousands of books written on the subject of diet, and you may have a favorite one. I would only recommend that you find a sensible diet that you can live with and follow it. Be open to change. Of course, if a diet author makes a great case for a cauliflower and potato juice fast, you may not wish to suffer through that at present. Don't make your diet another stress issue.

It is more important that you find the motivation to follow whatever diet you choose. You may have many reasons for wanting to change your current diet, and whatever they are, be clear about them and use them to get you going.

Be Aware

There are some common-sense guidelines that a consensus of nutritionists generally agree on. Take them for what they are worth to you. Much of the information points out the direct link between what we take into our bodies and our stress level.

Be aware of sugar. This is a major job if you eat packaged foods. If you cannot cut it out completely, at least cut down on foods in which sugar makes up a great portion of the bulk. Sugar has no nutritional value. It overstimulates the production of insulin, then drains the blood of its sugar. It creates an ongoing cycle of highs and lows, each depression triggering a craving for more. Jean Mayer, a professor of nutrition at Harvard, says simply, "I can find nothing good, nutritionally, to say about sugar." Most authorities are even less kind.

Be aware of coffee. The caffeine raises the blood sugar for about thirty minutes after drinking it, then lets you down in much the same way as sugar. It also raises blood fats and cholesterol. After stimulating the cerebral cortex, a burst of energy is soon followed by a lag. This stress is followed by the desire to regain another peak. Heavy coffee drinkers put enormous demands on their pancreas, kidneys, and heart. The Surgeon General has warned pregnant women on the dangers of birth defects from caffeine. It is also found in cola drinks, tea, and cocoa.

Be aware of alcohol. The dangers of alcohol are well known but so is its lure. The initial effect is relaxation and a release of normal inhibitions. But in the body, excessive alcohol does great damage by irritating the kidneys, causing them to excrete more water than is taken into the body. The pallid look of heavy drinkers or the red network of burst capillaries attest to its effect. Eventually it overburdens the liver, resulting in cirrhosis. Any number of other ailments are directly attributable to the problem of alcohol. Still, 10 to 12 percent of all drinkers become alcoholics.

Be aware of refined foods. Much of what we eat nowadays has been processed to the point where most of the nutrients have disappeared. During the milling process, for instance, refined and bleached white flour is stripped of not only its natural nutrients but also the bowel-cleansing roughage. Canned vegetables that have been cooked at high temperatures and are soaking in water cannot match slightly steamed fresh vegetables in nutritional value. Preservatives and coloring add to the attractiveness of food, but our bodies have no need for them. Eating whole food whenever you have the choice is much more sensible and healthy.

If you cannot cut these things out of your diet, at least cut them down. There is a tendency to eat, drink, and smoke compulsively during times of stress. Unfortunately, most of the things listed are addictive and debilitating. Gradually slow down your consumption. Limit yourself to two or three cups of coffee spaced through the day, and see if you can't go with four or five cigarettes instead of a pack. Your body will appreciate the rest.

Vitamins

If we could create for ourselves a balanced and natural diet, there would be no need for vitamin supplements. Fresh fruits and vegetables, whole grains, uncontaminated meat and fish, nuts and seeds are all that we need. But as a society we are into mass production and the quality, especially of food, has been diminished. What is lost in the spraying, washing, waxing, refining, processing, canning, and storing of food cannot be completely replaced by artificial means.

Most nutritionists agree that to fill in what is missing in our diet, a program of vitamin supplements is necessary. It is not just a matter of adding one or two. Vitamins, like most things in nature, work in a chain. They complement, balance, and activate each other.

Each authority has his or her special opinion about vitamins, and there are conflicting claims about dosage. I would encourage you to do some reading and investigation in this area. Ask your doctor or nutritionist for some advice. Most larger health food stores have a nutritionist on duty to guide people toward a program that best suits them. Check out the book section in those stores for materials on diet, and supplements for stress.

To eat well is to nourish yourself. It is *the* essential act of personal self-caring. If you have neglected the quality of your diet, seriously reflect on what that means. You are simply not being very good to yourself. Now is the time—in every part of your life—for nurturing. What you eat and how you feel are vitally connected. When you realize this fully, you will begin to give more attention to your diet.

SEXUAL NEEDS

For many women, one of the hardest things to do during the transition period of divorce is to stay in touch with their sensuality and sexuality. Again, every woman is different, but it is my experience that many women shut down that part of themselves. It is certainly understandable. As a relationship ends, there is an unavoidable, even natural, distancing of the two partners both spiritually and physically. The very nature of a healthy sexual relationship has to do with energy, excitement, and letting go. These may be the last things you are giving to or wanting from your husband right now. Good sexual relations are, in the best circumstances, a part of life requiring imagination and openness. Chances are that a failing relationship has either distorted or discarded both.

The problem is not in trying to revive what has been lost, but how to survive divorce feeling sensually alive. Shutting down one's sexual feelings is not a matter of simply taking a slice of life and saving it for the distant future. You are, by nature, sexual—sexual in the sense that the life force within you is in a continuous state of physical pulsation, and you need to nourish and affirm that existence and goodness.

This stream of essential life is unceasing. It is the very fabric of your being. It can be diverted, repressed, or denied, but it will be there somewhere. By shutting down sexually, the whole response of the organism to the world around it wanes. If you stop feeling in this vital area, all of your life is affected.

This is a genuine bind for a woman caught in divorce. On the one hand, there is a natural closing off of feelings toward her mate, and on the other, there is a need to remain a person tuned to her sexual needs. Women's options seem limited. For some it has meant numbing their feelings; others divert their needs into friendships that give caring and warmth; some women resort to fantasy and daydreaming to find release; still others have an affair or a series of sporadic ones, in an attempt to stay in touch with their sexual selves.

It is a mixed set of options. However, it is hard to create an interim life that fully answers a woman's sexual needs. To blatantly seek out sexual fulfillment from others is risky, in terms of your relationship. Indiscriminately seeking a sexual relationship in any form could be hazardous in today's environment. But if you can't always get what you want, for the time being, that does not mean that you must totally deny yourself. By continuing to give attention to the natural desires of your body, you are instinctively acting to protect the force that charges you with the spirit of life.

Male Companionship: Yes and No

Although women share many common things at the end of their marriages, there are wide differences when it comes to relationships with other men. Many women have had absolutely no intimate contact with other men; others have had affairs with several other men; for some, a particular man is the reason for divorce.

It is interesting that the affair she has with another man is often the turning point in a woman's consciousness of her marriage. Many women with whom I have contact have said that it was the first time, or the first in a long while, that they had been given real attention, had been told they were sexy and attractive, been made love to with caring and even style. This goes beyond the need for romance and adventure on the part of women. It gives them new confidence and reaffirms their self-worth.

Because there are so many conditions involving women and other men, it is impossible to suggest totally clear guidelines. But while I recognize some women's needs for male companionship, I also want to point out that having an intimate relationship with another man during the last few months of a marriage breakup is flirting with danger. The reasons are obvious and become more so when male consciousness is discussed in the next chapter. The decision in some situations is not an easy one. It may be that a woman has grown very close to her lover and feels dependent on his support through the divorce transition. Such a relationship may be her one link to some sanity. But it is still a hazard.

It is, of course, not for me or anyone else to say "do" or "don't." You must decide that. But recognize that there is a lot involved. Ask yourself whether or not you can delay your new relationship until some critical points in your present relationship have passed. In the meantime, at least consider some other alternatives.

Personal Satisfactions

You can give yourself pleasure. This may not be a new idea, but in the haste of life, you may have forgotten. We are by nature sensuous creatures, or put another way, creatures of our senses. We taste, smell, feel, hear, and see. We have learned, by conditioning or necessity, to use the senses for practical matters—eating, performing tasks, looking out for where we are going, and listening for information.

But our senses are pleasurable in themselves. Listening to music or feeling the wind on your skin or tasting an apple—these are good for their own sake. Getting in touch with yourself at this level is experiencing yourself sensually in a most basic way.

When you watch young children at play, you observe them in their sensuality. Playing with sand, they sift it through their fingers, over and over again, letting it trace in little mounds before them. If it is a puddle, they squish mud between their toes. Their uninhibited willingness to explore is their pathway to sensuality. Small children are unashamed in their pursuit of pleasure.

We, as adults, have that same desire and need for exploration but it is buried under years of prohibitions. It takes a conscious effort to regain some of our original feeling and expressiveness. When you see a grown person glowing as a child glows, it is a joy.

The following exercises are simple, and that is their beauty. In sensual matters, simplicity is the key.

- Allow yourself to get into random movement. Turn on some of your favorite music and begin to move to it. Forget about prescribed dance steps. This is not strictly a dance; it is *you* doing what *you* want to do with *your* body. Close your eyes and feel the music. Let the spontaneity of the moment and your senses dictate the flow of your movements. This may not come easily at first, but feel the points at which you restrict yourself. Be rid of that critical spectator in your head. Do it for yourself. Do it for fun.

- Go for a walk. If it is snowing, windy, raining, or sunny, don't block out or translate the experience. Simply feel it. Take in the environment in a purely physical way. Be aware of your skin and muscle response, the smell and sounds of your world.

- Wear something sensuous. Do this often. Put on a silk blouse or a flowing shirt over your naked skin and get into that luxury. Add a long, silky scarf and some musky perfume. Be sensually creative. Do things for yourself that just feel good, and don't make excuses. If physical satisfaction is not a highlight in your life at present, start small and give some to yourself.

- Take a sensuous bath. Do this regularly. The Romans had it together. Fill the tub with hot water and bubbles or scented oils. Turn on some soothing or erotic music. Light candles and put them close by. Choose a time when you will be free of interruptions and can bathe in leisure. Sink into the water and feel it both envelop and support you. Have a bathtub headrest to relax your neck. Rather than using a cloth, massage your body with your hands, feeling the smoothness of your skin. If you use soap, set aside a special aromatic bar just for your bath and wash your body with slow care. Spend time at the end simply floating, feeling, and relaxing.

After the bath, take some time to massage your body with oil or lotion, again slowly. If you are going to bed, sleep nude and feel the sensuality of the sheets against your body. Stretch and roll like a lazy cat.

SELF-LOVE

Sexual release is an expression of self-acceptance. This letting go is a final unblocking, the last stage in the flow of human energy. With it we join with all of nature in the process that creates the explosion of life, the force that brings plants to full flower.

Human beings, unfortunately, can complicate this natural function. Admittedly, it is difficult to find adequate sexual release with a partner whom you no longer love. Strong trust and good sex are bedfellows. Moreover, you may have found that there is too much tension in any extramarital affair to allow for total physical satisfaction. If that is true, consider (if you aren't doing it already) finding release in masturbation, or as I prefer to call it, self-pleasuring.

For some women, masturbation is a frightening word and a distasteful idea. For others it is a whispered activity, shrouded in secrecy and myth, but never confronted directly. However, more and more women have come to see that it is an activity which allows them a ready opportunity to honestly investigate their bodies while providing a natural and exciting way to discharge sexual energy. And in the process of achieving orgasm, they find the depth and variety of their emotional and physical needs. Contrary to the dark horrors that traditional religious teachings and medical practice have conjured up about masturbation, it can be and is a simple yet profound expression of self-love.

Sexual self-fulfillment is simply that. It is a healthy and natural way to treat yourself. Because you are sexual but like most of us have probably not fully explored your sexual potential, you may be curious about your basic sexual nature. You are obviously not the person you were five years ago, or even last year. Maturity deepens every experience of our life, especially our sexual expression. Discovering the range of your sexuality will not only give you renewed confidence with others but can afford you pleasure right now.

A cautionary note: If self-pleasuring is threatening, scary, or disgusting to you, don't feel obligated to investigate it at this time. You don't need more tension in your life. The conditions may not be right for you to test this experience. Nothing is wrong with not wanting this now and you may wish to explore it at some later time.

For those women who are interested, a lack of knowledge about their bodies often presents a problem. A surprisingly large number of women aren't well acquainted with their own genitals. It has not been a common practice for a mother to teach her daughter about the nature of female organs and show her the detail and function of them. This is vital information, but each generation is forced to struggle with its own ignorance.

However, realize that when you are investigating human sexuality, you are confronting your strongest, most deeply felt force. Dr. Alexander Lowen says of orgasm:

> The problem most people face is that the tensions in their body are so deeply structured that orgiastic release rarely occurs. The pleasurable, convulsive movements are too frightening, surrender too threatening. Regardless of what you say, most people are afraid and unable to give in to strong sexual feelings.

Although orgasm is a peak experience of physical joy, the intensity of the experience can churn emotions that are darker and more difficult. To choose sexual satisfaction means to risk coming to grips with the core of your being. Some persons are not ready for that.

Doing It

It is beyond the scope of this book to give detailed instruction on the art of self-love. There are a number of good and sensitive books on it, and I would especially recommend Lonnie Barbach's *For Yourself* and Betty Dodson's *Sex For One*. The two books discuss the subject with more complete detail than could be adequately achieved here.

Be patient with yourself. Each of us has our own rhythm, our own unique flow of sexual energy and timing. Oddly, you may have been thrown off by defining your sexuality in the same terms as men. Ruth Moulton, a sex researcher, notes:

> Many women have arrived at a greater enjoyment of sexuality when they gave up comparing their response to that of men and allowed themselves a sensation completely theirs. The development is only hindered by using the typical male sexual response as standard.

Self-pleasuring affords a good opportunity to find out what is special in *your* sexual nature. You may have been blind to many of your sexual preferences and wants during your marriage because you did not feel they were acceptable to your husband. Take another look at yourself.

In general, I would give this simple advice. As you already know, good sex takes time. Give yourself plenty of it, relax, and put aside the pressures of the day. Create for yourself a warm, safe environment in which to be. Sexual pleasure and self-excitation are best achieved when there is no rush. Part of the enjoyment of self-love is that it is a very personal act in which you control the intensity and pace of your feelings. In that sense, it is important to feel comfortable, private, and free. Enhance your space with anything that makes you feel good—music, candles, perfumes, incense, special lighting, pillows.

Find out about your body. Even if you already think you know it, look at and touch your body as if for the first time. Use a mirror if you wish, and take your time. While in a shower or when rubbing yourself with lotion, caress and touch your body all over. Find the spots that turn you on—the inside of your thigh or along your breasts. You are unique and have special places that are sensitive. Discover what feels good.

Above all, sexual pleasure is found in the body. And again, as in any activity of the body, breathing is the key. Letting go to deep and regular breathing both charges the body with increased energy and engages the muscle system in its rhythmic beat. To hold back your breathing is to restrain the full involvement of the organism. Don't be afraid or shy about your sounds during sexual release. They are your signature. Be as proud of your unique sexual response as you are of every other distinctive thing about you. Enjoy each plateau of excitation, and if full orgasm comes, let it be expressed fully in every part of your being.

Self-pleasuring can be an act of confirming your worth to you—that you not only enjoy pleasure, but that you deserve it.

Other Satisfactions

Physical isolation is a real problem for a woman who is separating. It is not easy to find a substitute for the physical closeness that a husband and wife share. Whereas masturbation may be an answer for some women during long stretches of emotional loneliness, often in the final stage of divorce even that does not fill their need.

When Peggy was in the last few weeks of her marriage, there was no "one answer" to her feelings of physical discontent.

> I don't remember feeling very sexual. It wasn't that I'm not a sexual person; sex just wasn't on my mind. I was worrying about negotiating about the house and then I was on the phone to my lawyer every day. I was working late at the office because of a change of management and when I came home I tried to put up a good front, be cheerful as possible. I was trying to take the pressure off everybody, but in the meantime I was *exhausted.*
>
> I was sleeping on a daybed in the TV room so that didn't give me much privacy either. But I don't think that's why I wasn't masturbat-

ing. I think that feeling sexual wasn't foremost in my head. I was very anxious.

The best thing that was happening to me at that point was that I had a couple of friends, my girl friend and her husband, and they were warm and physical. I could stop by after work or on my day off and spend an hour or so. They'd sit and hug me or just put their arms around me and reassure me. That really felt good.

Then at home I'd sit and watch TV with the kids, let them sit on my lap, or we'd play on the floor together. There was that kind of closeness that I really needed at the time. I was scared and I needed that.

Nonsexual physical contact is very important. A client of mine was feeling stiff and went to a chiropractor to get her back worked on. As he started to work on her, she broke into tears and had to admit to herself that what she needed was simply someone to touch her. We all need recognition, not just in conversation but in physical contact. It tells us that we exist. Having your arm stroked by another is not only feeling *her* hand, it is feeling *your own* arm. The touch outlines the boundaries of your body and, in that sense, gives you real definition. You literally know who you are. So often the person who is not in regular physical contact with others actually feels "spaced out," as if the limits of her body were not readily clear to herself. Touching provides a grounding and gives us a sense of self.

It sometimes doesn't take much to keep us going. Grand, passionate lovemaking is wonderful, but when you are up against the wall, a touch or a soft conversation can be terribly gratifying. This is a time when everything is magnified, so take advantage of the small but genuine experiences of life. Try these.

- Go out to your friends and family and get daily hugs. In fact, *ask* for physical warmth. You will find that people will be complimented and will enjoy giving you something that you are so open about needing. Make sure it is real contact and not merely a gesture.
- Hold and touch your children more. The increased physical contact can be good for both of you. Be aware however that it

is not compulsive, needy holding that says more about your problems than your love. But if the touching is done freely in warm caring and play, the children will have an increased sense of security. "Spooning" is fun. Lie on the floor, side by side, facing the same direction. Hold the person in front of you. It is a cozy and reassuring way to make contact.

● If you can afford it, get a massage regularly. If you can't, trade massages with a woman. Be straightforward about it. Tell her about your situation and ask if she would be willing.

Centering

Focusing on your physical and sexual needs is a centering of yourself at this most essential time. You have been pulled and pushed in many directions, and while some of it is inevitable, the danger is that it is easy to lose yourself in the process. Although you started with a clear purpose, you may feel at times that everything in your existence is muddy.

By coming back again and again to your physical self, you reaffirm the sense of your own value in most elemental ways. The world may be coming apart, but you are of one piece. It is there you must start and finish. In the end, your physical and mental well-being are so interconnected that the health of one is dependent on the health of the other. Feel and *be* that oneness.

CHAPTER 7

Husbands—and Leaving Them

When you get down to it, husbands are what this book is about. They are the core issue. Your history with your husband in the bond of marriage is what motivates your actions and, at the same time, is what makes it so difficult. For years you gave a great deal of time and attention to him.

Ending that relationship is not easy. How do you stop something that was so physically and emotionally involved? And if you have children together, what will be the nature and form of your future contact with their father?

Although such broader inquiries relating to your husband need investigation, more practical questions bear in heavily at this point. After all is said and done, you are still left with some very gritty considerations.

- How do I *tell* my husband?
- What will his reaction be?
- How, in fact, do I actually leave?

As much as we may want to avoid thinking in such detail, it really comes down to these points.

The purpose of this chapter is to help you assess your particular situation and point out some available options. The unpredictable nature of your husband's reaction obviously compounds the problem of giving universal advice. How can any common direction be given to both a twenty-five-year-old woman with four children whose husband is a combat veteran and works in a meat packing company in East St. Louis, and a childless forty-one-year-old woman clothes buyer from Boston who is leaving her alcoholic stockbroker husband? As usual, because of the divergent circumstances, any specific advice lays itself open to criticism.

Rather than walk away from the dilemma and fatalistically assume that there is nothing that can be said conclusively, and that, therefore, each woman must work through her trials without help, I do feel that certain information and general guidelines are worthwhile and can, in fact, be lifesaving. At the risk of sounding dogmatic, my experience with women going through this stage of a breakup indicates that there are some do's and don'ts. Naturally, you will have to take what applies to your situation, but don't discount any possibility until you have thoroughly considered it.

Leaving and Being Left

The game of life is, at times, a very serious one. This is one of those times. When you choose to leave your marriage, you are creating a structure of rules that will ensue throughout the rest of the divorce process. By initiating the divorce, you immediately become the controlling agent. The name of the game is "breakup," and when you create the rules, your husband is put into the position of being the unwilling player. The reverse would be true if he initiated the divorce.

And strangely, it is not always a matter of who has the stronger feelings that determines the depth of pain. Put simply, the person who acts first often suffers less emotional hurt. The truth may be that your husband has, for a long time, had strong reservations about the future of your marriage and has wanted to get out. But the fact that *you* chose to act first on the matter puts him in a defensive position. The same principle was first applied in teenage romance. You may remember, when at the end of going steady, there was a rush to see who would announce it first. Nobody wants to be left behind.

This is not meant to discredit your husband's genuine feelings. His hurt is very real. But a good part of the hurt and the anger that grows from it is not just the knowledge that you no longer love him enough to want to live with him, but that now he has no choice. You have made it for him. It is you who has chosen his destiny and he is helpless to do anything about it. He did not ask for this.

I draw this out in dramatic terms because there is never a time when feelings are more magnified. The incredible stress casts everything into distorted proportions. The person being left is suddenly bombarded with words that wildly run through his head—words like "abandoned," "deserted," "rejected," "unwanted," "dismissed," "dumped," or "trashed." Almost automatically a whole mind set comes into play, and it may well be the first time he has had to confront anything like this. It may substantiate old fears.

Realize clearly the ramifications of the structure you are creating. When you are the actor, he becomes the reactor. The method, the style, and the content of what you say and do will influence and to some extent determine his response. If you are thoughtless, impulsive, or insensitive, you may get it back in spades.

At the risk of being considered calculating, think carefully through this entire stage. It is the final giant step toward your personal freedom.

MALE ORIENTATIONS

I do not mean to stereotype men as a group, or your husband in particular. Labeling men has become almost a national pastime among authors lately. Men's consciousness ranges from Archie Bunker to Robert Bly, and it does everyone a disservice to make sweeping statements about "all men."

At the same time, men in this culture do share a common heritage. There are traditional male attitudes of "acceptable" behavior, and these ideas, as they filter into the consciousness of men and boys, can be cataloged and described. It is really no great secret. A boy who watches TV any time of day will be imprinted with the variety of styles and values that males are "supposed" to have. We live out our myths, and many men get permanently stuck in them.

Your husband must be considered individually. Nobody knows him better than you. You can't live with a man for years and not be in touch with his deeper levels. However, it is also essential to recognize that in a time of extreme stress, your husband may react in ways based on feelings and instincts of which even he is not fully aware. In preparing for this part of the divorce process, consider all possibilities.

How will *your* husband react? It is an important question. The answer will determine much of your conduct for the time being.

Men's Lives

Weston La Barre, in his famous book *The Human Animal*, sees the roots of man's nature as simply and as profoundly as this:

> A woman can give proof of her femaleness in a very simple and irrefutable way, by having a baby—but a man must always prove something, his manhood within a group.

There are two relevant points in this statement for our purpose—the phrase "a man must always *prove*," and the definition of the word *manhood*.

This striving to prove manhood is no trivial matter. Many men see themselves in a lifelong contest to do just that. The pressure is always on, whether in business or at play, to perfectly embody the attributes that guarantee his manliness. The nature of just how this is to be proved is never quite clear—perhaps by wearing a cowboy hat, or strongly voicing opinions about military tactics, or taking swift action at the office to undercut a competitor.

But in the end, who gives the final approval, the confirmation that he has *arrived?* And, of course, one achievement is never enough. It only raises the stakes, and the game gets tougher.

Television presents highly defined, prepackaged images of what it is to be a man. The Athlete is the premier representative: In sports there are winners and losers, but there are no quitters. Other stereotypes have emerged, the slate of characters presented in those forty-five-second beer commercials. Slick models can be found in the rough independence of The Cowboy; in the sex appeal of The Playboy; in the camaraderie of The Working Man; in the confidence of The Doctor; in the affluence of The Businessman. And although they neatly glide across the screen and into men's consciousness, the result is more confusion. Men in the commercials jostle each other in warm friendship and high spirits after a tough day at the mill, but real life never quite matches up. Neither does the average man's concept of his own manhood.

At an earlier time in history, the definition of manhood was much more simple, more cocksure. Whether he was hunting or protecting the family, the man knew his role and how to gain respect. Today, values are changing so quickly that definitions of manhood keep slipping just out of reach. Does he stay at home to raise the children, talk about his sexual anxiety, have a face-lift, wear jeans that hug his ass, cry? Twenty-five years ago there would be no question as to what he did. Now men are caught in a revolution of gender redefinition that has challenged and confounded most of them. The women's movement has pushed open the door.

Many men seem to be saying, "I'm not sure what I trust anymore," and are retreating into the fortress of macho thinking and posturing. In their eagerness for security, their adolescent definition of "manhood" is found in becoming simply the exaggerated opposite of what they imagine makes up "a girl." The deep-seated fear that heterosexual men have of being feminine shows up in every part of how they relate to the world each day. This attitude was implanted by parents and peers, teachers and textbooks, movies and television. The worst thing that a boy can be accused of is being a "sissy." (For a girl to be called a "tomboy" is rather cute.) In reaction to this, the boy typically denies all of his softer, more sensitive feelings.

By the time he is a man, he has been given the following messages again and again in one form or another:

- *Don't show weakness.* If you cannot be the biggest, strongest man around, you can at least present an unbendable character. If you give in to anyone, others will be quick to take advantage and in the battle of life, nobody wants to be labeled a "wimp."
- *Don't be dependent.* It may be hard not to rely on others at times, but don't get in a position of need or at least never show it. Once in a while you may slip in this regard, but be quick to reaffirm your precious independence.
- *Don't show your emotions.* This is hard but if you are constantly alert, you can keep what you are really feeling hidden from others. It gives you the upper hand when dealing with others because they never know your vulnerabilities.
- *Don't ask for help.* Asking for it is a most blatant sign of weakness. There may be times when you need things from others, even things like "good lovin'," but mask those requests in ways that others don't see your real needs. You may get relief in the short run, but later you will feel exposed.
- *Don't be hesitant.* Act on things quickly. You may not always know the outcome of what you are doing, but that's not the primary issue. It is worse to be thought of as wishy-washy. If things don't turn out, you can deal with that later. If you seem indecisive, others will run all over you.
- *Don't trust your feelings.* These are changing all the time and who knows where they come from. They actually seem to undermine your will. You are bound to have some at times, but it's not hard to find masculine ways of expressing them, by putting the energy into something concrete—your business, your car, a hobby—something where your feelings aren't easily recognized.
- *Don't accept losing.* In life as in sports, there are winners and losers. You may lose sometimes but never admit defeat. And never quit. If you get to be known as a loser or a quitter, the quality of your manhood is in serious question.

Whether it is an Axl Rose music video or a version of *Lethal Weapon*, the media's values subtly and incessantly shape the attitudes of boys and men. For some, this male posturing becomes a straight-jacket of behavior. In being "Successful," the search for manhood finds rest. It matters not whether the man is a short order cook or a petroleum geologist, if he considers himself successful, and this judgment is confirmed by others, his manhood is safe. For the moment.

A Woman's Place

Women constantly engage these character bents in men. Often men show some flexibility, depending on their level of acceptance and trust. But during the stress of divorce, they may well revert back to those most primitive guidelines and fiercely seek reassurance from them. And when certain male behaviors are carried to their extreme, they can be dangerous to you.

Men have, for instance, an affinity for idealism. The positive side of this is their desire to make things work better, to improve the quality of life by invention and organization. But the negative side is that they unrealistically seek out perfection. In their relationship to the female sex, this is especially evident. For the past thirty years, we have seen them create and re-create the "perfect" woman each month in the centerfolds of *Playboy* and similar magazines. But this is also extended to include the perfect bride (a virgin), the perfect wife (docile yet sexy), the perfect secretary (smart but respectful), and innumerable other "perfects." It is a fantasy world of absolutes.

The problem with idealists is that when their dream is shattered, they are plunged into seeing what they had chosen to beatify as "fallen." And so, for instance, we get the madonna/whore syndrome. On the one hand the woman is idealized as a madonna figure—saintly, untouchable, and captivating. But when she has fallen from grace, she becomes the whore—common, used, and coarse. A wife choosing to leave her husband is often condemned to the latter class by him, and treated accordingly.

The pressures and influences of growing up male are complex, but you should be aware that whatever basic values motivate your husband's behavior during his life in normal times, these will be tested and expressed in an intense form right now. It serves you well to know where he is coming from.

Men and Marriage

Everybody gets married for a different reason. Or do they? In their book *Husbands and Wives*, Anthony Pietropinto and Jacqueline Simenaur, after taking a detailed poll of thousands of married couples, found declining numbers of men and women were stating "love" as the primary reason for getting married. It had always, of course, been the "correct" answer.

Although love and companionship arc reasons men still give for marrying, one suspects that it is not that simple. And even if the word "sex" is substituted, it may not be getting deep enough into men's motivation for coupling. Despite the threat of AIDS, many men still seek out sexual satisfaction in a free-wheeling context.

Marriage does fulfill some special emotional gaps for men. In fact, it can become a kind of crutch in the sense that, as stated previously, many men are not at ease expressing deeply sensitive feelings, and they believe that marriage is a safe emotional refuge. Through women, they can at least vicariously experience a sense of emotional completion. If it is not OK for a man to cry, his wife can do it for him. If he is not comfortable being dramatic and excited, his wife gives him voice. He can lean on her to translate his inarticulate feelings. She can send the "thank you" cards and the letters of sorrow to relatives. She can verbalize his worries about the kids. Her contribution is perhaps best symbolized at Christmas. She makes it happen—her shopping, planning, and cooking. The husband is usually silently grateful for the warmth that a woman's caring brings. Most of them recognize that they would be incapable of pulling it off by themselves.

Many men find marriage genuinely convenient. It provides them with the creature comforts that have been so clearly and traditionally promised—a warm supper and a wife in charge of the details of life (laundry, shopping, cooking, entertainment, house management, child care, feeding the dogs, taking phone calls, etc.). Many women have been raised to provide these services. Of course, when growing numbers refuse this role, those same husbands often react in amazement, becoming totally disoriented. They have assumed that the very definition of marriage included these duties.

I know a man in his forties who got a divorce after twenty years. But he quickly got disillusioned with the single life after finding out that he had to do all of the daily chores himself. He went back to live with his mother. She was a good cook.

At some point, most men are willing to exchange the advantages of the single life for those of being married. Behind the choice, there is a massive subliminal pressure, a kind of unwritten social obligation, for a man to marry and raise a family. Marriage is a sign of success. Not to do so is shirking one's duty as a man.

Men and Divorce

If marriage is an affirmation of a husband's manhood, then divorce shows his failure. Even though a man may have long ago neglected his responsibilities to his family, the marriage still provided a socially recognized and approved structure for his life. When a wife acts to end the marriage, it is very threatening.

The most incomprehensible thing about the situation is that it goes directly against a firmly established role that had been almost universally accepted by men and women: *Men are the Initiators.* Traditionally, this belief ran through almost every activity in which men and women mutually engaged. It was the *man* who initiated the decision of which car to buy, when the house needed painting, in what part of the city to live. If his job took him to a different location, it was finally *his* decision. For many couples, these and other behaviors still constitute the role definitions of their marriage. Men are the ones who ask for dates, choose the restaurant, buy the theater tickets, drive the car. Furthermore, they are most often the ones to initiate sex. Some of this may not have literally been true, but most men *see* themselves as the person who must take action.

It is, therefore, an outrageous psychological affront when a woman independently chooses to initiate a divorce by herself and without prior approval. Her action redirects the course of not only her life but his as well. *There is no more radical act that a woman could possibly do to undermine the security of his "manhood."* Certain men are mature enough to hurdle this; many others are not.

Each word of La Barre's statement is significant: "But a man must always prove something, his manhood *within a group.*" Men play to other men especially. And when a man's wife leaves, it demands explanation, not only to himself, but to others. Furthermore, if she is recognized as highly desirable by his contemporaries, it makes him look very bad. And no matter how it is rationalized, there is an old saying that whispers: "He couldn't keep his woman."

A man's feeling of his sexual potency goes beyond the glamour of being thought of as sexy. He knows that he must *prove* it. In our culture, his sexuality is at the very root of his confidence, and the way he experiences himself sexually is reflected in every manner of his person. The rejection of divorce, as he imagines it to be perceived by others, completely undercuts his self-esteem.

A man's economic potency is also challenged by divorce. If women have ordinarily been seen as the *nurturers* in marriage, men have been the *providers.* Men have traditionally been the principal wage earners, responsible for the financial security of the family. It may have been something that he complained about—the thankless daily effort of going off to work each day—but the role of provider seems to fulfill a very basic need in many men. It is an external sign of his caring for his family, and also gives clear definition of his place.

But when a woman leaves, it again questions how well he has done his job. Another old saying, "He couldn't take care of his family," is a powerful indictment that he must respond to. And even though he may be able to show it was not an issue in the breakup, the very loss of the role of provider can be very unsettling. For years he may have gained satisfaction and acceptance from that role. Now he is no longer needed, at least in any formal sense.

In addition, divorce brings into sharp relief the emotional dependency of the man for his wife. For many men it may be the first time in their lives that they have to look deeply into themselves and question some very fundamental values and attitudes. A lot of men are ill-equipped to do this, lacking the introspective tools to make sense of what is going on and the kind of relationship with other men that might make it possible.

Over the past ten or fifteen years, many men have become much more sensitive, open, and self-aware. They have been able to somehow slip by the forces that formed traditional male consciousness. The crucial question is—has *your* husband?

LEAVING

The way in which your marriage breaks up depends on many, many factors. The history of your marriage together is probably the first place to look for indications of what to expect and, therefore, what to do. Obviously it is not easy to accurately judge just how your husband might react in a situation he may have never before encountered. But this is not a minor point of qualification. His response sets the tone for your leaving.

There are over a million divorces a year and the same number of special situations at the point of leaving. However, for the purpose of describing and understanding this period, three types of break-ups can be identified:

1. *Yielding.* Leavetaking for some women is a relatively easy matter, especially when the husband also recognizes that the marriage is over. There may be sadness, tears, and some pain, but the period is free of incidents of terrible conflict. For whatever reason, the parting is smooth.

2. *Aggressive.* Most divorces unfortunately fall into this range. Any number of issues exist that can be used to hurt and punish

each of the partners and no end to the methods used. At best, it is a hassle that is gotten through; at worst it can escalate or be suddenly triggered into the next category.

3. *Dangerous.* Because of the extremely volatile elements in divorce, the potential for physical violence is real. Moreover, a woman's decision to leave her husband moves their relationship into uncharted territory. There are enough recorded cases of abuse to warrant the warning. It is a possibility for which a woman must be alert.

In the following extended descriptions of these categories, you may feel that you recognize your situation. That, in part, is the purpose. But also remember that things at this time can change quickly, and that each day often brings a new surge of emotion. Be flexible in your assessment.

THE YIELDING BREAKUP: The Hope

Tony and I were always able to talk. That's one thing we *could* do, we could talk for hours on end. We had other problems, but communication wasn't a big one. We probably talked too much.

In one sentence, our relationship just ran out of gas. There were still ways we loved each other but they weren't near enough. We argued a lot at the end and it was clear to me for quite a while that our marriage was over. When I told Tony that I wanted out, he had seen it coming and resisted it some, but he really knew it was over too. We're still friends and are interested in each other's lives.

Sandy's account is about as ideal as one could hope for. They had no children, both worked, and lived in a small apartment. Both Tony and Sandy were twenty-eight years old and had a good deal of confidence in themselves and their separate futures.

Few couples have it that easy, but given the possible personal tragedies in breaking up, a number of women do get through this period in relatively good shape. Some of it has to do with an acquiescent husband, thoughtful planning, or chance.

The major reason why most breakups in this category end with some accord is that, for one reason or another, the husbands also tacitly want to get out of the marriage. Some of them will admit it when they are confronted with the situation, but others will use the potential drama of it all to protest every injustice they ever felt in the marriage. This is a safe and righteous outlet for his emotions, freeing him from the guilt of his silent feelings.

When Erica told her husband, Mark, that she wanted to separate, he reacted in such a manner. But his later response indicates the transitory nature of his feelings.

> He reacted very emotionally, like a child. I felt that the reaction was to make me feel guilty, or to make me feel sorry for him. It's like he was totally helpless. He banged his head against the wall and had a *tantrum*, really. It seemed so unreal, but it made me even more sure of what I was doing instead of less sure. It didn't make me want to reach out and say, "There, there—poor Mark."
>
> He gave me the divorce. He said, "If you want it, *you* do it!" And so I went ahead. But I still compromised in a sense and said that maybe we could spend three months apart to work on things. He agreed and left for Traverse City to stay with friends but within a week he had moved in with another woman. If there was an ounce of doubt, it closed the door completely. It really wasn't a terribly emotional time for me. The relationship had been harder for me than the breakup.

A common element in the previous stories is that no children were involved in any of the marriages and, therefore, leaving was a matter of two individuals working to free themselves of a relationship.

Even in a more complex situation, the transition can be relatively calm. One factor that seems to be paramount in achieving this is if the husband is successful in other parts of his life. Or rather, if he *sees* himself as successful. A strong sense of self-esteem will usually override irrational and extremely vindictive behavior. Milt was a senior pilot for American Airlines. He and Eleanor had been married for eighteen years when she told him she wanted to leave. Because they had two teen-age children, it was a very hard decision for her. When I asked her if Milt was surprised, she said no.

> He knew it was coming. After, we actually started communicating better than we had in a long time. He was very out front with his emotions—he was in tears. I had rarely seen him so emotional, for such a sustained period of time. I was steadier because I had gone through tons of anger. He really didn't know what to do; the divorce was breaking up the family.
>
> But he was never verbally abusive. That's not his style, though it probably would have been better if he was. He was afraid of anger or being angry.
>
> About the most he did that could be called abusive was that he went around to a lot of our friends and gave his side of the story. He told them it was my fault. That I had done this and this, and that he really didn't want to leave. But he was also very busy flying and it is a thing he loves to do. I know that helped.
>
> He's still angry in some ways. We had to have the house reroofed a couple of weeks ago and I went away while it was being done and he came by. While he was here, he cut back a lot of the foliage around the house. I was furious. I felt violated, exposed—too much light was coming in. The masculine self had come in and overcome the feminine. And I realized that he was still pissed on some level. He said, "I knew you wouldn't like it," and I said, "You're right; I don't."

Getting through this period successfully is a matter of knowing how to handle relationships, and in particular, the temperament of your husband. There are some subtle skills that work. Earlier in the book, Adrienne told the story of her life as a waitress, a mother of three, and of her studies that led to her becoming a dental hygienist. Her husband had been an alcoholic for years and had given it up under pressure from Adrienne. However, their marriage was still on the rocks.

Jerry had taken a job as an electrician for a traveling carnival company which worked the Midwest, and he was often gone for a month at a time. While he was away one time, Adrienne met

another man and the experience totally awakened her to the fact
that she had to get out of her marriage. Adrienne used both her
intuition and her verbal skills to get through what might have
been a very harrowing experience.

I told him I was leaving over the phone. He was on the road at the
time. We had talked about it earlier. But he didn't believe me because
in the past when I had talked about divorce many times, it just went
over his head. He was seeing other women on the road but gave me
that line about me being his number one lady.

So about a week later he called again and I told him that I was
filing for a divorce. He was quiet, then said, "OK, if that's what you
want." But he really didn't think I was going to do it.

When I did file, he was shocked. He's been in a state of shock ever
since. He is depressed and he cries and asks why? Over and over.
The wounded puppy syndrome—following me around and telling
me I'm causing unhappiness for the children, that he thought we
had more together, that I've ruined his life, that his dream is shattered, just on and on—trying to lay a guilt trip on me.

But I really didn't argue with him about it—I just listened. Because I've learned enough in psychology and in dealing with people.
So I would feed it back to him, "So are you saying that you feel
angry about what I've done?" Then I'd tell him I'm sorry—that I
was doing this for *me*, that I wanted to be free.

He couldn't argue with that. I'd say, "I need to be on my own, to
try my wings, and I need it now. Maybe years ago I didn't, but I
need it now." The thing to do is talk about where *you* are at, not
where *he* is at.

These are some examples of separations that were compara-
tively nontraumatic. Whatever underlying principles that were
working which made the woman's announcement finally acceptable are hard to label—and I hesitate to do so more than I have
here. Because the factors that make one divorce seem civilized,
can in the next case be a signal of danger.

For instance, the fact that the husband is a "nice guy" is no
guarantee that his behavior will continue to be that. As Bach and
Goldberg, in their fine book *Creative Aggression*, point out:

"Nice" behavior is not reliable. Periodically, the "nice" person explodes in an unexpected rage and those involved with him are shocked and unprepared to cope with it.

Everyone has anger and everyone has his breaking point. The husband who feels his reputation demands that he be a good guy in every situation may be a greater risk than the man who has learned to express anger regularly in nonviolent ways. The authors clearly show this in their book and document the tragic results.

No one can say for sure what grace gets some couples through divorce without being psychologically or physically scarred. Your intuition—but more, your common sense—may be the best guide. Act with confidence, but be on guard. A man who starts out looking like he will yield may suddenly turn aggressive, or even dangerous.

THE AGGRESSIVE BREAKUP: The Reality

On the subject of divorce, Rose DeWolf, in her book *The Bonds of Acrimony*, says:

> If some kind of annual prize were to be given for sheer nastiness, it would undoubtedly be awarded—well, at least nine years out of ten—to someone involved in the breakup of his or her marriage.

The expression of divorce seems to bring out some form of aggressive behavior for many couples. It may not be new to them, but it now intensifies and spreads. This is especially true when women choose to leave. As Warren Farrell, author of *Why Men Are The Way They Are*, observes, "Men feel that they are being pushed to the wall. They don't know how they are getting there. The only thing they know is to come out fighting." Whether it is fighting about the kids, whose fault it was that the communication wasn't better, or who gets the lamp in the bedroom, most marriages end in battle.

If there is no shortage of subjects to fight about, there is also no end to the number of ways in which the hostilities are acted out. The most bizarre incidents are not uncommon when couples break up. Stereo equipment gets deliberately broken, tires are slashed, the phone rings at odd hours, antiques disappear, private correspondence is published, thinly veiled novels written that tell all—you could add to the endless list of ways spouses have found to harass each other. They could be said to fall into three general areas.

1. *Psychological abuse.* A most common form that women report is "badgering." It is that constant stream of verbal nagging, the continual requestioning of the woman's motivations and actions by her husband, either over the phone or as he follows her from room to room complaining and pressing for "an answer." Any method is used—from appeals for sympathy to pushing all of her guilty buttons to making dire threats—anything that will get a response.

2. *Financial abuse.* Many husbands crack down on a woman where she is the most vulnerable. Some hold back money so that women and children are put in a position of having to beg him for help or go to court. Even then, there is almost no limit to the worries he can cause. Some men systematically hide the joint assets, others threaten financial suicide, a few skip out with the bank deposits.

3. *Legal abuse.* Couples can always get someone else to do the fighting for them. For a price, lawyers will find innumerable ways to make a partner's life miserable. The very cost of their service is a starter. If your husband wishes, he can find ways to delay almost any action or complicate situations that could be sensibly solved.

When a woman chooses to end her marriage, she can usually expect some amount of abuse. The man who has depended on her emotionally will react to the loss. In his state of panic he may see her as his sole source of support, love, and caretaking. Facing the future alone is frightening. If, in addition, he sees his age as limiting his opportunities, his fear is compounded.

And yet he doesn't allow himself those feelings. They are "unmanly," after all. Instead, he often attempts to cover his insecurity and control the situation in any number of ways—from being cajoling to being menacing. The net effect for the woman is a constant feeling of pressure.

Remember that when we are considering this behavior, it is not only during the few days or weeks of physically leaving each other. The harassment of divorce can linger for months or longer. If your husband really wants to be a nuisance, he will try to find means to intrude into your life before and after you leave. As long as there are some channels of contact, there is always the chance for him to take another tack.

Voices

The nature of this behavior is perhaps best brought out by random comments taken from longer interviews of many women contacted in the research for this book. Only the tips of the icebergs are given here, the anger and frustration running much deeper in every case. Submerged psychological abuse can be heard in the voices:

- *Gary started asking me questions like, "How could you do this?", or "What do you expect me to do—move out—go live with a friend?" They were questions with no good answers, and we had been over them a hundred times before. But he kept asking them. If I was doing something—cooking dinner or doing the laundry, he'd just stand there. Then the argument would start again. I guess he hoped I'd get worn down and give up the idea of divorce.*

- It would be back and forth. Sometimes Bill would be sad or understanding, and other times cold and abusive. It wasn't as though I could count on him being one way. It was like there would be this buildup, and then there would be the Dr. Jekyll and Mr. Hyde.

- *One time Tommy made the remark—something like, "Well, you're not going to peddle your ass all over town and then think you're going to come back to me." So what he was reducing my leaving to was having some kind of fling. Well, that was trivializing everything. It was deeper than that. He'd get nasty about stuff like that—he thought I was going to go out with millions of guys. That was when he was the nastiest.*

- Dick was really strange. He'd go for a long time not showing any emotion and then the littlest thing would go wrong and he would have an absolute fit, throwing things down, stamping around, and slamming doors. Then he would brood.

- *When Stewart dropped the kids off last Sunday, he said, "Hey, you're screwing up the kids emotionally and it's all your fault." I thought, "That's a bunch of bull. It's not all my fault."*

- So when I got home he called me in the middle of the night and that's how it started and went on for two weeks, with him calling every night until I got smart and unplugged the phone so I could get some sleep.

- *Manny said that he won't pay for the kids' college, the ones under eighteen. He is indicating to them that I'm taking him to the cleaners and he won't have any money after that.*

- After listening to Howard tell me, for years, that he hated me, hated the sight of my fat body, that I never understood him, treating me like an acquaintance for whom he had contempt instead of as a wife—now I get a letter from him saying he's sorry I feel the way I do, that he loves me, that I was always his best friend and that I'm important in his life. And how he's sure we can work things out if we could just learn to communicate. I feel like telling him, "We *communicated,* all right."

- *Then later Lenny came down and told my girlfriend he didn't know what to do with me, that he was trying to make the marriage work and I'm a real shit. All the time the kids are sitting in the back seat of the car, listening.*

- Vince just showed up at my apartment unannounced and then he immediately went all through the house, checking *everything,* looking into things, and although he was saying nice things, he was checking everything out. Maybe looking for shaving lotion in the bathroom or something.

● *I had to go to the beauty shop and Gene just came into the bedroom. He said, "Come on, come here!" and grabbed me and came over me and got me on the bed. All this time I'm saying, "No, I don't want this—please Gene, no!" And he's saying, "It's OK, it's all right." And I thought he was going to rape me. He was forceful but didn't seem angry. I just kept protesting, "Please don't—don't do this because it will be an ugly scene." So he just held me down and wouldn't let me up from that position and said he wanted to talk to me. When I wouldn't look at him, he'd yell, "Look at me! I am talking to you. Look at me!"*

● I left, spent the night with a girl friend. When I came back on Thursday Jim didn't say very much. But Friday in the bedroom he grabbed me, looked very hostile and asked, "Who did you spend the night with? Were you shacking up with somebody?" The kids were right outside the door. He was pretty abusive and said, "If you don't tell me who you spent the night with I'm going to drag you out of this house!" And he started toward me and I yelled for one of the kids. Later he denied being aggressive and hostile and said it was my imagination.

Examples of the spectrum of aggressive behavior could go on and on. The variations on the theme become draining. But perhaps by understanding the process that is taking place, some of the conflict can be avoided or, at least, tempered.

Common Reactions

Earlier in the book, divorce was compared to dying. Dr. Elisabeth Kübler-Ross has outlined various psychological stages that a person experiences when facing his or her death. She isolates five distinct reactions that most people go through: First *Denial*, usually followed by *Anger*, then *Bargaining*, *Depression*, and finally *Acceptance*.

Much the same thing can be observed in divorce. The stages may be masked in a number of ways, but they are surprisingly similar. There may be some jumping back and forth, say between Denial and Depression; or Anger may be expressed only long after the separation; or a man's pride may block him from Bargaining. But in general the signs are remarkably present in the response of men (or women) when they experience their partner leaving. The following is a sample of how your husband might react when confronted with the announcement of the end of a marriage.

Denial. It sounds like this: "I can't *believe* you're doing this to me (or the kids, or the family)." Often the husband did not hear what you were saying when you talked about divorce, or he claims he didn't. Or later he treats it lightly, as if it were a whim: "Boy, you sure were in a bad mood the other night," or, "Have you come to your senses now?" In the denial stage, the man may engage himself in avoidance behavior—changing the subject by being gay and charming, or by plunging himself into his work, or by just staying away from the house. If he is a drinker, he may resort to that. Nothing, however, completely blocks out the shock of the new reality.

Anger. A man's anger is reflected not only in *what* he says, but in his tone of voice, his temperament, and actions. The way men show anger depends on their particular backgrounds and the conditions of their life. For some, it is all verbal. Others displace it in fast driving or hostility toward others. Some react physically toward their wives, and when that happens, the situation suddenly can become dangerous. You can expect anger to be directed at you in some form.

Bargaining. This stage is major in the process of divorce. Whereas the act of bargaining is an illusion in dying, in divorce there *seems* to be real hope. The man feels that if he can only make a strong enough case to convince his wife this one time, everything can be saved. He has been successful in other less important times, so hope exists.

The bargaining may be a change in attitude and style. He buys flowers and presents, dresses differently, promises to give up outside activities, or even to lose weight. He might promise to "let" her go back to school, or to stop drinking, share the housework, perhaps suggest that she go on vacations by herself. Anything that works.

The greater and more relentless the bargaining, the stronger an indicator this is of his desperation. This is not to say that he is insincere. He may well be totally convinced of his own earnestness. But there is an inherent bind in such bargaining.

- If you accept the promised changes, it may create just another stage in your relationship that makes neither of you happy. You may feel you were coerced into this choice out of sympathy or some wild hope. But as the first flush of reconciliation subsides, you feel compromised, having gone against your deeper needs. Later, he too feels that whatever was pledged was done under duress and that now you hold a loaded gun to his head. His changed behavior was unnatural and he would never have done it except under your threat of leaving.
- If you refuse his promises, it is one more rejection. A very clear and unambiguous one. Because he has so exposed himself by bargaining, he may resort to anger or more forceful means.

Bargaining usually doesn't work. It is something like a kid trying to be spontaneous when he knows his parents are watching.

If two people are really serious about starting over together, and the shock of divorce awakens *both* of them to some truly undiscovered caring, a new start is possible. But if the offers of change seem to be too good to be true, you're probably right. Real change usually occurs in more gradual ways. Bargaining is more often a ploy by the husband to gain time, the underlying hope being that when the woman comes to her senses, things will again be back under control and "normal." And that is what most women wish to escape.

Depression. For many men, depression comes from the feeling that with this divorce, they have lost their last chance. Age is an important factor here. A man in his forties or fifties may feel that the end of his marriage is the visible symbol of the decline of his potency and creative abilities. The apparent signs are a loss of appetite, long crying spells, withdrawal, and indications of suicidal thoughts.

With men of any age, depression is something to be watched. Below its surface are a lot of feelings, and some can be explosive.

Acceptance. This parallels the yielding stage that was discussed earlier, in the sense that the man, in the face of an inevitable situation, lets go to it and accepts the new conditions. Some men are able, for one reason or another, to either get through or bypass the other stages and rather quickly accept the reality of separation. This does not mean that at some later time he may not experience the feeling levels of other stages. A delayed reaction of depression, for instance, might happen.

A few men never totally accept their divorce, harboring resentment for years. It is important for a woman to realize that the man's final acceptance is *his* issue and not hers.

THE DANGEROUS BREAKUP: The Fear

The word *dangerous* is not used to be sensational. And yet in investigating what happens when women leave their husbands, it would be dishonest and irresponsible not to address in some detail the possibility of physical danger. It occurs with enough regularity to discuss it as a genuine hazard for women. A man and a woman who are separating live on the raw edges of decisions, and their ultimate actions will be life-altering. Some persons do not cope with that pressure and strike out in physical violence. And while I do not want to exaggerate the chances of that happening to you, the plain truth is that many women have experienced this at the end of their marriages.

In the aggressive type of breakup that was just described, the seeds of real physical danger could be sensed. But at that level, the abuse was primarily in the psychological realm. Men's behavior was controlled by personal and social codes. Here, the man goes out of control.

A central problem in analyzing any of this is that you can never be sure of exactly what *is* happening. When a wife announces that she is leaving, a man might react by being upset and hostile, but his behavior seems to be within the limits of how a reasonable person would react to the stress of the moment. A false security may exist in this. It is difficult to say with any certainty just what suddenly triggers a man to physical violence. But it is also vitally important for the woman to be alert to its impending signs.

The problem is like that of a woman who regularly takes the New York City subway. For years she may have traveled safely to a distant station on the line and never been personally molested. Then one day she gets on the train and as she sits watching other people, she senses trouble—an ugly scene. The best thing that she could do would be to get off the subway immediately—at the next stop—rather than disregard her intuition and hang on until her destination. Why take the chance? Unfortunately, life nowadays comes down to trying to balance out feelings of paranoia with legitimate concern over what might happen in these disturbing times.

In the case of a woman leaving, she is not misinterpreting the possibility of the situation when she is extremely wary of strangeness in her husband's behavior, and is quick to ensure her physical safety. When you have a choice, *err on the side of caution.*

Abuse

Wife-beating is not a phenomenon that is experienced only when women leave relationships. Tragically, it happens to some women throughout their marriage. For the most part, it is an invisible form of violence that takes place behind the closed doors of the home. Accurate statistics on the frequency of such abuses are hard to get because it is estimated that up to 90 percent of them are never reported to the police. However, reports indicate that a woman is battered every eighteen seconds, and one fourth of them are pregnant. Even with the vast majority of women not reporting attacks against them, 20 percent of aggravated assault cases happen between married couples. Many more women than that suffer in silence.

However, enough cases come to the surface to get some idea of what is going on. Every city in the country, for instance, has some form of social service dedicated to this specific problem. By whatever title—Women's Crisis Center or Battered Women's Center—our society has come to recognize the permanent need for shelters where women can find refuge from the threats and acts of physical violence by their mates.

The researchers of long standing with regard to family violence—Suzanne Steinmetz, Richard Gelles, and Murray A. Straus—studied over 2,000 families to find out the rate of spousal violence. They discovered that about sixteen of every one hundred American couples engaged in at least one incident in which either the husband or wife used physical force on the other.

> As you might expect, most of the violent acts were minor assaults, such as slapping, pushing, shoving, and throwing things. However, just over six out of every hundred husbands and wives were involved in a more serious act of violence, such as kicking, punching, biting, hitting with an object, beating up the other, or using a knife or gun. Applying this to the 47 million couples in the United States suggest that serious violence of this type takes place in almost three million American homes a year. Clearly, the typical husband or wife stands a much greater chance of being assaulted in his or her own home than in walking the streets of even the most crime-ridden city.

A stream of examples could be given here to dramatize the truth of this passage, but you can check out the sad reality of this in your local newspaper almost daily. Granted, only the most spectacular abuse cases reach print, but they represent hundreds of other crimes of family violence. In fact, police become immune to these calls and are reluctant to respond to reports of violence directed toward a woman by her husband. They are often labeled "family squabbles" and passed over.

From judges to lawyers to the cop who arrives at the door, a general apathy is evident when a battered wife seeks relief from immediate or ongoing acts of violence from her husband. It goes so far that in some cities, law enforcement has come up with the "stitch rule." Murray A. Straus notes in an article titled *The Marriage License is the Hitting License*:

> In general, the police seem to share the belief in the legitimacy of spousal violence, provided the resulting injuries or destruction are within limits. Some police departments have informal "stitch rules" whereby the wound requires a certain (high) number of stitches before an officer makes an arrest.

The prevailing cultural attitude is still probably best summed up in a hundred-year-old ruling by a judge in North Carolina.

> If no permanent injury has been inflicted, nor malice, cruelty, nor dangerous violence shown by the husband, it is better to draw the curtain, shut out the public gaze and leave the parties to forgive and forget.

The curtain, for some women, is never open, and what happens behind it is beyond the interest or, in effect, the scope of the law. Women's rights are usurped under the banner of "the sanctity of the family."

You may never have experienced physical abuse from your husband. In fact, the whole subject may seem quite foreign. It is the stuff featured in the *National Enquirer* and other sensational publications—the picture of the bruised and bandaged woman whose celebrity husband attacked her during an argument in the parking lot of a famous restaurant. Or it may be what that crazy drunk who lives down the block does to his wife every Saturday night. You might not be at all concerned about that kind of extreme behavior happening to *you*. Until now, the confrontations between you and your husband may have been vitriolic, but have still fallen far short of being physically violent. However, before you reject the notion, consider a few things.

First, what has been your husband's attitude regarding physical violence toward you? I have found, for example, that women
tend to either discount or actually forget times in their marriage
when their husbands have physically abused them. Perhaps because there was no permanent damage, the violence was forgotten when the pain went away. Not long ago I interviewed a
woman about her marriage breakup. At three separate times I
asked her whether she had experienced any physical abuse, and
each time she said no. Then she suddenly remembered—"Oh,
my gosh! Well yes, one day after we were arguing he pushed me
down a flight of stairs." It was as if such things almost did not
count.

Look at the actual behavior of your husband and see if he has
not been prone to use physical means to control or punish you. If
it has happened during arguments over grocery bills or petty
jealousies, the chance is great that this abuse will become more
intense and encompassing during what he sees as the cataclysm
of divorce.

Another point: In the family, just as in society, the person or
group that is dominant will often react with violence when its
authority is threatened. Husbands have traditionally seen themselves as the head of the household and, therefore, the women's
wish to leave is viewed as mutinous, or worse. When they find that
their wives cannot be persuaded with promises or threats, some
husbands resort to physical violence.

Almost any act of assertive behavior by a woman can bring down
the wrath of certain husbands. Lenore Walker, in *The Battered
Woman*, tells that when she began working with her clients in
assertiveness training during transitional periods in their lives,
their mates, in response, became more physically abusive. Women
seeking a divorce are, by definition, in a hazardous position.

ELLEN'S STORY

Ellen's experience was not exceptional. For other women who
have experienced physical abuse, her story had many common
elements. Crueler and more seriously damaging stories could be

recounted, but the idea is not to shock you into panic but into awareness.

Ellen and Jay had been married for nine years when she began to have serious thoughts about leaving. Whatever attraction brought them together in the beginning was long gone, and nothing had replaced it. They had two children—Sue, age ten, and Fran, age six, but Jay had shown only a passing commitment to the family. Still the children loved him and a breakup would be hard.

Jay had held many jobs throughout the marriage and was currently managing a large pet store. Ellen had blindly gone along with most of his failed schemes but grew to distrust both his judgment and his character. She went back to school at night to get a realtor's license, and although she was enthusiastic at first, her interest began to fade. Their life together seemed directionless. In fact, she felt washed out.

This lack of energy bothered her. She had always enjoyed her strong sexual nature, but in recent years her life with Jay had reduced her desire. At thirty-three years of age, Ellen wanted much more out of life than she was getting. She tried to tell Jay this in many ways, but he wasn't listening. It was not easy to pinpoint just where Jay's interests lay—in his work, in his car, in sports on television.

Finally, the idea of divorce that played on Ellen's mind for years began to take over her thoughts. Beginning a new life became a topic of discussion with some of her close female friends, and as the ideas shaped, she became impatient. She decided to tell Jay.

I was out, over at Wendy's, and I knew that I had to tell him. So I rushed home and put the kids to bed and waited for him to come home. I remember it was a Thursday. I was scared to death. We had argued a lot and I knew how mad he could get, but I felt that the best way to tell him was just to *do* it.

I walked in and said, "I'm getting a divorce." He said, "What?" and I repeated it. He said he didn't believe it and didn't want to talk about it. He just sat on the couch and wouldn't say anything. Later, he went to sleep there.

I didn't know what to do next. He didn't say anything for the next two days. I got really frightened. He had never really beaten me up but he talked about beating up guys sometimes and I knew how hot his temper could get. It was strange. He kept his eye on the kids for the next couple days, as if he didn't want them out of his sight. I thought, "God, he's going to blow up or something." I tried to talk, but nothin'. I went out for a while and when I was gone he told the kids I was going to leave and they were really upset. I spent the rest of the night settling them down. Jay seemed to be in another world.

On Saturday he said that he wanted to go somewhere with the kids and that if we were a family it would work out. I had to get a haircut and when I got back he was already gone with the kids. He left a note saying, "I'll be back later. We'll go out and we'll be a family." The note didn't sound like him. For one thing, he just wasn't accepting the fact that I was saying that I wanted to end it. They didn't come back so I went out with Wendy to the deli and for a long time we talked.

When I got home he was standing out in front of the house. I walked up to the door and he said, "Get the fuck out of here! This is my house and these are my kids." I said, "I'm goin' in!" and I pushed past him to get in. He really grabbed me and just started screaming, "Get your fucking ass out of here!" and he pulled and dragged me across the lawn. I couldn't believe it. He pushed me up against the garage door, then tried to cram me into the car. I was crying and screaming. He was really rough. I thought he'd twist my arm right off.

I finally got away and got in the back door with a key. It's very vague. I was so scared and all I could think of was that I wanted to get back to the kids. But I couldn't just drag them out of bed. Then he started screaming again, saying I'd better get the hell out of there, and I said I wasn't going. He was in a rage and yelling that I wouldn't see the kids again. Then he went in the bedroom and I sat on the couch trying to think about what to do.

He came out with this wild look in his face and grabbed me and started forcing me down. I was really mad and fought back, but he was so goddamn strong. He raped me. *He* may not call it rape, but I call it rape. He *forced* me to do it, I didn't do it willingly. It was like his final power over me, like he was saying, "You belong to me and I'm going to take you. See how good I am!" It wasn't sexual at all.

Then he just went in the bedroom. The next thing I remember it was five o'clock in the morning and he woke me up by pulling me by the hair from the couch to the floor. We fought some more. I was exhausted. I had black and blue marks all over, my arm and hand was cut and my back hurt so much I could hardly stand.

What was really strange is that we were supposed to have breakfast with my father at a restaurant that morning—and we went! I don't know why we did that. But when we got there, Jay was real freaky. He just paced up and down in the restaurant, walked outside, then came back to the table and cried. My father didn't know *what* was going on. He asked me, but I couldn't say anything in front of the kids.

Later that day, we were at home and Jay went to the store, and that's when I packed up a few of the kids' things and left. I went to Wendy's house and stayed there.

He came over later but Wendy wouldn't let him in. He stood in front crying and she went down to talk to him. He went on and on about me. Then he left for home and just wouldn't leave the house—for days. I talked to him on the phone and said that we had to get back in the house and he'd have to go. When we finally did, he had wrecked a lot of things. He had torn up all my pictures and broken the frames—torn up our wedding pictures and had pictures of the kids spread all over the house, like he had spent three days just looking at them.

In the past year since Ellen and Jay have been apart, things have not improved much. Jay still comes by the house regularly, often parking down the street to watch what Ellen is doing.

In the past few months, she has had a male friend who has been living with her most of the time. Jay has asked the young girls what Ellen and her boyfriend do in bed. On a Thanksgiving Day visit when Jay picked up the girls, as Ellen was kissing them, Jay put the car in reverse, slamming the open door against her and knocking her to the ground. Many more incidents could be told, but the point is that she has been a victim of ongoing physical abuse. "I tell him how he had beaten me and how terrifying the situation was, but he claims it never happened that way. He says he doesn't remember. I can never *forget* it!"

The purpose here is not to criticize a particular marriage breakup. At the time, we all do what seems best. Nevertheless, were there things Ellen might have done to make her transition less dangerous? The sections that follow give some information and guidelines suggesting other options.

Predictions

Human behavior is seldom easy to figure out, and it is nearly impossible to predict accurately if your husband will respond to your desire for divorce with physical violence. There are, however, several indicative areas of your husband's personal makeup that may give strong hints of what to expect. Although no one thing is conclusive, if your husband has a history of the following influences, be cautious.

If he was abused himself as a child. There is a good deal of research to back up the proposition that children learn physically aggressive behavior from their experience at the hands of their parents. Researchers into aggressive and violent behavior have found that parents who attempt to control a child's aggression by using severe physical punishment are teaching the child to behave in a hostile manner. That child will play out those early woundings in further combative outbursts at some other time and place. Most men who batter their wives were abused as children.

The tragedy of this cycle of abuse has been well documented. Social workers and family counselors deal with the results of early childhood abuse on a regular basis. A sense of fair play or even the threat of law are not deterrents to a man with this history who wants to vent hostility. Divorce seems to justify physical punishment toward the offending wife. Although this kind of physical response may have been dormant for years, it is a behavior that has been learned and is stored for the moment.

If his values are fundamentally distorted. This can be the case without the man exhibiting so-called "antisocial" thinking. In fact, this distortion may be gained by simply taking in all of the media messages that during the years of a man's life come through television, magazines, and the rest.

For instance, much of the media promotes ideas and images of male dominance. Television continually tells the story of the man of action with his docile but attentive woman at his elbow. Whether it is a commercial or a teleplay, women are constantly pictured as window dressing for the real message—it is a male-centered world. The whole idea of woman as a "possession" is encouraged and spread in the multiplication of these media images—she comes with the sports car, with the new suit of clothes, with anything that sells. Women come as neatly packaged and displayed as a product in the drug store.

The reality of a woman acting independently in *her* best interests is a shock to many men. Possessions don't have rights. Objects do not have a will of their own. They can be admired and taken care of, but the thought of them living outside the sphere of the husband's protection is inflammatory—"not *my* wife!"

Divorce and infidelity are often linked together in the man's mind, even when a woman may not have been unfaithful sexually. What is most troubling is that his possession is not under his control. Del Martin, in her book *Battered Wives*, explains, "If he suspects that his wife has a will of her own without actually having proof of her infidelity, the husband may nevertheless suffer a profound insecurity at the *possibility* of her betrayal. If such insecurity invades the man's imagination, he might take pains to prevent *her* from living out *his* fantasies." And if your husband's values include physical violence toward a woman for behavior he doesn't approve of, be wary.

If his self-esteem is low. Again, a person's self-esteem is central to how he sees himself in relation to the world. Often at the time of divorce, things have not only gone poorly in marriage, but also other facets of his life are deteriorating. The hoard of negative events in his life brings out a last ditch effort to recover ground.

A study by John E. O'Brien, *Violence in Divorce-Prone Families*, shows that many men with low self-esteem are more violence-prone in their relationships with their wives. He found a combination of other things working at the time—they were often seriously dissatisfied with their jobs, their income was a source of conflict, they had dropped out of school in their past, they were usually less well-educated than their wives, and they held jobs of lower status than their wife's father.

Check out such items and see if the accumulated weight of his situation is too great for him. When a man sees himself as a loser—then loses his wife—he may make a final attempt to prove his potency through violence.

THE REJECTED HUSBAND

An initial impetus for this book was provided by Dr. Steven Bryant and his study "The Rejected Male." In this work, he outlines the unique factors that are involved in a woman leaving a marriage. Rather than paraphrase his conclusions, he is quoted here directly and at length. In an interview, he summarized his findings as follows.

The typical scenario is this: The woman tells the man she's leaving, but she's going to stick around for a month or two. The man goes to work every day, and every day when he comes home he expects her to have changed her mind. Each day her failure to do this is a new rejection. So what she is doing is piling on top of the rejection of leaving, a new rejection every day based on her failure to change her mind. And so if he wasn't ready to punch her out the day she told him she was leaving, he is getting more and more ready in the next three, four, or five weeks.

It may seem to be a reasonable compromise to stay around for a few weeks to help him get little things straightened out so it won't be quite so traumatic, but I think that is a mistake. That four-week period is fraught with danger. No matter what surface indications there may be of an amicable acceptance on the part of the male, I think that there is a tremendous risk that inside he is seething with resentment and will explode. In other words, he's a time bomb.

I can't see any way that being around is going to do any good, unless your being around can change the things in his life that are bugging him. For instance, if you can stay around long enough to make his business succeed and, therefore, allow him to have a better self-image and so on, that would be fine. But clearly, if that has not happened by now, what chances are there that it's going to happen?

Remember, these are traps. For example, at the time the woman says she is going to leave, the man may make all kinds of promises of changing his ways. So if he has been defective about the way he functions in the outer world, he'll get on the ball and start doing things right. One of the reasons why the woman is leaving will then have disappeared. If he's been an alcoholic, then he's going to stop drinking. If there's been violence in the marriage, then he's going to stop being violent. And it never happens, it just plain never *happens*. The frequency of that kind of reversal is probably so low, that from a woman's point of view, she can neglect the possibility. So the idea of sticking around long enough to patch things up for him in order to make the leaving tolerable—I think that is just ridiculous.

Women compound the problem by being so attached to all the physical things they have accumulated—their worldly possessions. They spend the next month or two with the man simply for the sake of packing up and getting things together, moving furniture, and deciding what belongs to whom, and the whole process is exacerbating. They are worried about comfort and convenience and economics, and what they should be giving actual first priority to is survival. The whole process is just reemphasizing her rejection of him.

There is a danger in familiarity—the woman thinks she knows the man. She feels, "Oh, I can handle it." But this is also a trap, because he is not the same man. After you have told him you are leaving, you are not dealing with the same individual anymore. So whatever predictability his behavior had for you, with reference to how he will react, it is not the same.

What it comes down to is that most women are very poor predictors of their spouse's behavior *under this kind of stress*. Because this type of stress is a discontinuity in the life of the individual. So you might have been perfectly able to predict as to what he would do— what kind of movie he would like, innocent things like that. But that doesn't say that you would be able to predict how he would behave, let's say, in combat. Or how he would react to being tortured in a concentration camp. Now what we have here is an *extreme* situation, that's the thing that's not understood—it *is* extreme. You are looking at a man in extreme.

First of all, separation itself is traumatic. Look at the situation with older people, when one person dies and the other dies several months later. What is that but separation? Now here you're taking a situation where you have separation plus rejection, plus in many cases the rejection being a magnification of his low self-image. One thing is piled on top of another. So what you've got is separation, rejection, and then failure. So you are dealing with a jump discontinuity in the man's life. And that's why the woman's predictions of what he is going to do are off. The guy is in a pressure cooker.

Of course, the specific history of the man gives some clues about the chances of violent behavior. If, for example, the man is an alcoholic, the risk is higher. If the man has a previous history of violence, the risk is higher. If there has been violence in the actual marriage, then of course the risk is greater.

But in our study we found that there are cases of complete surprise, when there was nothing in the past behavior of the male to indicate that he will act violently upon being left by his wife. He nevertheless *does*. There are cases of the perfect husband—a surgeon with no past record of anything—and he comes apart and shoots his wife's attorney.

From everything I have read, I believe there is a ten percent chance of violence if a woman stays around her husband, in the physical proximity of the man over any extended time after she tells him that she is leaving. I can't say that I have solid proof of this, but from the case histories we took and the available literature, I would estimate that the chance of violence is at least ten percent, and could be as high as thirty or forty percent.

Even if you know all of this information, it is very tempting, almost seductive, to feel "I've got one chance out of ten"—like drawing straws. But people who gamble a lot know that one chance in ten is something to be taken seriously. Things that have one chance in ten, a ten percent chance of happening, *do happen*. And one of the problems here is that you don't *know* what the chances are.

Of course, the other thing that he can do is psychologically harass you with an implicit threat of violence, and while it may never actualize, it has the same effect on your nervous system. In fact, it would almost be a relief, in a sense, if he one time punched you and got it over with.

But again, the real cure is complete physical separation.

TELLING HIM

After listening to and analyzing thousands of accounts about the experiences women have when they leave, it is not difficult to ascertain what works and what does not. Of course, *you* must decide the best course of action. But it is with confidence that I pass on the following suggestions, which summarize the information I have gained. Take what is useful to you.

Before You Talk to Him

How to tell your husband begins with the preparation you make before you say, "I'm leaving." You already have given much thought to your divorce. Take more time now to think through the steps you will be taking at this stage. Don't act in haste or out of impatience.

- Ask yourself if it isn't possible to have an amicable divorce. If so, what can *you* do to allow that to happen? The difference may be as much in your *attitude* as your action.
- Don't deliberately create situations that will foster an argument. By now you know what they are. Avoid them; they become an addiction in their own right. Take a look at the arguments that you have had in the past. What was your part in them? Don't make sweeping accusations about him. This is not the time to bring up old resentments.

  I am not asking you to hold in everything. Vent your feelings, but do it with a friend or therapist. Give up trying to win the battle of words.
- Before you tell your husband you are leaving, be sure you have arranged for a place, or several places, to stay temporarily. In case he reacts intensely, you will need to remove yourself from the situation immediately. Check out a friend's house, your family, a shelter, an efficiency-motel apartment. *It is important that you create a backup system for yourself in advance.*
- Ideally there has been some gradual buildup to your announcement of divorce. Most often it is "in the air," so that the topic

is not totally foreign. There have been enough statements like "We can't go on like this" to make divorce at least a possibility. I seriously question that the husband does not have *some* idea that something is going on.

But in some cases leaving is a complete surprise. These situations must be handled with extreme care. The lawyer Sandra Morris says, "One of the worst things I can conceive of is having someone walk up to the door and hand out papers that say, 'Get out of the house; you've lost your wife; you've lost your kids; you've lost your belongings.' I mean, that is a terrible shock. People have *done* things like that." You can't predict behavior when things are done "out of the blue."

The Moment of Truth

Some women are very frightened to tell their husbands they are getting a divorce. Many have been in a traditional relationship, having spent most of their lives deferring to their husbands and subordinating their opinions and needs to that of their spouse. And even if you haven't, it is still one of the very hard experiences in life. When it gets down to telling him, it is easy to be confused.

What should you actually say? That depends. I would suggest keeping it as simple and direct as possible. As Dr. Paul Brenner put it to me in an interview, "What *is* there to say? 'I'm leaving.' " Although it's not *that* simple, the other extreme is to devise a long, involved speech. It is not the time for a full-blown discussion of "what went wrong." After an initial announcement of wanting to leave, the chances are that your husband will not be listening well, and such a discussion can quickly dissolve into making accusations, then name-calling.

I sometimes encourage women to practice the situation beforehand if they are feeling insecure about it. This may seem contrived, but the manner in which this critical event is accomplished can set the tone for your future relationship with your husband. The idea is not to be perfect but simply to be more at ease.

It is best to use "I" messages, rather than "you" messages. "You" messages only invite a hostile response: "I'm leaving because *you* never gave me a chance to grow in the marriage"; "*You* always dominated the conversations"; "*You* gave up on our love life"; "It was *you* who forced me into this decision." Avoid this approach.

Express yourself in the first person, using strong, clear statements—"I want to live alone"; "I really need to be on my own and find my own strength"; "I have changed in the past few years, and I'm not happy in the marriage anymore." Such statements affirm your feelings in a positive way, without being an attack on the man.

Don't use your announcement as a way to hurt him or be vindictive. It will come right back to you in a stronger form. When telling him is also an attack, you can't expect him to say, "Yes, dear, you're right." Cooperation begins by not shattering each other's dignity with hateful arguments and acrimony that could be avoided with some forethought.

Choose a time in the daylight hours, morning preferably, to tell your husband. Psychologically it is a more positive time for people; they are apt to act more rationally. It will give him the entire *day* to think about what you have said, and even afford an opportunity to contact other people if he needs support. Nighttime brings back childhood fears of being alone and frightened.

Ask him to go with you to a somewhat public place, where there is also a good degree of privacy—a park, the beach, walking down a quiet residential street. The desirability of this is obvious. Being in public encourages both of you to be more civilized and react more responsibly than you might in the enclosed privacy of your home. It may be your insurance against an ugly scene and a safer environment in which to get his initial response. Don't tell him when either or both of you are under the influence of alcohol or drugs. That is asking for trouble.

The *worst* place to tell him is in the bedroom, at night. Several studies have shown this as the most common site of violence between a husband and wife. The bedroom is a reminder of all the intimacies you shared. If your sexual relationship together was strong, he now knows it will be ending; if physical intimacy has died, he will likely feel inadequate and frustrated. The bedroom is symbolic of the marriage, and holds real memories of intense emotions.

It is important to meet him as an equal. This may not be as easy for some women as for others. If you have often seen yourself as a victim, the chances are that you will express that to him now. It is a position that invites him to exploit you.

Body language is as telling as verbal language. Don't put yourself in a victim position—that is, in an inferior position in which you must physically look up to him when you talk. Your posture, what you do with your hands, your ability to retain eye contact— all say something about your confidence.

By the nature of it, the meeting with your husband will have tension. But stay in touch with your breathing, and take two or three deep breaths when you feel keyed up. Constricted breathing changes the tone of your voice and cuts off your words. Part of staying out of the victim's role is not sounding like a little girl. An apologetic tone only invites him to pounce on you.

Give your husband reassurances about the children. At this stage he may feel that he is losing everything and his reaction may be to declare his rights as *father* of the children. Acknowledge the continuing importance and necessity of his role as their father. Attempt to make your concern about the children a mutual expression of caring rather than a point of contention. Be clear in your own mind what you want, but do not make the details of custody and visitation rights a major issue now. These can be dealt with in a cooler atmosphere of negotiating.

Afterward

Suggest to your husband that you spend the next few days apart to think about what has happened and to process it. Later you can get together and discuss more permanent living arrangements. If you have children, it would be easier if he were to stay with a friend or at some other location. If he refuses, strongly consider relocating yourself and the children for a short while. In doing so, you will avoid many needless confrontations.

After a few days, it will be necessary to discuss a longer-range living situation. Again, my recommendation is to stay apart. In the best of circumstances, living together is a strain. If you have determined that it would be best for you to stay in the house, then ask him to move out.

Should he offer resistance, suggest that this does not have to be a permanent agreement. The house, and who stays in it, are open to negotiation as part of your settlement. This is a temporary agreement.

One of the drawbacks of staying in the house that you once shared (especially if you jointly own it) is that he probably will claim that it is *his* house. He may have put work into it and it has come to be proof of his success in life. As a result, every time he visits the house to pick up the kids, or whatever, he may experience a new resentment because *he* had to move out; *he* had to find a new place and establish a new routine. It looks to him as if you have had it pretty easy.

From this point onward, how you communicate with your husband will make all the difference. Encourage his sense of self-worth by recognizing it. Acknowledge the difficulty of his position, while giving him information about your needs. For example, if he says to you, "I'm devastated by this—I can't believe you would do this," instead of seeing that as a challenge for rebuttal, allow for his feelings. "I'm sorry that you are hurt," or "I can see that you really are upset by all of this." But also tell your needs: "I have to do this for myself."

Stay clear of getting into major discussions in the house where you both lived. When you meet to discuss things, again, do it in a public place—a restaurant, in a park, at the attorney's office.

Don't create a *new* occasion for anger. Remember, although you are no longer together, psychologically you still have connections that may only gradually dissolve and until they do, the nature of your communication could be erratic. Don't try to prove he's wrong. This isn't an issue you will "win."

See if you can't arrange a cooling off period, a stretch of time in which you both agree to put off discussing the core issues of custody, visitation, property settlements, and financial arrangements. The first few weeks are too full of charged emotions that only make such discussion more upsetting than it has to be. Once you have made a split, don't feel rushed to obtain a final settlement.

If you are seeing another man, even though you are now living separately from your husband, be discreet. That may mean, for instance, not having the other man around when you know that your husband is going to stop by to pick up the kids. In general, it is best to have that person keep a low profile, period. If he spends time with the children, they will probably tell their father. Use your best judgment in this regard. In the first month or so, everything is new and it may be asking too much of your husband to not only accept his rejection, but also his replacement. One woman interviewed spoke of her husband's fury over another man, "sleeping in *my* bed, taking a shower in *my* bathroom, eating at *my* table." This is a reality that he may eventually have to accept, but it's best not to force that on him the first month or two. And it doesn't matter if he's doing the same with another woman—he still may see you as *his* wife.

It is difficult to give specific guidelines in regard to communication with your husband. Some men are more cooperative and easygoing than others. Some good rules of thumb are:

1. Keep contact with him to a minimum, especially at the beginning, both by phone and in person. Most women I have worked with come away in worse shape than when they began the discussion.

2. If he gets off the track with questions like "How can you do this to the kids?" don't get drawn in. Gently but assertively bring the discussion back to the reason why you are meeting, and ignore the barbs. This is a time to bite your tongue.

3. Don't let his negative comments about you get you down. Women leaving are commonly accused of being cold, mean, selfish, rotten, a bitch, and a whore. So don't stick around for the barrage. Leave the room or hang up the phone. Let it be known that you are willing to discuss issues but will not listen to verbal abuse.

4. Some women report being harassed by phone at work, at

home, at all hours of the night. You have to draw the line some-where and pull the plug. Have someone else answer the phone, or get an unlisted number. If these measures don't work, contact your attorney.

5. Be aware that most of his desire to speak to you will be in order to vent old anger and not to negotiate a problem. Whether it is a discussion about the furniture, how to pay the lawyers, or who gets the crystal, the husband will often use the opportunity to say something about a past grievance. Again, let it pass.

6. Advice from lawyer Sandra Morris: "If you get to an impasse where you can't talk to the man, *don't!* There is always the last option, and that is don't talk to him. Let your attorney talk to his attorney."

THE DESPERATION FACTOR

Earlier in the book, the situation was described in which all the factors playing on the life of the woman are in the extreme and when immediate action is called for. If it is a clear matter of physical safety and survival for the woman and children, the sub-tleties and qualifications of the suggestions for leaving must be bypassed, and straightforward action taken. Some husbands are blatantly violent men who will respond to a woman leaving by physically attacking her or the children, not only during the initial announcement but *at any time later.* When all the signs clearly point to that, the only advice that can be given is this: *GET OUT NOW.*

1. *Don't be caught totally unprepared.* Find a place to stay before-hand—another house or apartment of a friend or relative. If that isn't possible or if secrecy is of the utmost importance, check with your local battered women's shelter, Salvation Army, or church-affiliated help service.

2. *Safety is the first priority.* Take every precaution to keep your whereabouts unknown to your husband. Create a physical dis-tance between both of you so that there are no chance meetings with him at the local quick mart. Shelters operate under a rule of secrecy in order to protect the women and children.

If your situation is truly desperate, strongly consider moving to another city, even to another part of the country. It is an initial disruption, but the reward is peace of mind.

3. *Be sure to gather up your important papers and all of your identification.* Get together as much money as you can get, and assess where you can get more if you need it.

Pack enough clothes for you and the children, and put them away where he won't find them. At this point, you can't afford to worry about your furniture or other possessions. That can come later.

4. *Pick a time to leave, and go.* You can leave him a note explaining why you felt compelled to take this kind of action. Reassure him that you will be in contact with him soon, when you feel the situation is stable. You may want to write a letter further explaining your action. It is a good way to communicate rationally and be reasonably sure you are being heard.

You could talk to him on the phone, but if you do, realize that it will be very stressful. Stay calm and in charge. He may try to get you to tell where you are staying by being remorseful. Tell him that you need complete privacy right now but that you will stay in contact if he wants. In the most extreme cases, even this much contact may be unwise.

5. *It is a problem if you have a job and he knows that he can find you there.* Some husbands harass their wives at work with phone calls, appearing there, or following them home. If things get bad, let your employer know and seek out help from your fellow workers. Leave work with someone. If it gets very bad, you may have to change jobs.

6. *If you haven't contacted a lawyer yet, do so now.* It will give you a sense of support, and you will want to check on getting a restraining order. But as any social worker at a shelter will tell you, if a husband is really wanting to be violent it won't stop him. The best protection is keeping your whereabouts secret.

7. *Take some very practical steps.* After you are on your own:

- Keep your doors and windows locked. Get a guard dog, if necessary.

- If possible, don't live alone. Stay with friends, or get a roommate.
- Don't travel alone, especially at night—at least for a while.
- Later on, if your husband is awarded visitation rights for the children, and you have ascertained that it is safe for them to see him, arrange that the children be picked up at a neutral place, away from your house. If you still fear him, have a friend take the kids to him to avoid direct contact.

During my contact with women at the battered women's shelters, the most common reaction of women who had left their husbands was to be unwilling to have *any* contact with them. They were especially fearful that their husbands would use the children in a vicious way.

For instance, one battered wife I interviewed had arranged to meet her husband in a park with her two youngest children (the older ones refused to go). During their meeting, he grabbed the baby and said he was going to take the kids and she would never get them back. She managed to calm him down and get the baby back, but since then has refused to meet with him at all.

Again, so much of this is very individual. Do not underestimate the danger, yet realize that what has just been described are *desperation factors*. Any advice along this line runs the same risk as of a mother telling her daughter not to talk to strangers. It may be good general advice, but in reality personal subjective judgments have to be made.

CLOSURE

To give balance to the chapter, it is necessary to recognize that many couples do not end up in a hateful, alienated place—and many more wish they could find another way. Because of the bitter arguments and damaged feelings, both of you may have become vindictive, unfair, or downright nasty at times in the past few months. The experience may be very uncharacteristic of your normal behavior with others, and it is leaving a rather bad aftertaste. No matter how understandable it may all be, it is a concern that negative conduct can swiftly become habitual.

In addition, some men and women still believe in the worthwhile qualities of their mates, and even though they no longer are husband and wife, they do not want to lose complete contact with them. Yet there seems to be no viable way of healing the wounds without risking that the effort would be mistakenly construed as encouragement towards reconciliation.

Your marriage began with an official, perhaps elaborate, ceremony. I'm not suggesting you end it that way. However, when two persons part after years of being together, it would seem that there could be some manner of leaving other than a slammed door and a muffled curse. What is needed is a method of closing the relationship.

Consider this: If you are *both* willing, set up a meeting with a third person, preferably a psychologist or family counselor, for the purpose of formally ending the relationship. Granted, this would be fruitless if your husband objects. But if you are both convinced that your contact will continue in some form, and it *will* where children are involved, then it is in your mutual interest to exercise good intentions around closure. Even when a couple will have no future connection, such a meeting can serve as a more desirable ending.

First, be very clear with each other that the purpose of it is to wind down the relationship, and is in no way a search for renewed communication toward saving the marriage. This is an essential understanding. What often blocks one of the partners from opening to the other is the fear that any sign of compassion or caring will be mistaken for a change of mind. You can stop being cold when you know that letting down your defensive posture will not mean that you will be taken advantage of.

The session is best when the focus is on an appreciation for each of you as separate individuals now going in different directions. The emphasis is not to rehash the past or figure out what went wrong, or even dwell on the nostalgia of the good old days. But if you can reassure each other of your respect and begin to establish a basis for trust, a bridge to the future can be built.

The key to leaving with less rancor can be summed up in two words—*be generous*. It works best when both of you exercise it. This does not mean that you don't seek out your fair share of what is rightfully yours. It may mean, however, that in the great number of small encounters with each other, you both exercise letting go in areas that are nonessential. Generosity is spiritual as well as practical.

This can be a meeting at which you once more experience each other in a human way. It need not be overly dramatic, simply a civil and warm method of drawing your relationship to a close.

Again, this is an ideal and most couples will be unable to cooperate well enough to effect this kind of closing. You can only do what you can do. Look into yourself to find that strength which has served you so well in your move toward personal freedom and know that you will survive any course of events.

CHAPTER 8

The Children

When I ask women why they did not leave their marriages earlier, a common response is "for the sake of the children." Many women stay in failing marriages several years after they know there is no hope for the relationship. They feel incapable of moving because of the kids. Obviously the entire question of children is charged with emotions that run so deep that to discuss them as just a practical issue to be resolved misses the point. The connection between parents and children touches into biological roots that defy rational explanation.

Yet divorce asks questions and presents problems about the subject that you as a woman may never have had to confront, much less respond to.

- Can I take care of the children's physical and material needs alone?
- How will the role of "father" be filled for the children? Is it necessary?
- What will the psychological impact of divorce do to the children?
- What will the future relationship of my ex-husband, the children, and me be like?

- What if I were to give up custody of the children and pursue a career?
- Will I be carrying all the burdens by myself?

These questions, and more like them, are legitimate and must be faced. Some demands can be put off, but not those involving children. Just as empty stomachs must be fed and dirty diapers changed, the other problems of children don't just go away.

To begin with, although the questions concerning children and divorce are fundamental and weighty, the subject need not be approached with a gravity that assumes disaster. Divorce, as it relates to children, is a serious matter, but it holds positive as well as negative prospects. As with most things in life, the outcome depends on what you bring to the situation and how you handle it.

> One reassurance which modern child psychiatry can offer to parents is that a child can absorb and survive almost any painful experience, if he is sure of his family's love.

This statement by Dr. Louise Despert, in *Children of Divorce*, succinctly sums up almost everything that will follow in this chapter. Whatever trauma life might bring, human love is the healing balm.

Love is fully expressed in the interchange of human activity. For this reason, despite whatever directions might be given, the answer lies in the day-to-day experience of a mother and child actually working out their new lives together. Anita was thirty-five years old when she left her husband and began to live with her two children alone. It was a very difficult separation and she was frightened at first.

> I have never experienced so much emotion in my life as I have during my separation. I have had guilt, anxiety, fear, depression, anger, and failure before in my life, but put all these feelings together all at once and it's a lot harder to handle.
>
> I always considered my relationship with my children very close.

But I have become more than just a mom to them now. We are almost like friends, yet they know their mom is still there. They had to see me at my worst, and they came to my rescue. *They* were the ones consoling me, instead of the other way around. I couldn't believe how much help they were to me emotionally.

But when I grew stronger, they became weaker. Then it was my turn to console. Sometimes they would sit beside me and the three of us would just cry. Not much talking, just a lot of crying. Nothing needed to be said for we knew each other's hurt. We just held each other very close. It was sad but yet very good, because we were seeing each other as human with feelings and caring for one another.

Such accounts are not unusual. Out of each family member's difficulty, a new bonding can take place.

But before the resolution, the problems themselves have to be acknowledged. Every facet of the divorce process has its own set of factors to be understood. "Children in divorce" is especially difficult to discuss because of the complex and very individual nature of parent/child relationships.

Connections

A mother's responsibility and connection starts early, before the child is born. And the duty never lets up. That obligation spreads quickly for the woman from being sole provider of nourishment, to exercise coach, nurse, language teacher, moral guide, and interpreter of the world. Hand in hand with that load comes guilt, because as the responsibilities multiply, so too do the occasions for falling short or failing in them. Parents grow up feeling guilty.

As a mother, your guilt may reach back to prenatal days when you worried about not eating right. After, the guilt came when the baby woke every night and you wanted to sleep, when you didn't have the energy or interest in playing with her, when you got really angry over normal but unruly childhood behavior, when you neglected to take enough time to do all the "right" things. If the kids goof off at school, hit their playmates, steal candy at the store, or later on take drugs, get pregnant, or do whatever adolescents do, the mother, at some level, feels that she is to blame.

Divorce is an automatic source of guilt. Some women imagine it as the ultimate failure of a mother—the abandonment and dismantling of normal family life. The children's welfare is seemingly put in jeopardy by the act of divorce, and a score of feelings come up about that. You may have a general sense of where it is all going, but the security of a fixed married life is now ruptured.

It is a very real dilemma and one that doesn't disappear even after a woman has physically separated from her husband.

Pain

And it will be painful. This is one of the hardest realities for parents to accept—the pain that divorce causes the children. Ordinarily a major part of a mother's time and effort with children has been shielding them from pain—the discomfort of wet diapers or the threat that playing in streets with heavy traffic holds. We also guard them against the more unpleasant realities of life, knowing that those will come in time, but wanting first to create an environment free from physical and psychological suffering.

But no matter how protective you are, there is always pain. The child *does* catch his finger in the door, is tormented by the big kids down the block, has a young playmate with a fatal illness, wakes up crying from bad dreams. Distress is a part of life that cannot be avoided. It is, in fact, inevitable and probably necessary. However, there is also a point at which the mother is *not* responsible for everything that happens in the child's world, and therefore need not feel guilty about it.

As much as we may not wish to admit it, even young children are independent agents in the world, with thoughts and personalities all their own, and abilities to cope with life, even pain. And by this I don't mean mere survival—they can flourish. Human beings are more resilient than we imagine. The good intentions of some mothers to create a pristine world in which everything is pleasant and totally secure has its own stifling effects.

Separation and divorce are painful for everyone involved. There is no getting around it. You may as well admit to this fact and move on to the next step. You feel it as a wife; they do as children. But remember that your separation from your husband did not *begin* the pain. Whatever hurtful things that have been inflicted on the children started in the marriage. Those months or years of hot arguments and cold silences were not lost on them. Jenny's experience is not extreme as she tells what her marriage was doing to her children.

> I had vowed that I would make a good home for them because they were adopted. But we weren't living up to it. My husband and I fought all the time and it was really getting unhealthy. I was a basket case. That's no life for kids. When you have a five-year-old say, "Mommy, don't cry anymore. Please don't cry anymore," and your little boy is saying, "I'm going to hit Daddy if he makes you cry again!" you begin to think about the atmosphere you have been living in. That's when I knew I had to make a decision.

It is difficult to believe that divorce will be more agonizing than such scenes.

Marriage vs. Divorce

In relation to the net effect on your children's lives, you have to ask this question: *By getting a divorce, just what am I breaking up?*

Your children have not been immune to what has been going on around them. Angry voices seep through thin walls and tension cannot be confined to the front seat of an automobile. If divorce has its traumatic elements for children, a destructive marriage has many, many more.

We often go out of our way to give children the best we and the world have to offer—good schools, health care, vacations, nourishment. But their lives are also strongly influenced by the models of behavior that they experience each day in an ailing marriage. Dr. Lee Salk, in his excellent book *What Every Child Would Like Parents to Know About Divorce*, explains.

> A child growing into adulthood in the midst of an unpleasant but intact marriage ends up with a far more negative attitude about

marriage than one whose parents were divorced and then entered into another relationship that was substantially more fulfilling. Your child, seeing you work out the problems of your life, as unpleasant as it may be during the process, also gains the experience of realizing that problems can be solved and that people grow as a result of dealing with them.

For parents to stay in an unhappy relationship is to teach the children that they have no options in life. Ending such a marriage, on the other hand, opens children to the realization that a person is never totally locked into an unchanging and cheerless destiny. It is important for children to know that it is possible to take charge of one's life.

A not untypical remembrance of childhood came from Maria, a woman quoted earlier. Her parents never divorced, but the effect became part of her attitudes.

> I don't ever remember my parents kissing or holding hands or touching very much either. In fact they hardly talked or, if they did, they didn't do it around me. Oh, they talked some at the dinner table, but nothing really interesting. My dad would tell my mom what he did at work that day.
>
> My mom talked to us a lot. She seemed to enjoy being around us and having fun with us. I can remember wondering what love was like when I was little and I remember thinking—you're only in love when you're young; when you get older and you're married, then you just live together, but it's not lovable and fun.

Parents who stay with each other "because of the children," then subject them to the misery of their lives together, are doing a favor to no one. By now, it is almost a cliché to observe that divorce is better for children than continuing in a bad marriage. It's true. More and more, researchers into the subject can show that divorce in itself is not a major cause for emotional upheaval, and certainly is not as harmful as living in a family that is hostile and unloving. A study of 1,800 delinquent children found that only one tenth of the delinquent boys and one fifth of similar girls came from homes in which parents are divorced. Most of the children came from homes that weren't broken, but in which the parents were badly maladjusted. Again, Dr. Louise Despert says,

> It is not divorce, but the emotional situation in the home, with or without divorce, that is the determining factor in a child's adjustment. A child is very disturbed when the relationship between his parents is very disturbed.

This disturbance sometimes shows up on a physical level with children. Interviewing professionals on this subject, I was concerned about how divorce might affect a child's health. Certainly stress can take its toll on children as well as adults, and I could imagine any number of physical illnesses stemming from it. When I asked Dr. Paul Brenner, an obstetrician and gynecologist, about whether children get sick after their parents break up, he answered, "Sure. But a lot of children who have chronic illnesses get well too. It is very common, super common. A lot of illness in children is *cured* by divorce. And they also get well emotionally."

Your fear of what divorce means to children could be saying more about you than them. If, for example, your parents had a poor relationship, you may be repeating the pattern in your life. The answer may not be in staying together. The cycle could simply be repeating itself. Antonia was in such a situation, sticking with a nine-year marriage for her two girls' sake, but remembering the damage her parents had done to her. Fortunately, she had a friend with good advice.

> My friend said to me, "Hey, look at what you're doing here! Do you think that you're giving the kids something when they are around this situation? You are doing the same thing your parents did to you. By walking away from it, you're *giving* them a chance. You're not taking anything away; you're *giving* them a chance." He just kept repeating that advice to me and I finally realized it was true.

The message that comes through again and again is that as hard as divorce is for everyone involved, it is not as permanently damaging as staying with a marriage that is intolerable.

Before the Break

The parents' sensitivity toward the children's emotional state needs to start long before the actual separation of husband and wife. The children share in the negative atmosphere created in the months or years that preceded the break, and they witness much more than you might imagine.

Often husbands and wives are so engrossed in their private anxieties about divorce that they neglect giving attention to the emotional life of their children. Even if there are no fights in front of them, children are terribly aware of even slight shifts in the temperament of parents. Complicating things, parents usually try to cover up what is going on. Children know better and respond in a variety of troubled ways, depending on their age. Whatever the behavior, what is behind it is anger and fear. A parent may wish to attribute the distress to a stage of development the child is going through, but it is more than that. Dr. Lee Salk comments:

> I cannot tell you how many young patients I have seen whose parents had tried to protect them from knowing about their marital discord. Invariably these children suffered from increased anxiety. They reacted subconsciously to their parents' marital problems and had to bear the burden in silence. A child whose parents are open and frank feels far less responsible for family problems than the child whose parents conceal the gravity of the situation. There is no human way human beings of any age can be fooled over a long period of time into believing that a tense situation is anything other than a tense situation.

It is not necessary to tell the children that you are considering a divorce in the first stages of decision-making. You may not be sure yourself of what will happen, and it would be unfair to burden the children with the fluctuations of the process. But it would be helpful to them if you *acknowledge* that you and your husband are not getting along, and that you are doing your best to work it out.

As in every case, much of what you say depends on the age of the children. You don't have to analyze the problems in detail.

But be as honest as you can with them. Rather than shutting them out, draw them to you so that they can at least balance what they are sensing with the security of your personal caring for them.

This period, even more than the actual breakup, is a time that parents most often look back upon with regret concerning the children because, although nothing was yet out in the open, a great deal of unspoken suffering was going on. Involve your husband in reassuring the children of your mutual love for them.

TELLING THE CHILDREN

Meeting with the children is a difficult moment. The situation can be more easily handled if you have your husband's cooperation, if he joins you in telling the children. By doing this, the children are presented with the fact that *both* of you are acting in normal, caring parental roles. It also discourages the children from doing two things: creating a fantasy that they might be able to get the parents back together again or playing one parent against the other. In showing that together you have arrived at a decision, the children are encouraged to accept the attitude and spirit you bring to the meeting.

You may be tempted to put off telling them of your divorce for fear of upsetting them. However, your delay may only result in blowing the situation even more out of proportion, making it seem more frightening than it is, and inviting misinterpretation of what the consequences will be.

Discuss with your husband beforehand what you will be saying to the kids, just how you both want to explain what is occurring. It may be hard to be in agreement on what you both feel comfortable telling the children, but find out if there isn't some common ground that will make sense to them and not misrepresent your position. If you cannot agree on what to say, at least indicate to the children that you and your husband want to do what is best for them, given the circumstances. The main thing is that neither of you openly express hostility toward each other during the meeting with the children, if at all possible.

Set aside a quiet time and place where you can be sure that the meeting will not be interrupted. Early in the day is probably the best time, as it affords the children time to think over things and to talk with you more if they wish.

Your *attitude* is more important than your words. If you are talking to them from a personally secure position, it will come across and they will feel confident in you. Choose a day when you feel stable. If need be, meditate or give yourself a tranquil period to get in touch with your strength. Strength here does not mean a lack of emotions. Being "strong" is not the same as being stoic. It is believing that it is OK to have the feelings you do, and the courage to express them. Despite whatever happens, they will learn that you are going to be a constant in their lives.

Sit close to them, within arm's reach so that you can be physically expressive and consoling to them. The way in which you are physically present with them is indicative. Some children may want to be held. Be open to what is needed at that moment.

What you actually tell the children will vary greatly depending on the ages of the children. Needless to say, how and what you tell a five-year-old will not be the same as a ten-year-old, and different again for a fifteen-year-old. But age is not the only factor. Every child is an individual with a special temperament and sensitivity, and only you can judge how to translate the events of your current life to her or him. Moreover, you may relate differently to each child.

Therefore, any advice in regard to what you could say has to be quite general, with the hope that you will find some of the ideas that follow useful and be able to apply them. For instance, if you have children of widely varied ages—four- and six-year-olds and a thirteen-year-old—it might be better to talk to the older one alone first, and then the younger ones. In attempting to discuss the issue with them all at one time, you would probably end up talking over the heads of the small children, or in a childish way to the teen-ager. Later, it would be good to bring them together to discuss things as a family.

It's hard to find the words. There is no single way to say anything. For the most part, keep it simple. Try on some of the following ideas and see if they correspond to your situation.

- It is good to confirm to the children what they already know—that the two of you haven't been getting along. Say to the children that they may have noticed that you and their father have not been happy lately. The arguments and bad temper that they have experienced are signs of this.
- Be straightforward and calm. Talk to them about your original hopes and dreams, that both of you had ideas about life and marriage which seemed to be the same. But after years of marriage, it just hasn't worked out the way you thought it would. You and their father have changed and grown in many ways and now realize that you want very different things in life.
- Some parents may want to acknowledge that they have made mistakes in judgment, especially in the way each of them dealt with their differences. It is healthy for kids to know that parents are not perfect. You will have to decide whether this is the right time for you to bring this up.
- "Rather than go on like this, we have decided to get a divorce, which means Mom and Dad won't be living together. We both love you very much, and just because we're not in the same house doesn't mean that we don't love you every bit as much as we always have. I will always be your mother and Dad will always be your father. That never changes. We will be there for you when you need either of us."
- Tell them that just because you and their father have not been getting along does not mean that they have to take sides. It is all right to love both of you equally, and they should feel free to express that love.
- Be ready to listen to *them*. Don't feel that it is necessary for you to get through this meeting quickly, and in the process cut off the children's responses. Let them come out with questions, fears, even accusations. They may need to express these things and get validation for their feelings. Let them know that you will listen to them, both now and later, that you will be available to them when they need you. Some children will have trouble

speaking up, which is not to say they have nothing going on inside. Others will not really *hear* what you have been saying about divorce, unconsciously blocking out that reality. Be patient; make your points clearly and slowly, sensitive to their reactions.

A Hostile Husband

Your husband may be unwilling to participate in such a meeting. He might be angry, depressed, resentful, or simply too upset. Or if he is extremely overwrought, you might decide that the meeting could work out better if you didn't meet with the children jointly. You don't want this very important and sensitive family meeting to be an encounter which dissolves into just another round of blaming, tension, and tears. Wild criticism and denunciation—"Your mother is ruining our lives!"—is totally out of place here and can be devastating to everyone involved. *There is absolutely no reason to leave permanent scars for the sake of trying to create an "ideal" situation.* If you believe this could happen, go ahead with the meeting by yourself.

Later on, at a more reflective time, explain your husband's reactions as best you can to the children. In a frank manner—without derogatory inferences—you might enlist their understanding for what is going on with their dad, if that situation applies.

Bleema Moss, divorce counselor and child custody mediator, suggests the following:

> There is a fine line here between explaining to the children what has happened to their dad and maligning their father. It's a good idea to talk to the kids and explain things, but try to be as factual as possible: "You know, the reason I left Daddy was because of problems that Daddy and I had, they don't have anything to do with you. Daddy's very angry with Mommy for making that decision. He might say some things to you that make you uncomfortable—things about me—and I want you to come and talk to me about it whenever that happens and I'll try to tell you what I think. You might hear two

different things from Daddy and I. As you get older, you'll decide for yourself what you think."

This gives them the right to make up their own mind, and the right *not* to decide that you're right and their father is wrong. It also helps them understand that there are two sides to every story.

Don't use this time to make negative remarks about him, no matter how angry you are. It may be hard, but your children don't need any more negative input. They are very perceptive. If your husband has acted poorly and done undesirable things, they have been aware of it and will make sense of what you are saying.

Dr. Lee Salk warns of the other extreme.

> I am not suggesting you be dishonest or "whitewash" your spouse. Your child would only become more confused and find it difficult to deal effectively with his own feelings. I have known some parents who have even referred to their spouse in glowing terms in an effort to ease the child's apprehensions. This simply does not work. It serves to weaken your own credibility.

Again, unless you and your husband can come together in *some* harmony concerning the children, it is better to tell them in your own way, alone.

CHILDREN'S FEARS

Earlier in this book, the woman's emotional response to divorce was considered. Children have their own set of psychological problems. The range is just as great, but the nature of their distress is often subtle and easily missed by parents, either because children can't articulate their feelings in adult terms, or their parents are simply not listening.

It's really my fault. Almost all authorities on children and divorce agree on this point—that a major fear of children is that *they* were the cause of their parents' divorce. It is surprising to most parents when they discover the depth of the child's concern about this. In that regard, Earl A. Grollman, in his book *Talking About Divorce*, writes:

> The child may believe that he must be responsible for the separation. After all, in his limited experience, unfortunate things happen when he is naughty. So he searches for the terrible act that caused the breakup. To him, divorce must be some punishment for wrongdoing. An unreasoning guilt drives him into self-pity and even self-punishment.

No matter how far this fear is from the fact of the matter, the child often has misinterpreted the overheard fights between the parents when his or her name was mentioned. The argument might have been about schooling, habits of television watching, or general behavior. The child may have been the visible point of contention, but the real source of conflict between husband and wife was much more personal and hidden. The child, however, only takes such things at face value and concludes that he himself is at fault.

The punishment for the child, as well as the adult, is guilt. It can be a terrific burden if the child or children are not able to express their deep concern about this. The children feel powerless to prevent the divorce process and anger often follows guilt. The close nature of family life has entangled them equally in the affairs of the parents.

The late Jerry Lynch, an outstanding family consultant and author of mental health programs here and in Mexico, explained in an interview a condition in which the children find themselves.

> A family is a set of triangles—interconnecting triangles—and everybody is involved and everybody is participating all the time. The child is usually used as a subtle communication device between the parents, positively and negatively, but often negatively. So that a lot of messages are directed at the child that are meant for the other partner. In a divorce, what you have to do is clean up that kind of communication between parents, so that the communication is direct.
>
> Some kids become the "shit screen" in the family. They are the ones who get the blame for whatever has gone wrong with the

dynamics between adults. So that when two legs of the triangle split apart, the third leg—the child—is bound to feel responsible or guilty. That's inevitable. It's just one of those things that happen.

The parents must be very clear in their messages to the children that whatever is happening, in terms of conflict between the adults, is not the fault or the problem of any child, and that the child is not a cause of what is going on.

Children will have to be reassured of this not only at the time of the first announcement, but periodically afterward. It may not be appropriate to broach the subject with the flat statement "you're not guilty," but certainly make it known that you both love them, and by positive reinforcement dispel the fear that their conduct in any way caused the divorce.

Who is going to take care of me? The fear of abandonment is a very early survival issue for most children, and it can become greatly exaggerated at the time of divorce. As Dr. Nicholas Putnam, professor of clinical psychiatry at UCSD Medical School, says, "Little children especially have this fear. If the parents can stop loving each other, maybe they can stop loving the child." Often during the divorce process, simply because of the press of events, the children's needs are neglected.

The fantasy world of children is sometimes a shadowy and haunted place. Many children who before the divorce were never upset when left with a babysitter suddenly get very apprehensive, worried that their worst fears will be realized. Being left at night becomes a type of abandonment in their eyes.

The children must be given the time and opportunities to regain the confidence that they had in their relationship with you. In the meantime, reassure them but don't overreact to their fear.

What will my friends say? We think that such worries are reserved for the parents, but many children are embarrassed and ashamed of divorce. They fear being ridiculed or even ostracized by their friends.

A woman I know found that her boy was having this problem.

It seems that some function came up at school and the teacher asked the children if their fathers could help out. The boy was downcast because his parents were divorced and his father was two states away. He didn't want to publicly explain this for fear that others would make fun of him. After she brought the problem to his teacher, school time was set aside to openly discuss the family situations of the class members. It turned out that ten other children in class had parents who were divorced. In fact, this was true of the boy's best friend at school.

The whole question may be too sensitive to discuss with the children right now, but it is safe to assume that many of them may be troubled by the social aspects of divorce.

What's going to happen now? Children, like adults, fear the unknown. The world and its future are, at best, a very great mystery to them. Because they depend on you to interpret much of it for them, there is also the fear that you are not letting them know the full truth. You might be holding back some awful news.

Children can be super-worriers, picking up on every anxiety around them and becoming enveloped in it. Their questions reflect these worries—"Where will we live?" "Will we have to move?" "How will we manage without Dad?" "Are you sure we're going to stay together?" Or the concern may be for the parent who is not living with them—"Will Dad have a place to stay?" "Who will fix his meals and do his laundry?" "Is he lonely?" For every answer, they think up two more questions. It is important to see how they are projecting their own insecurity in their concern for others. Their need is as much for reassurance as it is for answers.

On the other hand, children do need straight information. Bleema Moss observes,

> One of the biggest mistakes parents make is thinking that when a child is not asking questions or showing obvious problems, the kid must be doing fine and there is nothing to talk about. What you need to understand is that children repress their emotions, they don't talk about things because they sense you don't want them to. In the meantime, they have their feelings and they have their

questions. Some information is better than no information, except when it is explicitly hurtful.

Children need the security of reliable information. It allows them to regain a sense of structure and control in their lives.

CHILDREN'S REACTIONS

Behavior of kids is never easy to anticipate, especially during and after divorce. A few children seem unaffected and appear to take it in stride; others are confused and show it in everyday conduct and conversation. Many children do not verbally articulate feelings and thoughts. With younger children, it may simply be that they are unable to put into words the clash of emotions going on inside, whereas older children may be just too frustrated and angry to be coherent, and instead they fall silent. But rather than depending on what they *say*, it is better to look at what they *do*.

Whatever the children's ages, a radical change in their life will effect some kind of observable behavior change. This is normal and to be expected. It happens at other stress points in a child's life—when a new baby is born into the family, when the family moves to another city, if a family member dies, even the loss of a treasured and loved pet. And it certainly happens in the strain of divorce.

Naturally, the gravity of the response is measured by its intensity and duration, but what follows is a brief description of behavior that children often express during the process of divorce. The drama of it may range from being mildly disquieting to vehemently antisocial. In a broad sense, it is their attempt to communicate, to say something about what is happening. It is important to know what to look for.

Nervous, Anxious, Agitated Behavior

Sometimes the small things children do reveal what is going on inside. Restlessness, tense laughter, faster speech, and nail-biting are all signs that the level of nervous energy is on the rise. You can usually see and hear when a child is emotionally uncomfortable.

It may come in reports from the teacher that your ten-year-old son is having a hard time concentrating and is distracting the class with his uncontrolled talking. At home, he may ask a lot of worried questions, many having to do with the home or well-being of the family. The crisis is translated into fantasy: "What would happen if there was a tornado and it hit this house?" and they often go on to elaborately explain how they would save everyone.

Kids can get very demanding and anxious over the thought of losing you. Your older children complain that you didn't return home at the exact time you promised; a formerly secure five-year-old now cries when you leave her with a baby-sitter; even infants may become cranky and fitful or wake at odd hours and will not be easily pacified.

These actions are hard to deal with because no one of them is momentous and they may not *all* stem from the divorce. Yet as this behavior escalates, it can become a cause of concern for you.

Timidity and Hesitancy

Whereas the family tends to form a base of security for children, they often react by being less expressive and outgoing when that is threatened. The response is a subtle one and may only be sporadic for some children. A daughter may be more reluctant to stand up and recite in the classroom or be somewhat more timid in her relations with others after school. It may take the form of self-questioning in situations that before were comfortable. You might notice that your preschooler is less exuberant, more hesitant when meeting a stranger.

Some of this is to be expected. This is a time for the child to pull back a little, check out his world, and test the water again. Don't become overly concerned unless the problem intensifies.

Depression and Withdrawal

Offhand, it is hard to imagine a depressed four-year-old. We tend to think of depression as an adult experience. But if, as defined earlier, it is caused by a mix of unexpressed anger, sadness, and fear, then it is easy to see how young persons with an inability to adequately relate these feelings can withdraw and be depressed. What is sad about it is that they don't seem to have much choice.

Some children slide into it almost without notice. Instead of looking *at* the TV, they are looking *through* it. A zest for life is gone. A boy might lose his enthusiasm for playing on the baseball team. A young girl may spend more time by herself in her room. Change in appetite commonly accompanies this. If communication between parent and child was bad, at this point it becomes even worse. You may find yourself confronting an expressionless face that offers no way in.

But don't confuse this lack of energy with a state of no feeling. A depressed child is experiencing very powerful emotions that are, for the time being, locked up.

Despite this, a certain degree of withdrawal is not necessarily a bad thing. It may merely be the child's way of coping with a crisis. An introspective period of reflection and quiet may be just what the young person needs to recover equilibrium. Jerry Lynch comments, "Withdrawing is often an attempt to achieve a safe and sheltered place within. It is a kind of protection from allowing intervention from outside. A painful situation can wound a child so deeply that they will shut up, just to keep the world out and retreat."

As with the rest of the reactions, it is a question of severity.

Dependency and Regression

You may find that your six-year-old won't go out and play with the kids down the block after school, and instead stays in the house to follow you around. This clinging behavior can be annoying, but it is obvious that the child is feeling insecure and is attempting to find safety in close contact. But nothing seems to be enough; the simplest obstacles set off whining and expressions of helplessness. Older kids get into this too. Your teen-age daughter may become overly dependent on you and insist that you go shopping with her for shoes, an activity that before she was only too delighted to do alone.

Whereas dependency is bothersome, regressive behavior is confounding to parents. A preschooler, for example, may resort to baby talk, thumb-sucking, carrying her favorite blanket, or even wanting a bottle again. It is hard to ignore this kind of thing, and yet it should be recognized for what it is—an emotional panic to recapture a former time in the child's life when things were different and felt secure. In many ways it is a logical response and if the parent does not overly react and give it undue negative attention, it will pass.

This is sometimes difficult because other children see what is happening and make negative remarks. Quiet their comments by explaining the regressing child is needing to do that right now. "It helps her feel better. When she's ready, and doesn't need to be little anymore, she will stop."

In the meantime, reassure the child in an unrushed, mild manner. If the behavior is prolonged, see about getting professional help.

Hostile and Aggressive Behavior

One of the ways a child responds to being hurt is hurting back. The behavior may be quite uncharacteristic and cause you no end of apprehension. Your boy starts a fight with another kid during lunchtime at school and then is defiant to the teacher who takes him to the office. Your daughter picks on her younger sister, teasing her until she cries. A child's hostility can permeate a household, whether it takes the form of nasty remarks about the dinner you've cooked or belligerent back talk when asked about housework.

Often the antagonism has nothing to do with the issue at hand but clearly says something about the waves of confusion beneath. Despite the fact that you sense this, it is hard not to be drawn into responding with an equally aggressive edge. Very soon, the whole cycle of behavior becomes a drain on everyone caught in it.

A couple of things to remember: Some children take out their hostility on the parent they see as being at fault in the divorce. Then again, sometimes that aggression is directed at the parent with whom the child *feels most secure*, because they are not afraid of losing affection there. So that just because you may feel you are catching the brunt of crummy behavior doesn't mean you are hated by your children. You may be the safest target for the pain they are feeling.

That knowledge may not make life much easier, however, and you must set limits. Be firm and clear about what is acceptable behavior, even while letting it be known that you understand and recognize their anger. Help your children find ways to express what is going on inside and do it in ways that are not hurtful to others. Professional counseling, direct parental guidance, or simply making it OK for the child to cry may offer relief.

Anger

There is a distinct difference between expressed anger and the hostile, aggressive behavior just mentioned. When parents break up, a natural reaction of children is sadness and perhaps fear. Anger is there, too. After all, from their point of view, you and their father have suddenly changed the structure of *their* lives. They were probably not consulted, but simply caught up in it. The frustration comes from their helplessness in the situation.

It is healthy for them to express this anger, and you can help your children do it. Before it gets buried and turns into resentment, provide a nonjudgmental atmosphere of acceptance in which your children feel free to release whatever is going on inside. It may be that the anger will come out directly against you, but in the long run it is better to have this direct communication, even if it is impassioned at times.

Denial

Some children attempt to avoid the pain of divorce by denying the reality of it. They simply tune out the part of life that they feel incapable of handling. It is as if they are saying, "If I pretend it isn't happening, it will go away." Over the past months they may have learned how to effectively block the unpleasant things around them. When the subject of the divorce is brought up by parents or other family members, they shut down and acknowledge little or nothing in their verbal or physical response.

Initially, denial is a very human reaction to undesired change, and it is not necessarily negative. It is a method of buying time, the child giving himself or herself a more gradual opportunity to absorb and understand what is taking place. Again, patience is the most valuable asset you have right now.

Change in Health

A most common way of dealing with a stressful situation, both for adults and children, is to get sick. Don't be surprised if kids complain of stomachaches, headaches, or if they get a cold, nausea, or diarrhea. Sickness naturally causes genuine concern for a parent. It also creates a lot of guilt in her.

Some children become aware of their influence and get sick in the hope of drawing the parents together in their common worry about them. It is their way of staving off what is taking place. The attention also brings with it the nurturing that children associate with safer, more secure times.

It is always, for a parent, a question of how to give real health care and yet not fall into the whole syndrome of indulging the child's manipulation through illness. It is a matter of balance. As Dr. Putnam says, "With divorce, kids tend to be hypochondriacs. It's their way of asking for more attention and caring."

He goes on to recommend that you let them play it out a little, even if it means taking them to the doctor. It will make them feel better.

All of this may sound a bit overwhelming. At times children only have shadings of any one of these reactions. If you know what to expect, you can deal with it more confidently.

SOME RECOMMENDATIONS

There *are* some things you can do. Keep in mind that you are not dealing with a situation that lends itself to a perfect solution.

There will be some loose ends and pockets of resistance. But if you communicate your genuine love for your children and concern for their well-being, you can begin to re-create a base of security. It is a complex time of life, but probably not as hard as we make it. The following are simple yet often overlooked ways to make fruitful contact with your children.

Listening

Listening to your children is one of the most valuable things that you can do right now. Simply listen. Children should know right from the beginning that: a) You understand that they have a mixture of feelings and probably have a lot of questions about the divorce and their future, and b) You are willing and available to spend time with them talking about these things.

Like all of us, children want to be able to talk about a problem without someone giving them advice. They want to have time to vent their feelings. Listening to themselves talk out loud often provides whatever answer is needed. In his counseling of parents, Jerry Lynch stressed the importance of listening.

> Helping children starts with *listening* to them. A lot of things are done *for* children without stopping to ask, "Do you want this done for you?" or "What do you want?"
>
> And there are stages of listening. You have to be able to first be quiet around children long enough for them to feel free to say these things. A lot of parents assume they are listening when they are actually asking questions. Usually it's best to not ask questions at all. Be quiet and nonverbally open up to the child, saying with your body, "I'm going to hear you for a long period of time." The child will talk and tell you things.
>
> But children don't trust questions. They feel manipulated by them and trapped. So I wouldn't assume I was listening to a child if I asked him a lot of questions.

If you are willing and able, let your children know that you want to hear how they feel about the divorce. And don't be afraid of what they have to say. Many parents don't really want to know about their children's anger or disapproval and they communicate this to them in one way or another. They may accept sadness but indicate that anger has to be taken elsewhere.

If you agree to listen, do it without imposing your values on the child. This is not to say you agree with the way the child is interpreting what is happening, but an immediate critical or judgmental response, whether verbal or nonverbal, will only discourage openness. Remember that the child's world is changing almost as drastically as yours, only he doesn't have any control over it. It may be difficult for you to stay open to complaints, especially when they feed into your guilt. If this is happening and it is proving to be a strain, ask a sympathetic friend or relative to help you in providing a safe outlet for the children's feelings.

Children also need to be able to cry and know that it is all right. It may be hard for older children, and even the younger ones sometimes hold back because they aren't quite sure what it is they are crying about. Patricia had four-and-a-half-year-old twins when she was at this stage of her separation, and the girl, Avia, would get very upset about the things happening around her.

> The twins were bothered by it, especially Avia. She'd see me crying and she'd get upset. I did what I could to comfort her—I'd hold her and explain to her that I was OK—that the problems would go away. And I told her that I was sad, and she talked about being sad, and I'd just hold her and let her cry.

Out of this kind of shared experience new bonds of love can be made. Parents have the opportunity to show children new ways of working things out, but they must be willing to risk as much as the child. Such openness can last long after the pain disappears.

Don't be overanxious about always being there at the right moment for the kids. Trust that, in general, they can take care of themselves and let them sense the confidence you have in them. There is a trap in "fishbowling" them—watching their every move for signs of disturbance. Neither you nor your children are acting normal under those circumstances.

However, be available for them. Parents often have the best

intentions about getting together with their kids but never manage to set up specific times to do it. Instead, they rely on chance—perhaps they might talk during a drive to the supermarket or while doing dishes. A good conversational interchange is best ensured when adequate time and a place are made available.

Set aside periods several times a week that you will give exclusively to talking with your children. It doesn't have to be more than fifteen or twenty minutes, but it should be reserved just for that purpose. A good time might be just before or after dinner, or maybe at bedtime. Find a place in the house that is comfortable and let them know that they have, for a definite period of time, your undivided attention—no phone calls or other interruptions. This brief coming together will have more beneficial results than hours spent taking them to movies. With infants and toddlers, it may simply mean relaxing with them each day, reading a book, or talking to them in a soothing voice while holding them.

When children know that they can count on your being there and listening to them, for even a short time, it provides a secure center. It can also be a graphic example of what your future can become.

Accent the Positive

Every new set of circumstances has good and bad parts to it. Without being blindly sanguine, stress to your children the bright side of their future. Choose positive things to talk about, the stable, continuing aspects of their life—that they will be in the same house, have their same friends, be at the same school.

If this is not the case, give them a sense of adventure and excitement about their new life. One of the hardest things to do, for instance, is to explain to children the nature of what life will be like after the separation. The attitude you bring to this will greatly influence the way your children respond.

Patricia had to tell her twins about their new living arrangements and found a simple, optimistic way.

We told the kids that Dad was going to live in his own house, separate from Mom's. And we played up the positive side of it—that instead of having one house, now they would have *two*. Dad would live in one house and I would live in the other. You know they were only four-and-a-half and it was pretty hard to explain much to them. They seemed fine about the idea. They loved going over to Dick's and staying overnight. He got a place only about a mile away, so for a while they even forgot he didn't live with them anymore because they would see him so much. I moved later, but the transition was pretty smooth.

With older children you have to be more frank, and yet there are reassuring things to be said in almost every situation. This is not being phony. But being realistic does not require that you be gloomy. Change can be frightening enough in itself, but if you treat it with some lightness and good spirit, the children will see a model they may choose to follow.

Seeing a Counselor

I don't recommend that you run to a therapist the minute something goes amiss, without trusting your intuition and judgment and without giving it time to work out. You know your children better than anyone, and you know your situation. But because of the intense nature of what is going on, children and parents often need some help talking about divorce and sorting out everything that stems from it.

If the child's reactions are excessive, or of long duration, consider seeking professional help. Some children just aren't able to speak openly with their parents yet. Still, their need to express a storehouse of thoughts and feelings is strong. Explain to the child that the therapist knows how to listen and talk to kids, and that this person is one that he can count on. Sometimes child psychologists can act as an advocate or mediator for the child, helping him let out the confusion and desires that otherwise would have no coherent outlet.

Other Things That Help

- *Inform the teachers at school of your divorce and also check on how the kids are doing.* Explain the changes in your home life and ask for the teacher's support and patience with the children. Often attitudes and feelings that are hidden at home are played out in the classroom. A sensitive teacher can be a great help in providing additional attention to the needs of your child during the trying months that follow divorce. Most teachers will appreciate your thoughtfulness in exchanging this information.

- *Make sure your kids eat well and get plenty of rest.* The extra strain that these events cause must be taken into account, and children may need extra sleep. Their diet may also suffer at this time. Proper nourishment is the bottom line in terms of both mental and physical health. If you find yourself on a new daily schedule, it is sometimes easy to let your children's routine slide. Watch out that you don't, for the sake of convenience, get into the fast-food habit. It may save time but because of the high sugar content in such food, you may find yourself exhausted from the hyperactivity of the kids afterward. You are doing them a great favor by staying with a healthy diet.

- *Don't make promises that you can't keep.* In an attempt to compensate for your part in the divorce, you may be tempted to exaggerate the future—how you will be spending all kinds of time together doing fun things. Realistically, you may find that you have even less time for those things than before. And by promising more than you can deliver, you are setting yourself up for more guilt by not giving your children what they have come to expect.

- *Be ready to admit that you don't have all the answers.* It's OK for the kids to know that. You can simply say, "I don't know what's going to happen about this or that, and I'll let you know when I do." You can say this without appearing to be weak and directionless. The idea is to bring them closer to an honest assessment of what is happening and still retain their confidence and respect.

- *Don't be afraid to enlist the aid of aunts, uncles, grandparents, a family doctor, or clergyman for their support and guidance.* They may be able to give the kind of help the children need but you are unable to provide right now. Sometimes an uncle can be a temporary stand-in for the loss of a male that the children are feeling in their life. Such caring can give children an umbrella of security to live under during this transition.

- *Set up some playful ways for your children to get rid of their anger and aggression.* One woman told me of getting an old canvas laundry bag, filling it with rags, and hanging it from the rafters of her garage. The kids used it as a punching bag. When they would get mad, she'd send them off with the bag. They usually came back smiling. Let them blow off steam. In the car at the end of long trips, we used to let the kids take three minutes to scream and yell, just to work off the stifling effects of the drive. It was chaotic for a few minutes, but it was also fun and a relative peace followed. They could use such tactics now to release tension.

- *Everybody needs a day off.* Don't be afraid to give your kids a "mental health holiday" from school. It's better than their manufacturing an illness to get away. If you can, arrange some time with them that day. It doesn't have to be elaborate. Eating popcorn and going for a walk in an interesting place may be all that is needed.

Time to Adjust

In general, what the children need from you is understanding, comfort, patience, and enough time.

You have already had months, perhaps years, to adjust to the idea of a divorce. And even though it was your idea, it was still very, very hard. Your children also need time to accept and work through all of the implications of divorce. The pace at which this will happen is impossible to predict, and it will probably be erratic. Four children may react in four different ways. There may also be delayed behavior or abrupt turnarounds. Again, remember that they are separate individuals from you—you are *not* responsible for everything.

Whereas your sensitivity to their emotional state is important, you have to believe and trust that time will heal. Human nature is extremely adaptive.

The questions about divorce are not going to end after the initial announcement of it. There will be further testing and inquiries. They are sincere usually, but children can also use situations for their own purposes. If a child feels that in the past you have been unfair in some way, he may take advantage now to even the score. Keep this in mind.

Think ahead. A year from now, your children will have incorporated the changes into their life. Whatever the divorce meant to them will be a part of life and they will handle it. Most likely the situation will be better than the one they had in the past, simply because they will no longer be caught in the endless struggle of their parents.

THE DESPERATION FACTOR

Emergency situations have been discussed earlier in the book. In these cases, your options are limited. Because of the potential of physical or extreme mental abuse from your husband, any subtleties or gradual revelations about your desire to leave are curtailed. You have to move and move fast.

When it comes to the kids, this presents special problems. All of the precautions and preparations described previously still hold. But children make the process especially difficult because you must deal with their sensitivities regarding their father. On the one hand, you may not like acting in what seem to be arbitrary and unnecessarily secretive ways; on the other, you need to protect yourself and the children. If, for instance, you were to tell the children about your plans for leaving several days ahead of time, or even a few hours, they might divulge that information to your husband, directly or indirectly. This could lead to a blowup involving the entire family and become a very dangerous situation.

Afterward

Emergencies are a part of life, and in the end you may have to rely on your wits. Fortunately most of us are survivors and manage to make it through. Getting your children out of the house under the intimidation of a hostile husband and retaining a semblance of normalcy for the children is a challenge—don't expect too much of yourself.

Still, there is the problem of explaining your actions to the children. They may be fairly bewildered by the sudden change in their life and be wondering what it is all about.

Again, it's not easy to recommend an all-encompassing formula of what to say, but Dr. Nicholas Putnam has witnessed this dilemma quite often in his practice and his suggestions make sense.

> These kinds of relationships have constituted a real danger for the woman and her children. Therefore the woman should be able to say to herself and the children, "This situation was dangerous, was frightening, and I had to do this. And I know that it's very hard for you not seeing your dad." The two things she should make clear repeatedly are, first, that there was a danger and that his behavior was unacceptable and she couldn't tolerate it; and, second, that the children be reassured that when it is safe, they will be given access to their father. But she is not sure at this time when that will be. That's something that she is going to get some help with and she'll be talking to them about, but it may be a long time.

Unfortunately there is not much more you can do or say at this time, given the extreme nature of your position. It is not an ideal situation and there are no ideal solutions. However, despite the shock, your children are well aware of the fury in the relationship with your husband. They may be more accepting of your action than you might suspect. In fact, many children are relieved and thankful.

Some Further Points

- You may feel it necessary to contact your husband to reassure him about the welfare of the children. If you cannot do this directly, you might wish to use a third party—a mutual friend or a lawyer.
- Don't divulge your present location if you suspect that he will come after you with violent intentions. You are only setting yourself up for punishment. Again, give him some time to adjust, while protecting yourself and your children.
- If you feel it would help, send a letter explaining the reasons for your action. Be sure not to use the letter to accuse or rehash old arguments, but simply use it to explain the genuine concern you have for the welfare of the children and yourself. Reassure him that you are not running him down to the kids.
- Indicate that you are willing to consider establishing some visitation rights under certain conditions that guarantee the safety of the children and yourself. Check out with a social worker or family counselor if there are places available where you might meet under protective surveillance—a family counseling center, for instance.
- Unfortunately there are a few extreme cases where even these guidelines cannot be applied. In those cases, the woman must, for all purposes, disappear.

CUSTODY

Who will take care of the children? The question is vexing. Even in relationships that have been torn by profound disagreement, the nature of marriage implies that the care of children is a dual responsibility. In actual fact, women normally spend much more time in the guidance and training of the young. But as a particular marriage settles into its daily practice, the responsibilities of each parent become understood, even when not heartily accepted. It happens without being spoken.

With divorce, however, lines must be clearly drawn. Because you and your husband are no longer living together, everything regarding the children must be accounted for. Unfortunately, these issues frequently are the central focus for contention between husbands and wives. The subject of child custody is often so charged with rancor that it easily becomes the final battleground in the dissolution of a marriage. The subject pulls together all of the fear, righteousness, guilt, and paranoia that the divorce has not yet exhausted. But whatever real or forced difficulties are imposed on the situation, the truth is some agreement must be reached. If a mutual understanding is not reached, the court will intervene and decree a solution. And it may not be one either of you like.

In any custody agreement, the options for living arrangements and child rearing possibilities are nearly endless. Each couple must assess its individual circumstances and make an educated projection of what the future is likely to hold. The physical proximity of the couple after they split, the complexion of their new relationship, the individual needs of the children, the father, and you—these and so much more will have a bearing on what is worked out regarding custody.

In general, custody arrangements fall into four broad categories:

1. *Sole custody with one parent.* In some extreme cases, one parent has the children; the other parent has no rights regarding the children.

2. *Primary custody with the mother.* This is by far the most common practice in divorce. The father has visitation rights.

3. *Joint custody.* A rapidly growing arrangement, it allows for each parent to share in the rearing and care of the children in roughly equal amounts of time and effort.

4. *Primary custody with the father.* This is getting more attention, but is still an extremely limited practice in this society. The mother, of course, has visitation rights in this case.

The point must be made that when the word *custody* is used here, it refers to *physical* custody; that is, which parent actually has the children in the house with him or her. The courts differentiate between *physical* and *legal* custody. You could, for instance, have physical custody of the children, but share legal custody—a situation which the court encourages in most cases. Legal custody determines which parent shall have the right and the responsibility to make decisions relating to the health, welfare, and education of the child. If you shared legal custody, you would share in these decisions.

Children as Hostages

The ideal situation would be one in which you and your husband cooperate, separating your past hurts and differences from what is best for the future welfare of the kids. Parents fear that they will be alienated from the children if they are not *physically* living with them. Both parents usually feel that they have invested a lot of loving time and energy with the children. Hours spent teaching and talking, playing and worrying can never be adequately counted up. And although many women can rightfully claim more time spent in these things, the man, for his part, often is convinced of the worth of his contribution. What is called for is shared understanding of each other's needs and a willingness on both sides of seeing that some necessary, if hard, compromises must be made. As often as not, it doesn't happen.

Just as likely, the children are used as hostages. We all know by now what this kind of manipulation and blackmail generates. Whether it be an international crisis or a showdown between separating partners in a marriage, both sides feel totally justified in their demands and are willing to go to extremes to prove it. The issues then shift, changing to face-saving and revenge. The well-being of the hostages—the children—becomes a secondary concern.

The children are not unaware of what is happening. To be the object of bartering is a hardening experience. Instead of being the object of love, the child may see herself as a commodity. It is a dehumanizing experience for the child to hear herself argued over with the same emotions and in the same terms as the fight about the family car and the stereo equipment.

When the situation is carried to this length—as too often it is—

everybody loses. The children pass from one parent to the next, depending on who can bring in the biggest guns. In the process, the husband and wife destroy each other's dignity.

Rather than submitting to destructive patterns so common in custody fights, ask yourself some tough questions. Then see if your husband won't join you in thinking about the answers.

Who Is Better at Parenting Right Now?

Dr. Lee Salk sets down a logical but somewhat unorthodox first rule: "I do not believe that mothers or fathers should be given custody of a child based upon their gender." The challenge of this flies against custom. Gender, specifically the female gender, has been the determining factor in the vast majority of custody cases. The mother gets the kids—period. Most court rulings go this way. But even without legal enforcement, it is the assumption of the vast majority of married couples.

There are strong traditions for this thinking. Most women were introduced into the psychology and duties of child rearing very early. Young girls barely old enough to hold them are given dolls to "take care of." Later on, younger brothers and sisters who require baby-sitting, as well as other chores, are assigned to the little girl, complementing and teaching her the role of "mother." Boys are not given the same intense modeling to be "fathers." By the time a woman is eighteen or twenty years old, the shape of her implied vocation is cast. She has the fundamentals of homemaking.

So that now, after years of marriage and at the moment of divorce, any requestioning of that ingrained role seems almost sacrilegious, not only to others but to the mother herself. Yet if the best interest of the children is the primary purpose, then every part of your current life should be open to reevaluation.

An accurate assessment is not easy. To be objective about children and their needs in the best of times is hard. Now responses are triggered almost unconsciously. The very question "Who is better at parenting right now?" may automatically put you on the defensive, demanding that you *prove* your case. It is a question loaded with responsibility—and potential guilt. But it must be responded to honestly by you and your husband.

The following thoughts provide a place to start. No one of the items holds the answer. And even if the majority of them point in one direction, the emotional and practical weight of a single consideration may be deciding. For the moment, don't censor your thoughts. Let yourself know what you are feeling and what your needs are about this. It's not just a matter of love—that is assumed. The harder question is about what is *best* to do.

- In the past, which of you has shown more interest in caring for the children? How is this translated on a day-to-day basis? Which of you seems to derive more pleasure from contact with the kids?

- In a very practical sense, who is likely to have more time to spend with the children in the foreseeable future? Whose schedule is better suited to allow for the kind of personal care-taking and monitoring that children need?

- Considering the age of the children, which of you is better suited to fit each child's needs? The necessities of a toddler, a preadolescent, and a teen-ager are very different. The accepted wisdom says that younger children do better with their mother, whereas older children's requirements are less definite. Early ages need a teacher; older kids need someone to set guidelines. Which of you does better at these?

- The sex of the children is most relevant. Boys and girls look to parents as role models during their growth. Considering their age and sex, who provides this better? Does your husband have such glaring personality flaws that you feel it would be detrimental for him to act as a role model?

- Each child is an individual. His or her personality bent may work better with one parent or the other. The reasons for this may be obscure, going beyond logical reasoning. The ties between a child and one of the parents can be very strong. Do you recognize any such special bonds between the children and either you or your husband?

- Who can better financially afford to take care of the children?

Realistically, what are your chances of receiving regular child support payments? As you project your future money situation, will you be able to adequately provide for the physical needs of the children? Would your husband do it better?

- After the divorce, which parent will have a living arrangement most conducive to the needs of the children? Who will move? Will the new living situation give the children access to decent schools, recreation areas, and friends? With which parent is this most possible?

- Temperamentally, who is better suited to take care of the children right now? What about in the long run? Which of you has the stability and energy to carry out the daily activity of raising children?

- What do the *children* want? This is not meant to suggest that the children become full participants in the decision making. But children often have a strong desire to be with a certain parent. You should have that information. Obviously, it is impossible to ask infants, but even preschoolers can give indications. It is important, however, not to put a child on the spot so that the inquiry appears to be the question "Who do you love more, Mommy or Daddy?" Then, too, any indications have to be filtered so that passing moods and unrelated factors aren't taken as the real need of the child.

    Strongly expressed desires of teen-agers have to be considered seriously. Forcing a sixteen-year-old to be with one parent when he wants to be with the other brings nothing but resentment. Even the courts recognize this. When custody cases go to court for settlement decisions, most judges will ask what the *child* wants. Obviously, avoid the hand of the state if you can.

- Which of you really *wants* to take primary charge of caring for the children? Apart from the first automatic response of most parents, what are the long-range implications for your life? Husbands, for instance, often quickly respond that they want full custody of the children; some threaten to steal them if necessary. But when emotions sober and a "get even" attitude calms, many come to realize that they don't really want the full-time responsibility of caring for children.

Many women, on the other hand, would like to have their children with them, but are at a loss to figure out how they can work a job or train for a career, and still manage a household with children. Other women simply have an overriding sense of responsibility and are candid enough to know that they would not be happy unless they fulfill the traditional role of mother. One woman put it simply, "I want someone to come home to. It would be too lonely without the kids."

Social pressures, your personal upbringing, fears of the future, or the competitive challenge from your husband will conspire to complicate the issue of custody. But the central question is still— "Who is better at parenting the children at this time?" Don't let the issue become one of winning and losing. One of you may be clearly better suited to have custody of the children at this point in the children's lives. Be open to facing every possibility.

When Dr. Mary-Alice Isenhart left her husband nine years ago, she also left him with their two children. Her intention was to go back to college and then pursue a career in counseling. She was thirty-nine years old at the time; her boy was fourteen, her girl twelve.

I had begun thinking about changing my life at least five years before. And divorce was part of that change. I also knew that I couldn't take care of the children the way they wanted to be taken care of, and do the things *I* wanted to do. I *knew* that. Given the financial situation, I knew our lives would just turn into a spiral of looking for money—hunting, grabbing, struggling, and being angry with one another.

I also knew the kind of person that I was. At the time I wasn't psychologically able to take care of them. I was still immature and very undeveloped. I'm not sure my husband was ready for it either, but at least he had money. He had a good job and income, and was from a wealthy family. I didn't have anything. He was not the kind of person who was going to support us. We had always fought over money, and the idea that we would not fight about it in divorce was ludicrous.

I had to ask myself, "What do I want the children for? What do I want them with me for?" And the answers kept coming up, "So I won't be alone. So I'll have someone with me." And these were not good reasons! There wasn't anything for the *kids* in that. It was all for me.

My advice would be for women to really evaluate why they want the children with them, or why they want the children with the spouse. Be very clear about what it is that you are doing; really think it through. Talk about it with other people; get help in making your decision. I made the decision by myself and it was very hard.

Whichever agreement you finally work out, know that it will probably not be a perfect situation. Complications spin out of the details of any custody arrangement, especially at first. Don't get ruffled even though a new set of rules is beginning to govern your life and those around you. The attorney Sandra Morris observes:

There is no such thing as a permanent custody order. Until the child is eighteen, the court retains jurisdiction to modify the orders in the child's best interest. You can write anything you want into your agreement providing it is not illegal. The courts are very happy to have parents design their own personal divorce. The only time they intervene is when the couple has to submit the issue to the court for a decision.

You and your husband have the choice of restructuring your lives and the lives of your children. Whatever you choose, the decision is not set in cement.

A NEW START

The great majority of women do keep their children with them, and the changes happening in their lives provide a unique opportunity for starting over. Whatever disruption divorce has brought, this time can be seen as a chance to rethink and make over your choices for the future.

Everyone, whether happily married or not, can look back with some regret at how they raised their children. There were times when too much was expected of the children; periods when they wanted more attention than you wanted to give; there were the mistakes.

It is rare in life to have a fresh beginning so sharply defined as it is now. That sense of bright prospect should be evident in your person and imbued in your kids. They will be looking to you for clues on how to respond. If their new life seems to them simply a continuation of the past, then a chance to rethink your relationship with your children will have been passed over.

SINGLE PARENTING

Taking full responsibility for the care of children is a challenge. Although the problems of it may readily jump to mind, there are many promising, even exciting, parts to it. You are, for instance, free to make your own decisions without conflict or second-guessing your husband. That may be a very new experience. It can also mean that you and the kids could have a much cleaner communication.

But if you were like most parents, your present relationship developed out of a combination of half-thought-through ideas, the "lessons" of your husband's and your own childhoods, and natural change. Now, as a single parent, you can take stock and redirect your lives together.

You will probably be spending more time with the children than with anyone else for the next few months. It can be an ideal period for finding out what you like about one another. You can draw together to discuss personal problems with new candor. It can be fruitful if you are willing to give some effort and take a few risks.

The biggest need most children have after the split-up is just to know that you love them, and that your love is constant. They need to *feel* that. They also need to know that they have a place in your life, and what that is about. Once they are assured of this, their lives can begin to take on a new shape. You may fear that by giving them special considerations and increased amounts of time in your life they will grow used to it and demand it permanently. This isn't so. When children sense that their lives have regained normalcy, they will let go of unusual dependencies. It is more important to offer them the security that they are asking for at this time.

Some of the hesitancy or rebellion you may experience from the kids is due to the different role you will play with them. This is especially true if you have switched from being at home a lot to working full time outside of it. The change in your normal routine, particularly if it was one that catered to their wants, is bound to draw some kind of unhappy reaction. From their point of view, it means less of everything; the next step may be the loss of it all. Again, it's a matter of reassuring them.

A more perplexing and wearing problem may involve your continuing contact with your former husband.

VISITATION

The question of parental visitation of children comes down to this:

> The whole problem hinges on the simple human principle that the husband and wife can be separated or divorced, but the parental couple cannot. They remain a pair of parents, biological in a sense, forever.

The truth of the statement by Dr. Nathan Ackerman in *Children of Separation and Divorce* may be disconcerting just when you thought you were free from your husband "forever." But when there are children, there is visitation, and with that, the reestablishment of some form of relationship with your husband. It may be a very narrow, restricted contact, but it is there. It needn't be a headache, however.

To begin with, the available literature on the subject concurs that children with divorced parents are most satisfied when they see both parents regularly. This continuing contact enhances a sense of safety and confidence in them, and it is primarily this consideration which makes the effort worthwhile.

Find ways to cooperate with your ex-husband. This may not be easy. Your relationship at this point may be acrimonious. Privately you may be accusing him of being a terrible father. But much of this may be based on the fact that you just don't like him. The truth is that a guy can act like a complete jerk to you personally, but be a perfectly able father and parent to the children. The two situations can exist exclusively of each other, and often do.

Your children's loyalties toward their father don't end with the divorce. Case studies point out that, even when parents have physically abused the children, kids still often retain devotion. It is confusing to children, as well as futile, to denigrate your husband. And in many cases it backfires. Even when the level of criticism is low but steady—grumbling to the children about his habit of buying them junk food—it works against everybody's best interest. Show the children that, even though you have had differences with their father, when matters concern them you can work through these problems successfully.

Cautions

- Don't get in the way. The visitation period is the kids' time with their father. They both need it. Stay away from complicating the situation with instructions or demands that impose you unnecessarily on what they choose to do together. You may have primary custody, but you don't "own" the children.
- Don't use the kids as ransom. Withholding or interfering with their time with their father in order to get him to make his payments on time, or to cooperate more, is not a good idea. It is unkind to the children and illegal in many counties. Most family courts will be unsympathetic with this tactic. Sometimes it is hard to be fair and civil in one part of your relationship when he is being a creep in another part, but keep the issue of the children's time with him separate from your feelings about other matters.
- Don't get into competing with their father, even in subtle ways, over who is the better parent. This can take the form of trying to outdo him in giving the kids gifts, special activities, or exhibiting flurries of "niceness." The children are not trophies to be won. They pick up that this is happening and their reactions will be

as unnatural as what is going on. Most children love both parents. They don't want to be put into the position of judging who is "better."

- Don't overreact if your husband is saying crummy things about you. Older children have a mind of their own and are well aware of adult games. Sooner or later they see through them. Younger kids are more influenced by the way you relate to them, and insidious remarks aren't going to change the way they feel about you. If the stories are blatant lies and are destructive, you will need to set things straight with both the kids and your former husband. But the majority of backbiting will go away by ignoring it.

- Don't use the time when the kids are being picked up or dropped off to convey information to your ex-husband that is potentially confrontational. These can be volatile moments, still times of mixed emotions, and things can easily explode. If you have something important to say to your husband, find a neutral place free from the presence of the children. Also, stay away from using the children as messengers. Because of the levels of hidden meaning that can be packed into even the simplest message, misinterpretation is common and the child ends up as the middleman.

You can expect your children to go through a readjustment period after they have visited their father, especially during the first few months. They may be morose at times because they miss him, in the same way that anyone experiences a letdown after leaving someone they love. Be sensitive to this, but not upset by it. When the children get into a new rhythm of living, they will develop a new sense of the intervals in their lives and will know that they are not saying goodbye to their father, that their relationship is ongoing.

Be considerate in the details. It's usually at this level that things break down and hostilities are renewed. For example, be on time. If you are going to pick the kids up at five o'clock, be there at five o'clock. If you can't make it, call.

If he is doing a good job, tell him so. Be willing to see him in his new role as an individual, the father of your children, and, hopefully, a friend.

Things to Do

The kids will be looking to you to see "what happens next." They may not be sure of your abilities at handling the household, a job, or even their lives by yourself. Again, time is on your side. The urgency you may have felt at the end of your divorce should not be carried over to your relationship with the kids. They will be with you for a long time, enough to work things out.

Some of the following ideas might help in pointing a new direction with your children:

Announce yourself to your children. This may sound strangely formal, but by this I mean *let them know who you are.* Not as part of a couple, or even as a parent, but you as a *person.* They already know you in the former ways, and your role as a parent will continue. But you have many sides that you may not have given the children access to. Give them the chance to know you as a full and complete woman; let them experience the "kid" side of you, that funny and playful part. Bring the children into your social life when it fits.

Share your feelings. Don't try to hide what you are feeling; you have probably done that long enough with the kids. Children are very sensitive to you and know when something is wrong. You don't want to burden them with details they would not understand or that would worry them further, but you can honestly acknowledge some amount of what is happening with you. When a person, young or old, is left in the dark, he tends to imagine the worst.

For example, if you feel frustrated and overwhelmed by your job, tell the children about it—that your job gets you down at times, but that's how life is. It may not be the same tomorrow, but right now you are having a hard time.

The one area that is best to hold back on has to do with their father. For the reasons stated earlier, it is not good to get into the habit of expressing negative feelings about him, even if they are honest and deserved. It can quickly evolve into a contest of "our side" against "his side." The subject is a delicate one and will call upon all of your discretion and common sense.

Maintain limits. Don't let guilt or any other feeling keep you from setting and enforcing boundaries of behavior. You are opening a Pandora's box if you feel that letting go of normal and reasonable expectations will win over the kids. They are quick to recognize this manipulation, and when that becomes the new basis of how you relate together, they have as many skills as you. There is no reason to overindulge your kids, whether with food, presents, or privileges. That's not what they need from you. Set up a sensible routine and stay with it.

You will probably need help. As a single parent, you no longer have another adult to rely on. The children can do a lot to fill that void if they are not infants. Their involvement in the daily tasks of taking care of the house and their personal lives should be encouraged. Helping is not necessarily seen by children as "work" unless it is presented as that. When kids feel that their contribution is needed, appreciated, and for a purpose, their response may surprise you. This activity can be a focal point for the expression of your new life together. Young children can learn to do such things as clear the dinner dishes, pick up their toys, and feed the pet. Older ones can take charge of cleaning areas of the house or apartment, doing the laundry, caring for the lawn.

Watch out that some children don't become helpless at this time. It's their way of testing the new system. Be understanding but be firm. The future is their responsibility as much as it is yours.

Do things with the kids, more than for them. It is the small, personal things that children usually benefit from the most. Spending thirty dollars on a day at an amusement park, or going to movies and restaurants may be fun activities for special occasions, but more often than not, they don't turn out to be the times of close and warm contact that you had hoped. More likely that can be found in playing games together, reading stories, baking cookies, helping them decorate their room. These are the simple things that bring you together as people and as members of a family, which allow for real personal interchange.

Allow each child to determine his or her needs and how to meet them. Don't get caught in the trap of believing that you must solve everyone's problems for them. It will only lead to feelings of inadequacy and guilt, because the task is futile to begin with. Your children are not helpless. They have the resources to get through the normal difficulties that life presents. If they are in the habit of turning to you, show them alternative ways of handling their problems independently.

Enlist the support of grandparents and relatives. The children can use all of the love and support they can get, and relatives give a very special kind. A grandparent or an uncle can be just the right person to temporarily fill the gap in a child's life. It also gives a sense of continuity to their lives because the kinship is not broken. In this regard, encourage the relationship between the children and the parents of your ex-husband if that is possible and desirable. These connections can help you to feel less alone in your responsibility, and can be useful when you need help with the kids.

Join in a single parents' group. Most communities have some sort of club which brings together women (and men) who find themselves in a similar situation to yours. It is a great morale booster just to be able to freely talk to others going through the big issues and the small hassles that you are experiencing. These groups can be very helpful by affording women the chance to share their common problems and solutions. The communication ranges from where to buy a good, cheap used car to how to handle an ex-husband who won't let you alone.

One group I know of plans regular picnics and dinners, each parent joining in the potluck affair as he or she can. It brings together parents and kids in a new sense of community, even family. The social aspect of this group is, in fact, its primary appeal. It is an important part of life to be kept alive right now.

Give yourself some time off. Don't try to be Supermom. Give yourself a break and get away from the routine of life. Depending on your individual situation, make some time that is yours. If your children are old enough, leaving them for a Saturday afternoon or staying in bed on a Sunday morning should not be difficult. When children are smaller, this is more of a problem but it usually means simply planning ahead.

This kind of relief is essential to your mental health and outlook, and can't be emphasized enough. There are always fifty reasons why you can't give yourself more free time, and guilt about why you shouldn't be out for the evening often dampens whatever pleasures you are finding. But see that "time off" is an important need—a right—without which your life will suffer.

Take care how you handle a "new man" in your life. An entire chapter could be written on this subject. In terms of the children, a new man in your life is a replacement, and the very idea causes difficulty. In a real sense, the biological father cannot be replaced. Even if they are glad that he is gone, there is a part of them that will usually resist any substitute.

If you do not have a strong need in this regard, you might consider postponing heavy involvement with a man, at least in the presence of the children, during the first few months after your separation. There is plenty going on already in the household, and the adjustments asked of everyone have been taxing.

Until your children have become acclimated somewhat to the new family situation, they will tend to be jealous of your time. This can be annoying should you wish to date men or spend some evenings in other interests. A subtle but dedicated competition may arise. The strategies to get rid of another man range from rudeness to ingenious plots to subvert the relationship. Typically, on an outing at which you include a male friend for the first time, the kids become totally obnoxious, making any normal conversation between you and him impossible. Some women fear going out with men because of the possible upset it brings.

This is not to suggest, however, that your children should not see you in a warm, loving relationship with another man when you feel the time is right. It is a natural part of adult experience. In many ways, such contact will draw out feelings and attitudes from you that the children may not have seen in your marriage. They can have the chance to experience you as romantic, animated, outgoing, or any other way you respond to a man when you're truly interested.

The other side of the coin is that your children may get attached to the man rather quickly, and if he is a person who is just "passing through," the children may again feel a sense of loss. It is one thing to date men away from home and quite another to include him on a family picnic. Give the latter event a little more consideration.

While reassuring the kids that they have only one father, you can introduce new men into your life and the lives of the children that will not threaten them, but it takes a sensitivity to their changing awareness. There is no reason why another man in your life cannot have a positive relationship with your children in his own right—if he chooses.

A CONTINUING FAMILY EXERCISE

There is a very simple but extremely effective daily activity that can work as a renewing source within your family. Family counselors give it several titles. Jerry Lynch called it "The Magic Circle." It goes like this:

- Set aside a period of time each day. Whether it is before supper or after supper or just before bedtime, make it a time when everyone can be counted on to be there. Treat this time as a ritual; that is, an important event in your family life that has a simple but observed structure.
- The purpose is to have a discussion. The subject changes each

time. Typical questions or subjects might be: Talk about one good thing that happened to you today. What is your favorite food? What bothered you today? If you could go anywhere you want, where would you go? (Keep the questions specific.)

- The meeting should not last over twenty minutes. It may be tempting to carry it on at times but resist the temptation. If it begins to be an ordeal in terms of the time, there will be little enthusiasm for it later on.

- Everybody is equal and will have an opportunity to talk. This is true for the five-year-old or the fifteen-year-old. It is one time when no one is shortchanged.

- There shall be no criticizing, no attacks, no judgments. Each person gets to state what is on his or her mind in any way each wishes.

- This is a small forum for *expression*, not argument.

- The emphasis is on *listening* to each other.

- You, as a parent, are merely the participant/moderator of the group. It is not up to you to comment on anything being said. The nature of what the kids talk about should not be geared for your pleasure.

- Nothing said should ever be "used" against the person speaking. This is a "free zone" in the day of the children.

The process is actually very effortless and informal. The beauty of it is that *it works*. Jerry Lynch had used it for years in his family counseling and said:

> The coming together should be a safe and sheltered time for the children. You're not going to solve any problems in any one session. The idea is not to lay all the cards on the table and have it out. That's impossible. It's better for them just to know that there is going to be a time when you're not going to be *on* them, no matter what they say. That you're not going to put them down, and they *trust* that. There may be other times when you're mean and nasty—you're not perfect—but there is also another time when they can tell you things that you are not going to hold against them.

This kind of exercise can become a model for your changing relationship with the children. Such activities are graphic examples of your intention to create a new life with them.

Making over your lives won't happen instantly, so don't expect too much either of yourself or the rest of the family. The passing of time is a natural healing process.

CHAPTER 9

Closing Words

THE POST-SEPARATION PASSAGE

After several false starts, Rod was supposed to leave that day. The car was packed—he was going. I went to work. And the whole day I was on pins and needles because I didn't know if he'd go for sure. My phone would ring and I would jump.

I came home with my ride who drives a little VW. And we came around the corner, and Rod's car was *gone*. I started screaming at the top of my lungs—"I'm free . . . I'm free!" My friend had never seen me act that way before, and he almost had an accident in front of the house, with me screaming and waving my arms. Then I stopped and looked at him and said very clearly, "I'm OK now," and he laughed. He knew what I'd been going through.

I don't know an adjective to describe the emotion I felt. I really—for the first time in my life—felt *free*. And yet I have spent a lot of time alone and free. I lived alone before I met my husband, and he'd be gone and I'd be free to do whatever I wanted. But I still felt tied somehow. It was my personal tie. It was being free of responsibility that was too hard to carry.

I went in the house and I remember that happiness. I remember I felt like jumping up and down, and screaming and yelling, but I don't think I really did.

STAGE ONE: FREEDOM!

At some point soon after leaving, the realization hits—*I am free!* And as Beverly describes it, the feeling is wonderful. The sense of freedom regained is probably the most euphoric sensation a human being can experience.

Freedom comes in small and large doses in a person's life. When you were a kid, it was felt during the first days of summer vacation in the gloriously lazy mornings of sleeping in; in later life, making the final car payment or seeing the kids off to school in September were small moments of renewed liberation.

But the freedom a woman experiences after having been tied into the life of a man with whom she no longer wants to live is exhilarating. And the relief isn't necessarily dependent on whether the ex-husband was a good or bad man. For most couples, marriage meant being intimately and irrevocably involved with the other person's ambition, time schedules, personal value system, style of communicating, sexuality, sense of the world and its politics, and so much more.

To be free of that now, to have broken that link, is to be suddenly faced with the simply beautiful question—"What do *I* want to do today?" The words are at once ordinary and yet so full of meaning, because now it is not just the rhetorical mumbling that goes on over breakfast coffee, but an expression of a completely new state of independence and expectation.

Freedom is the realization that the answer to that question has several options, and that *you* have the choice of deciding. Your choices may not be significantly unlike those that you would have made when living with your husband, but since they are the result of your thinking alone, it makes all the difference.

Most women tell of ecstatic feelings that spring from this realization. Whether or not they can define it in words, just the experience of having free choices is a tremendous high. They find themselves spontaneously singing in the shower, dancing around the house, listening to music at higher volumes, calling new friends on the phone or writing letters to neglected ones, filling rooms with flowers, buying good wine for candlelit dinners, buying that blouse that uncovers more. Life becomes smiling more, saying what's really on your mind, rejoicing in the moment, finding an inner quiet, feeling terribly alive.

Enjoy! You deserve it. Accept the feelings and celebrate in them. Granted, it may be a purely emotional state of release that you are passing through, but take advantage of such times and live them fully. There is much to take pleasure in, much to learn. Sides of yourself that may not have been exercised for a long time are now finding expression. Stay open and let it happen.

Put away the vestiges of your past—the rings, the dumpy clothes, the mementos—and give the *present* a chance. Breathe deeply, walk lightly, allow yourself to physically feel your freedom. Ask yourself what you will need to do, and how you will need to change in order to build upon this vivacity.

This is an emotional time. And because there are buoyant heights, there are also fluctuations. The low periods are often our fearful reaction to freedom. Part of us just can't stand the good times. We have not been taught, or allowed to feel, that pleasurable times in life can be experienced openly, for whatever they offer. No compensation is necessary. We often say that we like being happy, but deep down we expect to pay the price. Of course, expecting it usually makes it happen, and some women during this time bring themselves down, doubting that life can ever be this good, fearing that to experience an extended period of joy will mean feeling doubly disappointed if and when it subsides.

Naturally, life is never constant. Even when you were a child, Christmas morning had its anticlimactic side. It is true, there will be some letdowns. When they come, let them be. But don't deny yourself the joy of this time because you are afraid of what *might* happen. Look at your life. You are now released from a routine that, even though it may have been self-imposed, was determined partly by the needs of your spouse—dinner was at a certain time, social pleasures were predictable, your inner clock was set to go off at designated times. Being free of that now is stimulating, especially if the pattern is one that has gone on for years. You can wear what you want, think what you want, say what you want. If someone argues that you could always have done that if you had really wanted, it doesn't matter. Right now you *are* doing it, and it feels great.

The physical and emotional charge that your newfound freedom brings can be a great source of strength and motivation for other changes you may want in your life. Use that energy to your advantage. Whether it gives you the nerve to apply for a job that you normally would feel to be out of reach or to bridge your shyness about meeting new friends, view this time as a special gift that you have earned.

STAGE TWO: SECOND THOUGHTS

While it is true that a zesty sense of freedom may run through every phase of your life from now on, many women nevertheless do experience a later period in which they question their decisions. Accompanying this is a longer lasting emotional letdown. It is not just an afternoon of depression or a late night's loneliness but more a rethinking of the situation that you have chosen and find yourself in. Few divorces were the result of decisions made on clear-cut black-and-white issues. Therefore, it is almost inevitable that a woman will go through a time—usually several months after her separation—when she will have second thoughts about the choices she has committed herself to in life.

First, you may have doubts about the very "rightness" of some part of your decision. If that is not a problem, you may find yourself spending a good deal of time reevaluating your previous expectations. Life may not be turning out as you had imagined it would.

Regrets

For most women, the very idea of requestioning their decision about leaving their husbands is embarrassing. The road out was too rugged not to have strong resistance to this. But while few women outwardly second-guess their choice, an inner self may be disturbed by a list of gnawing doubts about what they have done.

Did I exaggerate the crisis in our life? Weren't the kids a lot happier before? Could my ex-husband cope better with some of their discipline problems than I? Were my needs really legitimate?

As time passes and blurs earlier events, some things about the marriage begin to look better. And if your ex-husband is still hurting and is saying he loves you and he's sorry, your guilt may merge with nostalgic affection to create even further doubts. The moments of regret become weighty, full-fledged dilemmas for some women. Of course in saner moments, going back to your ex-husband is recognized plainly as idealistic nonsense. Yet the doubts about your decision won't go away.

Most of the questions about your past are unanswerable at this point in your life, and speculation can go on endlessly. But what is most likely at the base of this requestioning is the issue of dependence vs. independence.

If, for instance, you have never lived alone before, if you have had to move to a totally unfamiliar location, or if you are supporting yourself financially for the first time, it is understandable that you may waver and feel confused. Whom *do* you call on now for help if you get sick, or rely on in a money crisis, or wake when you hear sounds in the house? Out of simple habit, many women automatically think of their ex-husbands. There was a familiar ease in relating to him; his idiosyncracies could even seem less bothersome. This subtle dependency takes on many forms. Some women, because of their loneliness and the easy availability of their ex-husbands, reestablish sexual relations with them. It rarely works out. Other women continue to expect them to do all the gardening or fix the car. The apparent security in keeping ties with him is tempting—and that's the problem.

Even when the divorce process demanded all of your individual resources, it may have been hard to see yourself as a completely independent person. Many of your actions took into consideration your ex-husband's reactions. Whether in conversation or in court, his adversary position became something you could count on. That's being dependent.

But now you are independent in fact as well as in fancy. The shock can be disarming at first. It is one thing to dream about independence and another to *be there*. When you have no one to turn to, or even to blame—when you are *it*—the fear of that reality often triggers doubt, then regret.

Check and see if your feelings of regret are not really a need for someone to lean on. Don't mistake that for love.

Unfulfilled Fantasies

What carried you through some pretty dark times were the fantasies of what life would be like afterward. The fantasies served their purpose in that they sustained you when you might have given up. The problem with these dreams is that we embellish them with such loving detail that we believe that they will inevitably come true.

In the months after separation, a woman too often finds that what she thought would be happening is not coming about—the glamorous, good paying job she had hoped to get wasn't there; the three-bedroom apartment complex she had planned to move into changed its policy on children; her ex-husband has still not adjusted to the idea of divorce, and the war goes on. If her plans have become unrealistic fantasies, if she is out of touch with either her capabilities or a reasonable expectation of life (in essence, that some rugged but understanding stranger would be waiting at the courthouse steps as she walked out in a properly conservative yet subtly sexy dress with her divorce papers in hand to be swept away in his black Jaguar), then she is headed for a serious disappointment. Her reveries will need an overhaul.

It would be a small miracle if all of your plans had worked out as you had imagined. After all, before your divorce, although you may have been working on the best information available to you at the time, you could not possibly foresee everything. In six months things change: the economy, your children's attitude toward school, welfare rules, the availability and cost of housing, your relationship with others.

Most of your expectations may have been sensible, even cautious, but the design of your future might have to be reassessed. At any time in life, but especially now, there is a continuous need to redefine what *is*, and what *can be*—and adjust accordingly.

Behavior to Expect

Your feelings may still be unsettled. Just as in your original decision to divorce, there is vacillation again, but now over a new set of concerns. Are you doing the right things with the kids? Are you dating men too much, or not enough? How much longer should you stay with your job? The single-mindedness that may have gotten you through your last stages of divorce now is challenged by less dramatic, but very important, choices. Emotionally, it is hard to regear again for yet more ups and downs.

It is tempting to hand things over to fate now. Reading symbolic meaning into everyday events is one way. If you are asked out for dinner by the man at work that you have had your eye on, it is seen as a sign of your change of luck and you are high. When the car breaks down on the way to meet him, you are depressed because nothing ever turns out right for you. Fatalistic thinking often grows out of the exhaustion of having had to make an excessive number of decisions. And it can put life on a roller coaster—one day is full of hope, the next is haunted by self-doubts.

Some depression and exhilaration during this period is to be expected. These delayed reactions come from the energy output that your divorce demanded. You may find yourself a bit out of control—talking too much, buying clothes you don't need, being overanxious with men, worrying too much about everything and anything. On top of that, you may find yourself plagued by second-guessing yourself, doubting the wisdom of your original plans.

Remember, you just emerged from a harrowing experience. The aftermath will not be immediately smooth despite the fact that by now you have the right to a time of external and internal peace. It will come however. This second stage of self-questioning and doubt will pass away gradually if for no other reason than you will get tired of it. The past dies slowly, but it finally does. In the meantime, you can learn a lot about yourself.

Grieving

Many women find it hard to grieve the loss of their relationship, and in fact never directly deal with these feelings. But most marriages, at one time or another, had worth. A sense of loss accompanied with feelings of sadness is natural. However, for a woman to recognize this, and then to allow herself to feel sorrowful, presents a seeming contradiction. How could she feel so bad about a marriage that offered so little?

Grieving the loss of a marriage is not the same as wanting to renew it. That is what is so confusing. You may feel badly that the marriage didn't fulfill its original bright promise, or that the years of struggle to make it work are now only half-remembered, or that friendship with your ex-husband is no longer happening.

Most women I have interviewed told of feeling badly, not about their now-ended marriages, but about what "could have been." They regret that the dream never came true. "If only . . . If only we could have communicated. If only he had gotten some help with his drinking. If only he hadn't been so jealous. If only we had moved away from his parents." Most women don't miss the *reality* of their marriage, but it will take some time to let go of the *hope* they had for it. Some of the sadness has to do with saying goodbye to that.

A time when sadness and bewilderment commonly occurs is at the actual moment of the divorce. Courthouses are cold, paper-shuffling places. The formal procedures and legal jargon block out the expression of emotion that might naturally be present. The marriage—those years of untold intensity—is suddenly ended by the flat proclamation of a judge. Even though you may have wanted this day very much, the mechanistic ease of it all seems to say that the years you spent together were meaningless. This feeling of negation comes first as a shock—"Is *this* how it ends?!"—and then moves into confusion and sadness.

It will be helpful for you to directly feel that hurt rather than trying to ignore or discount it. The feelings are a human response to the loss of what was once an important relationship. The problem is that these emotions occur when you are unprepared to cope with them. Changes are happening so rapidly that you can hardly digest them all. The last thing you need are more heavy emotions about your marriage, let alone soft ones.

And yet women and men who do not at some time come to grips with what their divorce has cost them emotionally are often hampered in later years with unresolved feelings and attitudes that can get in the way of creating healthy new relationships.

Feel the sadness and find a way to say goodbye to the relationship.

STAGE THREE: RESOLUTION

Things get better. As your life settles into a new routine, it will take on a stability and sanity. Peace begins to be restored as daily life falls into welcome predictability again. Whatever changes have come about are now becoming familiar, and it is heartening.

It can also be disconcerting. Because if you haven't given some serious thought to how those changes are affecting your life, you may discover that you are living a very different life from the one you had with your former husband, but one that is not substantially more rewarding. The purpose of leaving, for most women, was not to simply break from their husband but to find a new beginning and explore unrealized potential.

There are parts of yourself that you may have vaguely sensed and only hesitantly expressed. If your future is to be essentially happier than your past, it is important to get to know yourself better. Now is an ideal time.

Self-Discovery

I thought that as soon as I got away from Wes everything would be just great. He was the one making my life miserable. Now that I've

separated from him for six months, things aren't so great. I've had
to face the fact that lots of times I make *myself* miserable.

Margaret's observation is one that has truth for most everybody
leaving a marriage. Although it is obviously useless to go on blaming your ex-husband for your unhappiness, it is not easy to be
confronted with the idea of taking full responsibility for your life.
But until that happens, you will live in a world of diversion. The
discovery of deeper levels of yourself—the creative, the healthy,
the joyful—comes with not only your physical but also your psychological independence.

This discovery does not mean thinking about your problems
more. You've done that enough. It has to do with providing yourself with activities and personal contacts that are challenging and
different. This is a time to loosen those self-imposed restraints. It
is a time to test, to reach out, to stretch.

A New Identity

Again, the old question "Who am I?" comes up. But this time
it is in a rousing and demanding voice. For years you have spent
time gaining an identity. It may have come without your realizing
it—then you felt stuck in it. You were "Bob's wife," or "Peggy's
and Jimmy's mother," or "the good-looking married secretary."
Although such titles may be grating when you feel that is your
only definition, they do sink in after a while. You take on that
identity. The simplicity of it can even be seductive.

In fact, after your divorce, you may feel uncomfortable and at
loose ends when those labels change. In frightened response,
some women rush back into another marriage in which their role
is substantially the same as the one they left. The husbands are
exchanged; the package is the same. A new identity proves too
threatening.

Even when a divorced woman does not revert to this, she may
find herself following the worn but familiar paths of life. There
is no possibility of anything different coming into her existence.
She makes sure of it.

The alternative is to redefine yourself. First that means exploding some of your self-limiting myths. The "I am only . . ." kind of thinking: I am only a housewife; I am only a high school graduate; I am only another working woman in her late thirties.

You are not *only* anything! There are a hundred sides to you. Some of them are unknown to others; some are vaguely known to you. Let yourself *see* yourself. Disclose yourself—who you are and what you want to be—to others.

Socially, intellectually, and sexually, be ready to approach others with a knowledge of your preferences and needs, and be willing to express them. In your marriage you may have been coerced into going camping each weekend. What a great relief to be able to say to yourself, "I never *did* like camping!" and then refuse an offer by a well-meaning friend. Or to say, "I would really enjoy spending a Sunday afternoon in bed making love," if that has been a secret desire.

In the act of free and honest self-expression, your new identity will be discovered by others, and by yourself.

An Exercise: "What Do You Want?"

To find out who you are it is important to first find out what you want. It sounds so simple. But much of our lives have been spent denying our *wants*, to the point that we have grown ignorant of them. It is as if we bury them so effectively that we ourselves forget them.

To admit a *want* is considered self-indulgent. There is something almost superstitious about it—that you had better not get caught wanting something because it will ensure that you won't get it. And indeed there are those who, when they find what you really desire, seem to do everything to see you don't get it. Husbands and wives know this game well.

So we learn never to tell others what we want in fear that they will then have the power to withhold or block fulfillment. In the process, we dull our own awareness. A kind of internal self-censor takes over to check our longings even before they are fully felt. Instead of saying to yourself that you would like to eat at a good restaurant for dinner, a voice within censors the want with four "good" reasons why you shouldn't go: It is expensive, frivolous, selfish, and it will make you fat.

Expressing your *wants* is not the same as getting them. Many yearnings are just not feasible. But being free to express your wants gets these feelings out in the open, to be accepted or rejected. You may have had a suppressed attraction for some sexual adventure or a trip to a far-off country. To be able to simply say that to yourself is freeing. The reality of actually doing something about it is quite another thing. It may be appealing only as a fantasy.

Getting in touch with your *wants* can be instructive in terms of how you wish to live in the present and plan for the future. For too long, marriage replaced "I want" with "I should." We grew to know a lot about responsibility and too little about personal fulfillment. The more your existence is in line with your deep needs, the greater the chance for happiness.

Try this—it's fun:

- Get ahold of an adding machine tape, or pad. Carry it with you for two weeks and write down *all* of your *wants* as they come to you. The list can range from the most lofty ("I want peace of mind") to the most mundane ("I want a spot remover that *really* works"). The thing is not to stop yourself. Write it all down, no matter how outrageous, greedy, provocative, heavenly, ordinary, specific, repetitive, or trite the *want* may be.

  At the end of the two weeks, read it out loud to yourself (or to a close friend, if you dare). You will probably discover a great number of things about yourself. Look for patterns. When you get to know this part of yourself, you can then decide which of the *wants* are worth pursuing.

NEW RELATIONSHIPS

As you enter into this new phase of your life, one of the most promising and at the same time perplexing activities will be forming new relationships. In fact, this last section has been about forming a new one with yourself. When you get down to it, life is about people. Now that you are free of the habits and constraints of marriage, it is possible to remake your life in relation to others. The persons you choose as casual friends or intimate companions will be important in creating the tenor of your new life.

MEN

There is bound to be some confusion about men. After all, you have just spent a considerable amount of time, energy, and money breaking free from one of them. Your ex-husband may have been insensitive, irresponsible, and flaccid. And even though you may have been cautious during the divorce process not to attribute the things you disliked about your husband to all men, there is often a suspicion planted. You can know in your head that each man is different, but your gut resists it.

The intensity of breaking up has undoubtedly left some wounds, uncertainty about whether you want another relationship with a man, and if you do, how to get what you want from it. During the press of events, you may simply have not had time to process your feelings about all of this and these may be still unresolved.

Four Pitfalls

Growing out of the fears and fantasies that some women have about men are at least four attitudes that inhibit the chance of a good relationship with a man.

Searching for the ideal man. Not many women would say they are doing this, but that's really what happens. It is that eternal quest for a trouble-free relationship with the perfect man out there. Some women have a very detailed list of their ideal qualities, from his height and coloring to how much money he makes, to whether he likes sailing and making love out of doors. He is probably the man your husband never was. With this dreamboat, life would be wonderful.

There is certainly nothing wrong with knowing what you want

in a man, even if that means being able to write down specifics.
You may have a good idea of what you want and don't want. It
should be one of the real and lasting lessons of a broken marriage
for all of us.

But be sure that your list has those qualities that are really
essential to your happiness. Certainly if you just divorced a man
because he was a workaholic and you seldom saw him, you should
be wary of that personality type. But don't create a model that is
so impossible to find that it ensures never finding anyone. Some
women demand so much that they are bound to be disappointed.
The rigidity of their demands rules out almost everybody. The
guy might be out there, but he's probably living in Oslo, Norway.

Perfection is rarely experienced in this life. Don't look for it in
a man. Not every relationship with a man must be part of "the
search." Many men can be valuable friends, yet what they offer
may be limited. One may be a compassionate listener, another
very helpful with practical advice about finances, and another a
playful companion. Let them fill your needs without insisting that,
right now, one man must "do it all" for you. Don't use the myth
of the ideal man as just another way of avoiding intimacy with a
real person.

Believing all men are jerks. This is a tempting generality and no one
is more apt to make it than a woman coming out of a bad marriage.
The frustration is understandable. But when the next step is to
believe that because the experience was so damaging happiness
can never be distilled from a relationship with men, the result is
a radical realignment of values.

Many women have never had a decent relationship with a man.
They spent their first eighteen years feeling alienated from their
fathers, then spent ten or fifteen years in marriages with men they
didn't get along with. It is not hard to imagine that some women
are hostile and distrustful of men.

If you are feeling a degree of this, don't mask it. You really
can't anyway. The first step is to let yourself know and feel the
anger. Don't expect to have a full and lasting relationship with
another man until the air is more clear. If you are not drawn to

men, don't push it. Some women feel pressured to immediately pursue another relationship with a man, as if to prove they are not sour. In fact, you *may* be feeling just that.

I recently had a conversation with a friend who had just gone through a particularly painful separation. It was the end of her second marriage and she was very angry. She complained that she hadn't been able to meet any man that she would even give the time of day. "Where are all the decent, intelligent men?" In the next breath she was telling me about several men she had met in the past few weeks, and how each one had grossly unacceptable qualities. They were all, without exception, "jerks."

They may have been. But the point is, she probably should let go of the search for a while. She didn't need to have a relationship with a man right then. In fact, I don't think she wanted one. As she continues, she becomes more embittered.

All men are not jerks. But that *men* might be a trouble spot for you, at least until some level of trust is restored, is a real possibility. It may take more time than you think to regain a comfortable feeling with men.

Needing a man to take care of you. Again, few women would be so blunt as to admit this. But that is clearly the message they send out. They want a man to take over their physical and emotional needs, including those of their children. Most often the plight of the woman is real. The hard reality of a woman making it alone in the marketplace can be discouraging. When things get tough, the cry for male help is almost a reflex for some women.

My advice is to resist this impulse. First, it usually does not work. A person who is relating to others solely from her neediness usually finds that people feel the pressure and run from it. A man may be willing to take on the responsibility of a woman and her children, but only after their relationship has had time to mature naturally.

Second, chances are that if you are only driven by the desire to be taken care of, the man who chooses to rescue you will make equal demands on your freedom of expression, thinking, and movement. There is usually an unspoken trade-off in such cases, and you may give up more than you bargained for. You pay the price for dependency.

There is a little girl inside all of us who wants to be taken care of. It's OK to want that, and OK to get it too—but in an up-front way. Healthy relationships are *inter*dependent, and each person should be able to freely ask for special caring and nurturing in needy situations.

Wanting an intimate relationship and being afraid. This is a most common response of the newly divorced woman. You put your feelings out there not just once but repeatedly during your marriage, and it just didn't work. So how willing are you to take another chance? The hurts are still fresh and the disappointment not forgotten. You may be hesitant, suspicious, and judgmental—and for good reason.

Your experiences since your breakup may only confirm your reluctance to take a chance. It's not uncommon that a woman's first encounters with dating men are small disasters. The man you finally decide to take to bed turns out to be a complete dullard and you find yourself comparing him—unfavorably—to your ex-mate. Or the opposite happens. You have a fabulously romantic night with an attractive man who makes promises, but never calls again. For a single woman used to dating, either situation is more likely to be taken in stride. For someone just divorced, it can trigger a range of reactions, from distaste to renewed distrust.

Intimacy is a shared creation, and a rare treasure. It is never guaranteed. And it takes risks to possess. The most daring part of it is self-disclosure. Unless you are willing to once again take the chance of opening yourself to another person, you won't experience a healthy bonding. But everyone moves at her own pace, and it is all right to go very slowly right now. When starting over, confidence is gained by inches.

WOMEN

When you were young, your best friends were probably other girls. You spent a great deal of time with them playing games, going shopping, talking about school, sharing one another's hopes and apprehensions about life. Later, marriage diminished that close contact for many women. The isolation and changes of location which happen after a woman marries do not foster an environment for intimacy with other women. Then, too, husbands have a habit of continuing their own early friendships while discouraging any for the women with whom they live.

Now is a good time to rediscover women. You don't have to be a feminist to recognize the special links that women share with one another. It has to do with the way we experience the world around us, the way we see things. Without attempting to define the differences between male and female sensibilities, it is enough to say that we instinctively *know* how to relate to each other. And when we break through whatever competitive junk women sometimes fall victim to, very satisfying relationships can develop. The playfulness and ease of communication found in earlier years combine with the maturity of womanhood to form some exciting and fulfilling friendships.

It may be an ideal time to take a vacation from men, if only to get some perspective. Going out with close female friends may be a safe way to actively engage in social life without the subtle pressure of, ultimately, sexual obligation that seems to go with dating. A whole range of social activities—from movies to weekend camping trips—are regularly possible with a woman friend.

Some feminists think that the value of women connecting with other women runs deeper, that such communication is not only essential for personal growth but also for political awareness. In fact, the two cannot be separated. During marriage, many women become subject to male orientations, ways of interpreting life that reflect unique male values. Adrienne Rich comments in *Lies, Secrets and Silence*:

> Women's minds cannot grow to full stature, or touch the real springs of our power to alter reality, on a diet of masculine ideology. This is not the same thing as saying that we can use nothing of those ideologies, or their methods, or that we need not understand them.

But the common world of men cannot give us what we need, and parts of it are poisoning us.

This is a strong opinion worth hearing. Having rather innocently accepted so much of the ingrained male thinking that each day's experiences plunge us into, you may want to step back and reevaluate just what *you* really want out of life. Rediscovering other women is a way to rediscover yourself.

BY YOURSELF

If divorce means one thing, it means being single. And while your attention may have been wholly given over to freeing yourself from your husband, the other side of the coin is that you have created a situation in which you find yourself alone. It is like fleeing a noisy room only to find a deafening silence in the next.

There will certainly be times when you will want companionship, and it simply won't be there—the Saturday night spent alone with only a television and the kids asleep in the bedroom. At times you will wonder about your strength. Or your wisdom. If it was worth it all.

It is. The advice—*know yourself first and find peace there*—has been given before in this book and others. It isn't an original idea but it still holds true. When you learn that you are a self-sufficient person, capable not just financially but spiritually of living alone, a very primitive fear vanishes. You are no longer the frightened little girl looking for her parent. You can survive by yourself.

Writer Judith Thurman in an essay, "Living Alone," delves into some secret pleasures of the single life.

I'm really alone—in good solitude—in those rare moments I can only describe as pure present. They resemble grace. They are gratuitous. Suddenly, I become alone. Myself is individual. I don't stand back, critically, and take aim at me in the second person—"you're too fat, lazy, haven't had an idea in weeks, can't write. . . ."

There is no such static from my body, my ambitions, obligations, guilts, objects, from things I have left imperfect or undone. Seeing becomes simple.

ADJUSTING

You cannot expect to integrate the wealth of new experiences coming into your life overnight. All of it takes time. In the months and years after divorce, you will be weighing the importance and value of a hundred new options opening to you. Some will find their way into your daily routine; others will be accepted into your belief system; many will be rejected.

Keep in mind some of the following points about the nature of the change going on right now.

1. Leaving is letting go. You have left physically. If you haven't done it already, you must also leave emotionally. As long as you continue to harbor strong feelings toward your ex-husband, even justified negative reactions, you are still caught in the web of that relationship. "Letting go" may not be as simple as it sounds. Addictions come in a variety of flavors. You may find that you are still hanging on to the connection with him, even though now it is only in the form of fault-finding, complaining, and cynicism. None of it is doing you any good.

2. Independence is *learned*. It may seem maddeningly elusive, but don't get discouraged or scared. Most of your life has been spent being taught dependency. It is part of the lesson our culture imparts to females. Finding security in yourself will come in small increments, but it will come. Living on your own is not all fun and adventure. You are bound to experience times of doubt. Nobody ever said that growing up would be easy—but it is worth it!

3. If you find that you are dating a lot of men (or want to), don't be surprised. And certainly don't come down on yourself about it. For one thing, it is a very common desire for women coming out of confining and uncaring relationships. If you hadn't been with many men before your marriage, you may feel the need to experiment; if you had been used to dating many men, you may

want to experience that life-style once again. The considerations are, first, if you are dating to discover and express your sexuality, be sure to use safe sex. And second, think about whether the whirlwind of dates and accompanying drama is an escape from something that deeply pains you.

On the other hand, many women tell me that being asked on dates and experiencing the attention of different men has been very positive. It helped to build self-esteem in ways either long forgotten, or never gained. Having taken these considerations into account, know that it is likely you will find balance in your life.

4. You are no longer part of a couple, a unit. That takes some getting used to. Your old mutual friends may also have difficulty with it, feeling that there are certain subjects that are now awkward to bring up.

If you care for them, don't withdraw. Confront them with the issue and talk about the changes that are taking place. Most good friends will understand and give your new relationship with them enough time to find its way.

5. If you are feeling isolated, it is probably self-imposed. Seek out people who take the same interest and pleasure in life. There is an ever-growing number of women and men in the same boat as you. You are not unique; many others coming out of a marriage face similar desires and obstacles. A variety of social and special interest clubs are available in almost every community. Test the water.

6. Realize that the first time around, Christmas, birthdays, anniversaries, and the like can be especially hard to experience alone. In the best of times, these holidays touch on emotions that are not always understood. After divorce, these events may be filled with conflicting feelings for times past and a sense of loss. Recognize the emotional power they hold and discover new ways to celebrate these special days. A nontraditional Christmas, for example, can bring together the family in a mutual effort to make the day different from those in the past. It will take some innovation on your part, but chances are you will be rewarded with a fresh insight into the real joy of the celebration.

7. Learn to be the initiator. You have a good start already. Use what you have learned during your divorce in your attitudes toward your work and in other parts of your social life. You may want to enhance your skills by attending classes in assertiveness training or reading a book on the subject. This new way of approaching the world is challenging and can be very exciting. You can *make* things happen.

8. *Don't panic.* Katharine Hepburn once said, "If you haven't found the right man by the time you are twenty-six, consider yourself lucky." Being newly divorced, if you don't find "the right man" for a while, it might also be a sign of good luck. No matter how "ready" you feel in the near future, you will still be picking up the pieces from the divorce for some time. Much depends on when the recovery process starts. Certain women leave their husbands emotionally long before they leave them physically. In that case, the transition is made easier. But I caution against moving in with another man too quickly. You are in the process of tremendous change, and the person you are today is probably not the same one you will become over the next year or two.

9. Accept *yourself.* After my divorce and at age thirty-eight, I was confronted with relating to other men in a direct sexual way. I was very uneasy, mainly because I was self-conscious about my body. I had generally felt good about my physical looks, but suddenly I became concerned about my sloping breasts and mature body that had borne four children. Didn't men nowadays expect women to be like the green-apple centerfold beauties in *Playboy?*

In an intimate moment with a lover, I expressed my anxiety about this. He looked at me with caring and delight saying, "I like *used* bodies!"

I knew what he meant. My history is recorded there, and I am proud of it.

CHANGE AS OPPORTUNITY

What the post-separation passage is really about is *change.* And the changes that are happening in your life right now give you the opportunity to become literally renewed. Whatever your life has been to this point need not determine what you will be after. That statement may sound wistful, but it is as true as you want to make it.

Our first instinct is to resist change, to distrust it—the outcome is usually unknown. Some of the changes also seem to be beyond your control. But fundamental change is the very essence of what is happening at this period in your life; and though parts of it may seem frightening, it is also electrifying. This is one of those rare moments in life when all things are possible, or so it seems.

New Patterns

Everybody's life has a design. Some people's designs are fluid and efficient; others are haphazard, cumbersome, or unpretentious. It is hard to see your own, easier to recognize in other people. But at times like this, we have a chance to get a clearer view of ourselves.

Having reached the postseparation stage, you have had to seriously question most of your original assumptions. Your life before may now seem like a patchwork of attitudes and habits. When you got out of high school you *knew* what life was all about, and you fashioned an existence around these ideas. Marriage changed the shape of your thinking, and children changed it even more. The years brought further adjustments. Whereas at one time you may have seen marriage as a final answer to happiness, those presumptions gradually disappeared. Whether you were a victim of faulty information or bad luck is of little difference. The main task now is to reevaluate and restructure the way you live.

It is a perfect time to take a long, hard look at your life and remake it in positive, enhancing ways. Because so many changes have occurred, you are forced to rediscover what works for you now. If something in your life is not working, and has not worked, get rid of it.

What do you want to do next Saturday night? What time should you eat dinner, and what kind of food do you now choose to eat? Now that you have time to read a novel in the evening, does it really interest you? And how about that dance class you always wanted to take? The answers are the beginning of your new structure. It is the way in which you choose to "do" your life. If you don't like what you have been doing each day, then don't *do* it. Or at least seriously plan ways to change in the very near future. And if you can't change the realities of your life, you can transform your approach to them. You may still have to do the dishes but it doesn't have to be seen as the housewife's burden. It can simply be doing the dishes.

This is a time to look at your life with new eyes, and rather than be swept up in the jumble of events, take charge and lay down guidelines that make sense—to *you*.

MY STORY—A CONCLUSION

I must finish the story that I began in the first chapter. Leaving my marriage was the most difficult and spiritually exhausting thing I had done in my life. In the end, I was working on pure survival instinct.

After arriving in California with my two youngest boys, I felt relieved, satisfied that I had made a complete break. However, in the following months, I struggled with the same issues most women face—serious economic problems, accommodating to a new and insanely crowded schedule, the internal problem of shedding past habits, deciding my future, searching for "the real me," and simply finding time to recover.

And my break with my former husband was not as clean as I first imagined. I had two children with me in California; he had two in Illinois. The bonds of family did not easily or completely unravel. Even though he had come to accept the idea of our divorce and, in fact, had remarried soon after to a woman with children of her own, our contact was strained.

When our divorce was final, the question of the younger boys going back to visit their father in the summer came up. The phone conversations and correspondence with my ex-husband regarding the kids had become intense, even explosive at times. Legally, I had custody of the boys, but the fear that he would talk them into staying with him was very real to me. I considered not sending them. After having overcome so many challenges, I didn't want to slip back now. My ego was also involved.

Because of my concern, I consulted a therapist who also happened to be my friend. I still think about his advice. He asked me what kind of relationship I wanted with my ex-husband.

"Most of all, an honest one," I answered. "One based on regard for each other."

He said, "Then the way to get it is to trust him. You have to start by extending trust and by being trustworthy."

I cried. I wanted to finally be free of all the acrimony we had been through, but I didn't think it was possible. Yet I went home and called my ex-husband that night. I told him what I was afraid of, and I asked him not to try to keep the kids when they came back. He admitted that he had thought of it but decided against it. That single moment of honesty began a new phase in our relationship.

Later that year, the kids went to Illinois again to be with their father for Christmas. When they came back to me, they seemed discontented. The vacation had been filled with activities that they had missed—the contact and guidance of their dad, the "horseplay" with their brothers, ski trips, a more traditional family situation. They wanted to go back for a longer period of time.

I had very definite misgivings. I was unhappy with some of his values (as he was with mine). But it was not as if the kids had never been influenced by his attitudes; they had already incorporated many of them. Depriving them of their father's love was not the solution to that problem, and I never doubted his deep caring for the children. The family that they would be moving back into was solid; their stepmother is an outstanding woman. The children left and moved in with him.

For the first time in twenty years, I was free from familial responsibilities. It was disorienting. But my everyday life quickly filled with new activity. I began to write and teach. My relationship to the man with whom I was living deepened. Though life is never free of complications, it became an authentic test of my abilities.

As it turns out, my former husband and the family have since moved out to California and now live a few miles away. My relationship with all of the children has resumed, and it is different. It is better. My love for them has gained something very special. And as I think about it, I realize that the change has been in *me*. During the past few years I have been able to acquire new awareness about myself. Some of it came with pain and loneliness; much more of it came in my renewed enthusiasm for life.

My relationship with him is different, too. Having distanced myself from it all, I can again appreciate him as a person and also acknowledge my responsibility in the marriage not working. It's not as hard to do that now.

Nineteen years of marriage cannot be taken lightly.

During a support group for women in transition that I was leading, one of the members, Dee Cunningham, contributed this poem. She was coming out of a seventeen-year marriage. Like all good poets, her metaphors give insight into our very human condition. The poem may mean something to you.

New Story

I bought the golden stories you used to tell me

Of Cinderella, Snow White and Sleeping Beauty.
They were so much better than my own wilderness
Or the shallow face I kept
So I listened and you grew tall.
When I listened for my sisters
They sat in corners licking bread
To keep me from taking their simple share.
When I watched my mother
I saw only that she didn't slay dragons.

When my legs grew longer
You had boy faces
And I hid with you in dark caves
While the night combed vacant lots calling
Ollie Ollie Ox In Free.
I ran from the snakes

You wanted to put in my shoes
Laughed at the curious branches
You brought to make your bed
Knowing that only the most tender tips would do.
But together we knew the secrets of birds
Would my sisters have known?

When my hair grew long enough
To catch in the wind
I had grown enough to know the lines
Of my body through your changing eyes.
I let my self grow small when you didn't want to look.
By the time all my babies had names
You had grown a beard and climbed inside.
I disappeared when I could not find your eyes.
But I stopped believing in dragons.

It's then, clutching at my woman's body
I entered my own wilderness.
The sky did not fall.
When I listened I found
The voices of my sisters
And together we are naming this new place.
I'm late I know, like fruit
On the final edge of perfection
But I'm here, and it's here I tasted my own blood.

Acknowledgments

Every book is written with the help of many others, and this one is certainly no exception.

Dr. Steven Bryant gave us the very first inspiration for the book. His initial work was invaluable. At an early stage of development, Al Hillix and Ann Elwood also made important contributions.

We wish to thank Richard Anobile for his tireless energy in initially getting the manuscript to publishers; and our first editor, Ken Leish at Bantam, for his faith in our work. Our agents, Margaret McBride and Winifred Golden, have been wonderful and steadfast in their support. Special thanks to Susan Suffes for her help and patience on this revision.

Ideas and expertise came from many people. Martha Lehr, a professional career counselor, was the source of much practical advice. Dr. Avra Kaufman shared his insight into the dynamics of human relationships. The legal chapter could not have been done without the help of Sandra Morris, Marge Wagner, and Gordon Sinning. Marshall Caskey gave not only legal advice but warm, personal support. Medical and psychological insights were given by Dr. Michael Gerber, Dr. Philip Sanderson, Dr. Richard North, Chris North, Dr. Paul Brenner, Dr. Nicholas Putnam, and Stephanie Covington, Ph.D., among others.

Our special thanks go out to Adrienne Miller at the Battered

Women's Service (San Diego), and the Women's Resource Center (Oceanside, California).

Palomar College faculty and staff and students provided a wealth of experience and source material. Essential help came from Cynthia Poole, Dave Chittock, Martha Lehr, and Ben McCormick, and the many people connected with the Palomar College Women's Center, especially Caroline Theiss, Linda Fred, Randy, Patty, and Barbara.

The reference staff at the University of California at San Diego library gave us tremendous assistance during the year we spent there.

The wisdom of a writer's teachers and counselors is always somewhere between the lines. We owe much to Lucie King, Bob Popovich, Al Malone, Hedges Capers, Sr., Maureen O'Hara, Jacie Smith, Jerome Ashmore, Ralph Keyes, and Gay Talese. Pat Stein and Sheila Moramarco gave us ongoing encouragement and journalistic help.

The contributions of others cannot be easily categorized, but life was made easier by the continuing support of Carol Pharo, Patsy Peacock-Evans, Orson Bean, Carolyn Maxwell, Alan Bernstein, Diana Solar, Lily Turner, Alisse Suess, Gail Myers, Steve Watson, Stephanie Wadel, Gene Youngblood, Peter Bollington, Cheri May, Sue Frings-Raftery, Colleen Erickson, Letty Butler Brewster, Kris Mattioli, Diana Peacock, and Clint Walcott. Also, Jane Zimmanck for her motherly neckrubs and hot meals at odd hours. Arlene Mattioli, who gave us a hundred kindnesses, cheers, love, and the use of an office on the ocean.

Ada Jane Akin translated disheveled manuscripts into clean, typed copy with great care and attention, as did Sherry Eaton. The initial editing of Evelyn Fagerberg greatly helped us.

The fatherly concern and care of Earle Triere contributed not only to the health of four children, but created a peace of mind which was necessary to do this book.

Our children's lives were perhaps most directly affected by the long hours of our work. We truly appreciate their understanding, patience, and love—Eric, Tim, Tom, and Jim Triere; Jerome, Martin, Zeke, and Avia Peacock.

Finally, the book could not have been written without the hundreds of women who offered their time and stories to us. Most have been given different names because of what they had to say. But they gladly cooperated so that other women in similar predicaments might benefit from their experience and have it easier than they did.

A major problem for women in transition is the experience of isolation. A quarterly newsletter on divorce is being published in order to help women create on ongoing network of contact. The purpose is to share histories, anecdotes, and advice with others of similar experience. Naturally, confidentiality is respected. Write for information and subscriptions.

A private guidance course on Divorce: The Emotional Stages of Leaving and Being Left, *by Lynette Triere is available on cassette tapes, as well as a six-tape series that includes interviews with divorcing people and professionals. This course is for men and women.*

In addition, Ms. Triere regularly gives both lectures and Learning to Leave Workshops *to organizations throughout the country.*

She is gathering information for a new book on women, men, and divorce. Those interested in contributing their stories, please contact:

Lynette Triere
DivorceCare
P.O. Box 234265
Leucadia, CA. 92023

Recommended Reading

No one book can say it all. Although you may have found *Learning to Leave* useful, there are a multitude of books on divorce and the array of subjects that relate to it. This is not an attempt to list all of them. However, I have found the following books especially helpful with my clients and in my own life. Continue to search out solid information and guidance in books. They may be your best companions at this time.

CHAPTER TWO: INDECISION

Belenky, Mary Field; Blythe McVicker Clinchy; Nancy Rule Goldberger; Jill Mattuck Tarule. *Women's Ways of Knowing: The Development of Self, Voice and Mind*. New York: Basic Books, Inc., 1986.

The book describes the ways women learn and know the world. Despite the progress of the women's movement, many women still feel silenced in their families and their lives. This moving and insightful study explains why they feel this way.

Bennett, Madeline. *Sudden Endings: Wife Rejections in Happy Marriages*. New York: Morrow, 1991.

The author writes from personal experience. The writing is an honest look at what it feels like to be left, helpful to those who find themselves unexpectedly there.

Covington, Stephanie, Ph.D., and Leana Beckett. *Leaving the Enchanted Forest: The Path From Relationship Addiction to Intimacy.* San Francisco: Harper, 1988.

A clear, practical guide to recovery for those who want to understand the nature of addictive relationships and are ready to embrace genuine intimacy. A helpful guide for a woman caught in indecision.

Forward, Susan, Dr., and Craig Buck. *Obsessive Love.* New York: Bantam, 1992.

The authors present a specific program for breaking out of an unhealthy emotional connection. Very useful information here.

Jongeward, Dorothy, and Dru Scott. *Women as Winners: Transactional Analysis for Personal Growth.* Reading, Mass.:Addison-Wesley Publishing, 1976.

The authors offer very positive and intelligent prescriptions for a woman's life. The writing is directly to the point.

Lowen, Alexander, M.D. *Pleasure: A Creative Approach to Life.* New York: Penguin Books, 1975.

You may have to hunt for this one but it will be worth it. A rather profound insight into an ignored part of our existence. The book is both thoughtful and satisfying.

Norwood, Robin. *Women Who Love Too Much.* Los Angeles: Jeremy P. Tarcher, Inc., 1985.

This has been a life-changing book for many women. It shows the way out for the woman who feels burdened with the pain of love.

Schaef, Ann Wilson. *Women's Reality: An Emerging Female System in a White Male Society.* San Francisco: Harper & Row, 1985.

A crucial book that will enable many women to articulate previously vague but disconcerting feelings by clarifying their mental and emotional conditioning in this society. Most women find it comforting to have their reality named and described.

Steinem, Gloria. *Revolution From Within: A Book of Self-Esteem*. Boston: Little, Brown & Company, 1992.
   The first book on self-esteem which includes both the personal and political contexts that can nourish or squelch one's own inner worth. A blend of Steinem's own experience as well as the wisdom of others, the book offers practical ways of going within and healing the body-mind split.

CHAPTER THREE: EMOTIONAL PROBLEMS

Bridges, William. *Transitions: Making Sense of Life's Changes*. Reading, Mass.: Addison-Wesley Publishing 1980.
   The author points out that every transition begins with an ending. The point is made that even though we experience change throughout life, most of us handle it badly. A very useful book at this stage.

Burns, David D., M.D. *Feeling Good: The New Mood Therapy*. New York: Morrow, 1980.
   This books is a very comprehensive study on the subject of depression. It explains how to conquer depression by changing the patterns of perception that create and perpetuate it.

Chellis, Marcia. *Ordinary Women, Extraordinary Lives*. New York: Viking, 1992.
   The personal histories in this book are truly inspirational. The author gives detailed records of how some women literally turned their lives around.

Ellis, Albert, Ph.D. *How to Stubbornly Refuse To Make Yourself Miserable About Anything—Yes, Anything*. New York: Lyle Stuart Books—Carol Publishing, 1990.
   The founder of the Institute for Rational-Emotive Therapy

writes about anger, anxiety, and depression. The book outlines logical methods to acquiring mental health and happiness. The title says it all.

Faludi, Susan. *Backlash: The Undeclared War Against Women*. New York: Crown, 1992.

It can be helpful to study the larger context of issues for women at this time. This book gives a quick summary of where things stand for women in our society.

Glasser, William. *Control Therapy*. New York: Perennial Library, 1985.

This work defines "life scripts" and gives insight on how to rewrite them. Basic and useful psychological information.

Lerner, Harriet Goldhorn, Ph.D. *Dance of Anger*. New York: Perennial Library, Harper & Row, 1985.

An insightful and prescriptive guide that shows women how to turn anger into a constructive force for reshaping their lives.

Lowen, Alexander, M.D. *Depression and the Body: The Biological Basis of Faith and Reality*. New York: Penguin Books, 1972.

Lowen combines a wealth of clinical experience and a lot of common sense in this book about the roots of depression. If understanding a problem is the first step to liberation, this book will help.

Sanford, Linda Tschirhart, and Mary Ellen Donovan. *Women and Self-Esteem*. New York: Penguin, 1984.

A complete but somewhat scholarly study of the cultural and psychological roots of self-esteem in women. The subject is well worth the investigation right now.

CHAPTER FOUR: NECESSARY STRATEGIES

Bolles, Richard Nelson. *What Color Is Your Parachute?* Berkeley: Ten Speed Press, 1992.

The book is now a classic, a great no-nonsense work on the techniques of finding a job. It takes you from beginning to end rather painlessly.

Hyatt, Carol. *Shifting Gears: How To Master Career Change and Find Work That's Right For You.* New York: Simon & Schuster, 1990.

This is the first book to focus on the psychological aspects of career change. Hyatt covers patterns that comprise career transition, and defines a program for positive change.

Hyatt, Carol. *Women and Work.* New York: Warner, 1980.

This is a good "how-to" book with many practical suggestions about getting and holding a job.

Levinson, Jay Conrad. *555 Ways To Earn Extra Money.* New York: Henry Holt, 1991.

The author has put together a very clever and practical manual for methods of networking and moonlighting. It is full of ideas for surviving which may be perfect at this time.

Leeds, Dorothy. *Marketing Yourself: The Ultimate Job-Seeker's Guide.* New York: HarperCollins, 1992.

This book provides a great impetus for getting you going out there. It is full of specific, detailed help on finding your worth and starting over.

Schwartz, Felice N. *Breaking With Tradition.* New York: Warner, 1992.

This book reveals the reality of life for women in corporations, professional firms, academic institutions, and public life. The author tells about the hidden agendas and other issues in a clear and provocative account. Ultimately optimistic, this study comes out of the author's thirty-year dedication toward women's advancement in the workplace.

Porter, Sylvia. *Your Finances in the 1990's.* Englewood Cliff, N.J.: Prentice-Hall, 1990.

The author's reputation is well established, and this latest book gives useful direction to anyone interested in taking control of their financial future.

Wall, Ginita, CPA, CFD. *Our Money, Our Selves—Money Management for Each Stage of A Woman's Life.* Yonkers, N.Y.: Consumer Reports, 1992.
This money management guide focuses on women at financial crossroads. A comprehensive easy-to-follow book gives advice on budgets, life insurance, child care, education, tax problems, divorce, and more. Worksheets are provided.

CHAPTER FIVE: THE LEGAL PUZZLE

Belli, Melvin, and Mel Krantzler. *The Complete Guide For Men and Women Divorcing.* New York: St. Martin's, 1988.
The book offers authoritative and clear advice on all aspects of attorney relationships and the intricacies of settlements.

Brenner, Lois, and Robert Stein. *Getting Your Share: A Woman's Guide to Successful Divorce Strategies.* New York: Signet, 1991.
Brenner, an expert in matrimonial law, attended law school as a young divorced mother. The book, aimed at preventing women from falling into financial and emotional catastrophe, is compassionate and extremely practical.

CHAPTER SIX: PHYSICAL AND SEXUAL NEEDS

Barbach, Lonnie Garfield, Ph.D. *For Yourself: The Fulfillment of Female Sexuality.* New York: Doubleday, 1975.
This book on self-pleasure brings the subject of a woman's sexuality to light in an unashamed, informative, and exciting manner. The writing is straightforward and challenging.

Benson, Herbert, M.D., and Eileen M. Stuart, R.N. *The Wellness Book.* New York: Birch Lane Press, 1992.

This is an outstanding sourcework in the areas of stress, nutrition, and exercise. Very clearly presented information.

The Boston Women's Health Book Collective. *The New Our Bodies, Ourselves.* New York: Touchstone, 1984.

This encyclopedic work is a must for every woman's personal library. It draws together the best of tested medical science and real experiences which women have discovered.

Comfort, Alex, M.D. *The New Joy of Sex.* New York: Crown, 1991.

The author's work is a standard, and with good reason. He gives a balanced sex-positive approach to relationships. Well worth looking into for the future.

Diamond, Harvey and Marilyn. *Fit For Life.* New York: Warner, 1987.

This bestseller is a sane, effective, and reasonable approach to changing your diet over the long haul. One of the best in a crowded field of advice.

Dodson, Betty. *Sex For One.* New York: Crown, 1987.

Dodson's book is a delightful self-exposé that is more than a technical study of sexual release. It is the ongoing adventure of a truly interesting woman. And her drawings are wonderful.

Harkness, Richard, Pharm. *Drug Interactions Guide Book.* Englewood Cliffs, N.J.: Prentice-Hall, 1991.

This guide is for anyone taking more than one medication—prescription or over-the-counter. Easy to follow and essential for some women.

Quillin, Patrick, Ph.D. *Safe Eating.* New York: Evans, 1990.

Without being a doomsday text, this books teaches what the dangers of toxins in food today are doing, and how to avoid them. Our health starts with what we eat—and don't.

Roth, Geneen. *When Food Is Love.* New York: Plume, 1992.
The author writes from personal experience about the compulsive drive to overeat as a substitute for intimacy. A good cautionary book for this time in your life.

McIlvenna, Ted, M.Div., Ph.D., editor. *The Complete Guide to Safer Sex.* Fort Lee, N.J.: Barricade Books, 1987.
Produced by The Institute for the Advanced Study of Human Sexuality, this is an honest, practical, and ethically written primer for safe sex. It also addresses sexual health.

CHAPTER SEVEN: HUSBANDS—AND LEAVING THEM

Goldberg, Herb. *The New Male.* New York: Signet Books, New American Library, 1980.
To understand your husband, you must first understand the roots of male consciousness. Goldberg gives some brilliant observations about what to expect from men in a divorce situation. He knows his subject well.

Jones, Amy, and Susan Schechter. *When Love Goes Wrong.* New York: HarperCollins, 1992.
The book provides valuable insights into recognizing the many kinds of abusive relationships, and how women can find strength to protect themselves and their children.

Miedzian, Myriam. *Boys Will Be Boys: Breaking the Link Between Masculinity and Violence.* New York: Doubleday, 1991.
This book studies the societal roots that shape the lives of men and gives a blueprint for change.

Tannen, Deborah, Ph.D. *You Just Don't Understand: Women and Men in Conversation.* New York: Ballantine, 1990.
Tannen's book explores the gender-based communication styles in a recognizable and accessible way. This linguistics professor suggests that the communication between men and women is cross-cultural.

Tavris, Carol. *Anger: The Misunderstood Emotion.* New York: Touchstone, 1987.

When relating to your husband, the problem of anger is a constant. This surprising work studies the causes and consequences of anger and comes up with interesting conclusions.

CHAPTER EIGHT: THE CHILDREN

Bell, Ruth, et al. *Changing Bodies, Changing Lives.* New York: Vintage, 1988.

If you have children in the teen years as you go through divorce, this book will alert you to what is going on in their personal lives which is affecting their behavior and emotions.

Clapp, Genevieve, Ph.D. *Divorce & New Beginnings: An Authoritative Guide to Recovery and Growth, Solo Parenting, and Stepfamilies.* New York: John Wiley & Sons, 1992.

A comprehensive guide for parents to help them weather the divorce and build a new life for themselves and their children. Especially thorough advice on single parenting, the unique issues concerning stepfamilies, and insight into the emotional stages children experience.

Faber, Adele, and Elaine Mazlish. *How To Talk So Kids Will Listen and Listen So Kids Will Talk.* New York: Avon, 1980.

The authors have put together a timeless primer on enhancing your communication with your children. Essential information for you at this crucial time.

The Unit at the Fayerweather Street School. *The Kid's Book About Divorce, By, For, and About Kids.* Lexington, Mass: Lewis Publishing, 1981.

A great book on divorce from the children's point of view. It affords an honest and surprising perspective on what divorce means to the young. The point of view is one seldom given a voice.

Galper, Miriam. *Joint Custody and Co-Parenting: A Source Book for the Separated or Divorced Family.* Philadelphia: Running Press, 1980.

As a helpful guide through the difficults stages of parenting after the divorce. This book is frequently recommended by professionals in the field.

Ricci, Isolina. *Mom's House, Dad's House.* New York: MacMillan.
The outstanding quality of this book is that it gives parents very practical advice about how to share co-parenting.

CHAPTER NINE: CLOSING WORDS

Andre, Rae, Ph.D. *Positive Solitude.* New York: HarperCollins, 1992.
The author writes a quiet, thoughtful book about the pleasure found in living alone. It is a light and realistic piece of prose.

De Beauvoir, Simone. *The Second Sex.* New York: Knopf, 1953.
After forty years and thousands of volumes by women, writing about women, no one has said anything more profoundly nor written in better prose than Simone de Beauvoir. If you read one book describing the condition of women, it should be this.

Fields, Rick, et al. editors of the New Age Journal. *Chop Wood, Carry Water: A Guide to Finding Spiritual Fulfillment in Everyday life.* Los Angeles: Jeremy P. Tarcher, 1984.
Inspiration and practical wisdom in this guide for helping integrate the events of modern living into the quest for spiritual fulfillment. A combination of wonderful quotes and poems from the world's great spiritual teachers, as well as useful information on all aspects of one's life.

Fromm, Erich. *The Art of Loving—An Enquiry into the Nature of Love.* New York: Perennial Library, 1989.
This is fundamental reading by a renowned philosopher and psychologist. Now may be the time to investigate the deeper meanings of love and human relationships.

Hendrix, Harville, Ph.D. *Keeping the Love You Find: A Guide for Singles.* New York: Pocket Books, 1992.

A book aimed at putting marriage counselors and divorce law-yers out of business, Hendrix wants to catch people before they begin in order to increase the odds for a happy, healthy relation-ship.

Kahn, Sandra S. *Leaving Him Behind.* New York: Ballantine, 1990.
  The book helps the already-divorced woman recognize how she may still be trapped by a marriage gone bad. Step-by-step program of hard-nosed advice to guide the reader toward self-confidence and independence.

Helpful Organizations

National Representative Department of the
AMERICAN ARBITRATION ASSOCIATION
1730 Rhode Island Ave., N.W.
Suite 509
Washington, DC 20036
(202) 296-8510
For information and assistance in mediation, contact national department for address of the office nearest you.

BUSINESS AND PROFESSIONAL WOMEN'S FOUNDATION
2012 Massachusetts Ave., N.W.
Washington, DC 20036
(202) 293-1200
Focuses on improving the status of working women through educational assistance, research on women and work, and special library for women.

CATALYST
National Headquarters
14 East 60th St.
New York, NY 10022
(212) 759-9700

A job counseling service for women, with extensive catalog of pamphlets and books giving current information regarding work and careers. Complete self-guidance series available.

DISPLACED HOMEMAKERS NETWORK, INC.
755 Eighth St., N.W.
Washington, DC 20001
(202) 347-0522
Contact for information regarding office nearest you. Offers support and guidance for widowed and divorced women from long-term marriages who must reenter the world of work.

NATIONAL ASSOCIATION OF DIVORCED WOMEN
Pan Am Building
200 Park Ave., Room 303E
New York, NY 10017
Get information on how to start a group in your area, if one does not already exist.

NATIONAL CENTER ON WOMEN AND FAMILY LAW, INC.
799 Broadway
Room 402
New York, NY 10003
(212) 674-8200
National resource organization addressing poor women's issues in family law area. Provides technical assistance to poor women and their attorneys.

NATIONAL ORGANIZATION FOR WOMEN (NOW)
National Office
5 S. Wabash Ave., Suite 1615
Chicago, IL 60603
(312) 332-1954
Contact this office or your local chapter for information and referrals regarding problems of your divorce. Your local NOW will usually have a listing of women counselors and lawyers. This

group will also give you support and direction regarding women's rights, and is a source for consciousness-raising groups.

SALVATION ARMY CENTRAL HEADQUARTERS
120 W. 145th St.
New York, NY 10111
(212) 620-4900
Contact for location of shelter nearest you.

UNITED WAY
This comprehensive organization includes most of the help agencies in communities across the United States. Take advantage of their services. The "Information and Referral Service" will be able to assess your needs and direct you to the appropriate agency in the area. Their services commonly include day care centers, mental health facilities, child guidance clinics, many social services, children's camps, the Legal Aid Society, and emergency shelters. Don't hesitate to contact the office nearest you if you are in need.

Index

About the Authors

Lynette Triere is a lecturer, workshop leader, and a nationally recognized divorce expert. Ms. Triere has appeared on hundreds of television and radio shows, with repeated guest spots on *Oprah*, *Phil Donahue*, and *The Today Show*. Lynette has been working with divorcing people since 1978, following her own divorce from a 19-year marriage. She has four sons and one granddaughter, and resides in Levcadia, CA with her mate, Clint Walcott.

Richard Peacock, an Associate Professor of Cinema, teaches screenwriting at Palomar College, San Marcos, CA. He has authored the textbook THE ART OF MOVIE MAKING, as well as numerous articles on human sexuality, relationships, and leaving. He has gone through the divorce process twice, and not only survived intact, but learned something.